Book of Mormon Authorship

New Light on Ancient Origins

FARMS Publications

Teachings of the Book of Mormon
The Geography of Book of Mormon
    Events: A Source Book
The Book of Mormon Text Refor-
    matted according to Parallelistic
    Patterns
Eldin Ricks's Thorough Concor-
    dance of the LDS Standard Works
A Guide to Publications on the
    Book of Mormon: A Selected
    Annotated Bibliography

Periodicals
Insights: An Ancient Window
FARMS Review of Books
Journal of Book of Mormon Studies

FARMS Reprint Series
Book of Mormon Authorship:
    New Light on Ancient Origins

Copublished with Deseret Book Company

An Ancient American Setting for
    the Book of Mormon
Warfare in the Book of Mormon
By Study and Also by Faith: Essays
    in Honor of Hugh W. Nibley
The Sermon at the Temple and the
    Sermon on the Mount
Rediscovering the Book of Mormon
Reexploring the Book of Mormon
Of All Things! Classic Quotations
    from Hugh Nibley
The Allegory of the Olive Tree
Temples of the Ancient World
Expressions of Faith: Testimonies
    from LDS Scholars

The Collected Works of Hugh Nibley
Old Testament and Related Studies
Enoch the Prophet
The World and the Prophets
Mormonism and Early Christianity
Lehi in the Desert; The World of the
    Jaredites; There Were Jaredites
An Approach to the Book of Mormon
Since Cumorah
The Prophetic Book of Mormon
Approaching Zion
The Ancient State
Tinkling Cymbals and Sounding Brass
Temple and Cosmos
Brother Brigham Challenges the
    Saints

Published through Research Press

Pre-Columbian Contact with the
    Americas across the Oceans:
    An Annotated Bibliography

New World Figurine Project, vol. 1
A Comprehensive Annotated Book
    of Mormon Bibliography

Book of Mormon Authorship

New Light on Ancient Origins

Edited with an Introduction by
Noel B. Reynolds

Associate Editor
Charles D. Tate

FARMS Reprint Series

Foundation for Ancient Research and Mormon Studies
Provo, Utah

Foundation for Ancient Research and Mormon Studies
The Neal A. Maxwell Institute for Religious Scholarship
Brigham Young University

Printed in the United States of America
12 11 10 09 08 07   6 5 4 3 2

First published 1982
by Religious Studies Center, Brigham Young University
(Produced by Bookcraft, Inc.)
as volume 7 in the Religious Studies Monograph Series

ISBN: 0-934893-18-7

Contents

The Foundation for Ancient Research and Mormon Studies (FARMS)

The Foundation for Ancient Research and Mormon Studies encourages and supports research and publication about the Book of Mormon, Another Testament of Jesus Christ, and other ancient scriptures.

FARMS is a nonprofit, tax-exempt educational foundation, established in 1979. Its main research interests in the scriptures include ancient history, language, literature, culture, geography, politics, and law. Although research on such subjects is of secondary importance when compared with the spiritual and eternal messages of the scriptures, solid scholarly research can supply certain kinds of useful information, even if only tentatively, concerning many significant and interesting questions about the ancient backgrounds, origins, composition, and meanings of scripture.

The Foundation works to make interim and final reports about this research available widely, promptly, and economically, both in scholarly and popular formats. It is hoped that this information will help all interested people to "come unto Christ" (Jacob 1:7) and to understand and take more seriously these ancient witnesses of the atonement of Jesus Christ, the Son of God.

FARMS publishes information about the Book of Mormon and other ancient scripture in the *Insights* newsletter; books and research papers; *FARMS Review of Books; Journal of Book of Mormon Studies;* reprints of published scholarly papers; and videos and audiotapes. FARMS also supports the preparation of the *Collected Works of Hugh Nibley.* To facilitate the sharing of information, FARMS sponsors lectures, seminars, symposia, firesides, and radio and television broadcasts in which research findings are communicated to working scholars and to all people interested in faithful, reliable information about the scriptures. Through Research Press, a publishing arm of the Foundation, FARMS publishes several series of publications addressed primarily to working scholars.

The Foundation is independent of all other organizations and does not speak for any other organization. FARMS is supported solely by subscriptions, sales, and private donations.

For more information about the Foundation and its activities, contact the FARMS office at 1-800-327-6715 or (801) 378-3295.

Preface to the 1996 Reprint Edition

Fourteen years after the first publication of *Book of Mormon Authorship*, interest continues to grow in a range of Book of Mormon studies that address the authorship question in one way or another. While dissident or revisionist Latter-day Saints join cause with skeptical non-Mormons to advance new or revised attacks on the standard account of the book's origins, there has been a major boom in research by faithful Latter-day Saints that substantially refutes these attacks and sets out volumes of new insights into its ancient origins.

A year ago I began planning for a new volume of authorship studies that would reflect the current state of scholarship on these issues. In that process, we discovered that many people have wanted to obtain copies of the original 1982 studies, now out of print. Several of the papers in that original collection have turned out to be classic pieces and are widely circulated as photocopies. While we have gone ahead in the preparation of a volume of new studies to be released later in 1996, we decided to reprint the original volume first, making these important studies available again in a high-quality publication.

The 1982 volume was published by the Religious Studies Center at Brigham Young University as volume 7 in its Religious Studies Monograph Series. We express appreciation to the Religious Studies Center for permission to bring the volume back into print as a publication of the Foundation for Ancient Research and Mormon Studies and as a companion for the second volume, which will follow shortly.

I have decided against any effort to update or revise these authorship studies as published in 1982. While the new volume will present more recent scholarship on some of the same issues, none of the studies in this volume have been outdated or refuted by subsequent studies. The evidence and conclusions they put forward are just as persuasive today as they were in 1982. It is this lasting quality of the collection that justifies this reprinting.

A footnote to the 1982 Introduction would point out that the famous debate on the shroud of Turin has taken some major turns with the publication of carbon 14 dating in 1988 that appeared to establish a late medieval date for the fabric, eliminating the possibility that it could have been the shroud of the Savior. While there are recent rumblings in the scientific community about alternative analyses that might open this question again, it is generally conceded that the issue is settled. While a generation of new critics of the Book of Mormon would like to believe that they could settle the question of its authenticity in a similar way, the evidence continues to mount higher on the other side, supporting the book's claims of an ancient origin. And the critics lag further and further behind in dealing with a host of new studies that vindicate the claimed ancient authorship in a variety of ways.

While the book's critics claim to base their skepticism in scholarly studies, the defenders represented in this volume recognize that these are not issues that will be settled by scholarly effort. Finally, belief in the divinity of the Book of Mormon is a matter of faith and depends on the personal testimony of each individual. While testimonies may be reinforced or encouraged by scholarly studies, such works are not the foundation of testimony. Religious truths require divine witness to establish the faith of the believer. As believing scholars, we recognize that fully and would not consider exchanging our scholarly perspective for the gift of faith that makes these matters so interesting to us. We hope others will continue to find these studies useful in developing a more complete understanding of the Book of Mormon and in learning to appreciate the great strengths of its position as a book of ancient scripture.

NOEL B. REYNOLDS

Acknowledgments

I am grateful to *BYU Studies* for permission to include the following previously published articles. As printed here they include revisions that vary from minor word changes to major rewriting to accommodate subsequent thinking.

Welch, John W. "Chiasmus in the Book of Mormon, *BYU Studies,* Vol. 10, No. 1, Autumn 1969, pp. 69-84.

Bushman, Richard L. "The Book of Mormon and the American Revolution," *BYU Studies,* Vol. 17, No. 1, Autumn 1976, pp. 3-20.

Madsen, Truman G. "B. H. Roberts and the Book of Mormon," *BYU Studies,* Vol. 19, No. 4, Summer 1979, pp. 427-45.

Reynolds, Noel B. "Nephi's Outline," *BYU Studies,* Vol. 20, No. 2, Winter 1980, pp. 131-49.

Larsen, Wayne A., Rencher, Alvin C., Layton, Tim. "Who Wrote the Book of Mormon? An Analysis of Word-prints," *BYU Studies,* Vol. 20, No. 3, Spring 1980, pp. 225-51.

I would also like to note that an extensively revised and simplified version of the first Nibley article has already been published in the *Ensign:*

Nibley, Hugh. "The Lachish Letters: Documents from Lehi's Day," *Ensign,* December 1981, pp. 48-54.

I am pleased to list Charles D. Tate as associate editor of this volume as a means of recognizing the editorial contribution of *BYU Studies* in preparing five of the enclosed articles for initial publication. I have also appreciated the continual encouragement and support of Professor Tate in this project.

Stacey Burton, Mitchell Edwards and other student assistants here at BYU have helped me with numerous editorial tasks. The bulk of the final typing and correcting has been done by my secretary, Carma Nielsen.

Hap Green of Publishers Press and George Bickerstaff of Bookcraft have been most helpful in preparing the final volume. Inasmuch as the collection is the result of a number of individual efforts, my continuing thanks go to each of the essayists, who have taken this project seriously and made a special effort to be part of it. Their work speaks for itself.

Finally, the project would never have come to completion had it not been for the continuing encouragement and support of my wife, Sydney, and of many friends who have wanted to see the volume completed.

N.B.R.

Introduction

Even in an age of advanced secularism, we are able to recognize that the truly significant questions facing mankind continue to revolve around the existence of gods, the reality of the supernatural realm, and the relationship, if any, which links men to them. For many people, these have possibly never been questions at all. Presented from their youth with an authoritative scheme of gods and men in interaction as an explanation for all their experience, they may have lost, as adults, the power to conceive of alternative accounts of man and the world. But modernity is marked by the painful discovery that men are able to make perfect sense of their experience using widely variant authoritative accounts. And by suspending belief in the supernatural altogether, scientists have been able to transcend that cultural relativism and discover marvelous secrets of the world around us that had never been suspected before.

The claim of religions to divine authority has rapidly lost its appeal as these alternative views of the world have grown in both availability and attractiveness. Pressed by unbelievers, the faithful have tried to persuade the ambivalent with testimony, arguments, and evidences. For many, it has been easy to believe on the testimony of others who have seen or heard gods or messengers from the supernatural world. But not for all. To help the more skeptical the Middle Ages, particularly, produced philosophical arguments designed to show the faithless that their most cherished beliefs about reality logically required them also to believe in God. These arguments have fallen on hard times. Other arguments point to different kinds of evidence, including physical artifacts of divine intervention in the world. Of course, the question is always whether the evidence compels belief in the divine. In most cases of alleged miracles, the skeptics are able to find plausible alternative explanations. And certainly in no well-known instance is divine intervention an unavoidable explanation.

One possible exception arises from recent attempts of scientists to explain the Turin shroud, the alleged burial cloth of Jesus. These scientific inquiries have drawn a nearly complete blank; they have produced no coherent alternative explanations for the image in the shroud, and thus have only served to reinforce the case of believers. But there are sufficient unknowns in this matter that a positive conclusion may never be available.

Another even more striking but less recognized artifact of this genre is the Book of Mormon. This readily available volume was first published in the nineteenth century by a barely literate young farmer in western New York. As if these unlikely facts of origin were not enough, Joseph Smith went on to claim that the book contains the record of an ancient group of Hebrew exiles and that it expands for us the prophetic texts coming out of that tradition. He claimed the record was given to him for a season by a divine messenger, during which time he was able to translate it by "the gift and power of God."

Since 1830, millions of people around the world have read the book and have been convinced that Joseph Smith's account of its origins is true. But, on hearing the account, others assume it must be a fraud. This easy assumption may well explain why almost no serious scholarly attention has been given to the matter until very recently.

If the Book of Mormon were indeed a fraud perpetrated by Smith or any of his contemporaries, it would be a very simple matter for scientists to demonstrate; for the Book of Mormon describes a people, their culture, a thousand years of history, and lands largely unknown to the nineteenth-century world. But today we enjoy a relative wealth of information about those times and people. Thanks to the flood of texts that have been newly unearthed, there are any number of straightforward scientific tests which could help determine whether this book is also of ancient origins or whether it was written by nineteenth-century Americans.

One striking thing about the Book of Mormon is that if the tests confirm its antiquity, we have no plausible alternative to Joseph Smith's explanation of its existence. And that explanation asserts the existence of God directly. In other words, we are presented, possibly for the first time, with a claimed major miracle which can be readily subjected to rigorous public, empirical tests. This volume brings together a collection of initial efforts to mount such tests.

The first chapter introduces the reader to the Book of Mormon and the kind of tests that might be appropriate by relating the intellectual and spiritual struggles of B. H. Roberts. In a very readable style, Truman G. Madsen reveals for us the logic of Book of Mormon claims and the relevance of empirical tests for those claims.

Chapter two presents our first test of the hypothesis that the Book of Mormon might have been written in the nineteenth century. In this chapter John W. Welch presents the exciting discovery of extensive and elaborate examples of ancient Hebrew poetic forms distributed throughout the Book of Mormon. The existence of these particular forms in the Bible itself was not generally recognized until after 1942. The examples outlined by Welch not only argue for the antiquity and authenticity of the text but also contribute greatly to our appreciation of its literary elegance and spiritual teachings.

In chapter three Noel B. Reynolds draws on Welch's literary insight and shows how an understanding of those ancient Hebrew literary patterns illuminate, in a systematic way, the author's design in the first section of the book.

In chapter four C. Wilfred Griggs outlines the standard scholarly techniques for detecting forgeries, that is, texts which have been written in medieval or modern times and attributed to ancient authors. He then applies those techniques directly to the Book of Mormon and finds a particular set of Book of Mormon symbols which give evidence of authentic ancient Mediterranean influence.

The individual who has been most seriously and productively engaged in scholarly analysis of Book of Mormon origins

and for the longest time is Professor Hugh Nibley. In chapter
five he presents us with a pair of brief new studies which argue
powerfully and independently that on two very ticklish
questions on which accurate information about the ancient
world has not been available until recently, Joseph Smith shot
in the dark and scored two bulls' eyes—a feat which Nibley
finds impossible without access to a genuine ancient text.

In chapter six Eugene England reports a very simple experi-
ment in which the lengthy flight from Jerusalem described in the
Book of Mormon is carefully checked against our contemporary
knowledge of the Arabian peninsula. He finds that although the
Book of Mormon descriptions of that journey would seem most
improbable and imaginative in the light of nineteenth-century
beliefs about that wild and distant country, the account given
accurately portrays the ancient trade route without any dis-
crepancies and in impressive detail.

Moving to a different type of analysis in chapter seven we
present the findings of a team of statisticians who have
employed newly developed statistical techniques for author
identification. Wayne A. Larsen and Alvin C. Rencher find
overwhelming confirmation of Joseph Smith's claim that the
book was indeed authored by more than two dozen separate
individuals. Their computer-assisted analysis also reveals that
the authors of the Book of Mormon cannot even be closely
approximated to the nineteenth-century individuals who might
possibly have been involved in bringing the book forth.

In chapter eight a well-known American historian examines
the claim that the political ideas reflected in the Book of
Mormon text may be simply borrowed from early nineteenth-
century American ideology. Richard L. Bushman finds that a
careful and systematic review of the text refutes this claim and
suggests rather that the politics of the authors are more easily
identified with ancient patterns of kingship.

Chapters two through eight give examples of various kinds
of scholarly analysis that can be focused on the text itself.
Chapter nine presents the most recent work of Richard L.
Anderson as he continues his exhaustive historical study of the
men who gave this text to the modern world. The more closely

he examines the confidential statements between Joseph Smith and his closest collaborator, Oliver Cowdery, the harder he finds it to believe that there was any taint of fraud or even self-deception in their account.

These studies vary considerably in their focus, their style, and the conclusiveness of their arguments. As a collection they challenge radically the easy assumption of secular scholars and sectarians that the Book of Mormon simply must have been a fraud composed and perpetrated during the early decades of the nineteenth century. It is hoped that these studies will attract the interest of other scholars who have the ability and the preparation to pursue the questions raised here.

Finally, it must be clearly stated that all the essayists would quickly agree that the studies reported here do not begin to get at the most important features of the Book of Mormon. For if it truly is an ancient record as we argue here, then it bears a most important message to the entire world. For it reports that the same Jesus who was born in Bethlehem and crucified in Jerusalem also appeared to other peoples and taught them his gospel. It bears independent witness that Christ is the Savior and Redeemer of mankind, substantiating in every way the Bible accounts. Far more so than the Turin shroud, the Book of Mormon offers powerful modern evidence for the divinity of Jesus Christ. It will be difficult for secular historians to remain indifferent to Joseph Smith.

NOEL B. REYNOLDS

1

Truman G. Madsen

B. H. Roberts
and the
Book of Mormon

Truman Madsen, Professor of Philosophy, is a Fellow of the Religious Studies Center and holds the Richard L. Evans Chair of Christian Understanding at Brigham Young University. He received his B.A. and M.S. from the University of Utah, and completed his A.M. and Ph.D. at Harvard University. In addition to teaching at five universities, he has served on the editorial board of BYU Studies *and on numerous advisory councils. Among his publications are* Eternal Man, The Highest in Us, *several edited books, and frequent articles in Church magazines. Recently he published* Defender of the Faith, *a biography of B. H. Roberts, a Mormon intellectual and Church leader at the turn of the century. In this article Madsen introduces B. H. Roberts and presents a synopsis of his rigorous lifetime study of the Book of Mormon. Roberts approached the Book of Mormon from many different perspectives, all adding to his conviction that it was authentic scripture. The article explores these perspectives and suggests that B. H. Roberts's five-decade probing of the book was "shrewd," "ground-breaking," and faith-promoting. Through Roberts the modern reader can come to understand the kind of challenge the Book of Mormon poses for an honest inquirer and how one can try to deal with that challenge.*

INTRODUCTION

By its own account, the Book of Mormon is for doubters. It announces on its title page a clear purpose for all the hard labor of preserving records: "To the convincing of the Jew and Gentile that JESUS is the CHRIST, the ETERNAL GOD." That statement presupposes that there would be serious and searing doubt in the world and that even religious readers, whatever their Messianic expectations, would not only raise questions about the historicity of this or that segment of the life of Jesus, but about the whole religious enterprise.

Whether that expectation was obvious in prior centuries or not, the fading religiosity of man is a contemporary fact.

Among readers who came to the Book of Mormon with hard, skeptical assumptions, B. H. Roberts[1] is notable. He was capacitated by temperament and equipped by study for penetrating analysis. Moreover, at many junctures of his life he had profound personal reasons and emotional and spiritual stresses which might have led a man of lesser integrity to discard wholesale his religious heritage. But on his other side was his capacity for constant, patient study. This he brought (for more than a half century) to the Book of Mormon as he did to his work in history, never letting go, never fully satisfied with what he had written or said, and never unwilling to consider afresh the latest spate of difficulties.

We have no autobiographical account of his own conversion to the Book of Mormon. But he does provide us with the makings of an outline: He accepted it with only surface acquaintance in his youth in Britain, as had his mother, as part of the total meaning of the "new dispensation" (his favorite phrase for the Restoration Movement). Prior to his becoming a missionary he had also had an intuitive or spiritual assurance in response to the very spirit of the book and its impact in his soul. In the mission field he was immediately subjected to the assault and battery of stereotyped hostility. And early on he found himself in public debate in Tennessee with a notorious Southern States figure, "Parson Alsup." For three days this man deluged the inexperienced elder with an exhaustive and bitter denunciation of the Book of Mormon. (He later learned that each of Parson Alsup's arguments had been borrowed whole cloth from Alexander Campbell's *Millennial Harbinger*.) From the stress of those three days, Elder Roberts emerged the victor in three senses: First, a responsive audience came and stayed to listen. Second, after a discussion of pre-Christian knowledge of Christ, Elder Roberts took the advantage and Parson Alsup refused to continue the debate. And third, within a short time he had baptized and confirmed into the Church more than sixty converts of the local citizenry.

This was not a mere passing episode but a preview of the rest of his life. Cumulatively, he worked to get a fair hearing for the book in two full volumes and some seventy articles, reviews, and tracts, and hundreds of sermons.

Aside from probing the book itself (one of his heroes, Orson Pratt, had read it countless times word by word to separate it into verses and cross-reference it), B. H. Roberts spent much library time in great centers and collections. As a missionary in England, for example, he went daily on a five-minute walk from the mission headquarters to the celebrated Liverpool Picton Library. There he made "an immense collection of notes" on evidences of American antiquities and archaeological works. At the other end of his life, during his five years as mission president in the Eastern States Mission from 1923 to 1928, he went on weekends, and sometimes at other times, to the New York Public Library and pursued further research on Book of Mormon antiquities.

The purpose of this article is to present a synopsis of what B. H. Roberts wrote and said about the Book of Mormon from ten different perspectives. Our samplings will corroborate the judgment of Hebraist Sidney B. Sperry and historian Hugh W. Nibley that his work, though not fully scientific or linguistic, was "shrewd" and that in basic outlines he was not only a ground-breaking pioneer but, in light of what followed, was ahead of his time.

1. Roberts as Circumstantial Analyst

In his considerations of the Book of Mormon, B. H. Roberts held that the strictest canons of confirmation—including strict, inductive methods—apply. The Book of Mormon, after all, is a public document that can be examined by anyone, faithful or faithless. It is shareable, and its claims can be checked against historical data. Examination of it is repeatable in the most concrete laboratory sense. Of course, at this level one can hope only for probabilities, but before one can be convinced that the book is authentic, he must be convinced that it is plausible and, before that, that it is possible.

Roberts was not himself "softened up" to the possibility of miracle. The Mormon understanding of miracles which he embraced repudiates the notion that they are a violation of law, natural or otherwise, or that they involve the logic of paradox. "Miracle" is the name of something extraordinary or beyond conventional explanation.[2] Roberts dealt extensively with what he called "external evidences" for the book. But that was preparatory to the other side of the equation, not what is the evidence for the Book of Mormon but *what is the Book of Mormon evidence for?* At a distance one may say the Book of Mormon story is impossible. Roberts's response has been reworded in our time: "If it happens, it must be possible." Here is a 531-page book (English edition). Start by reading it, and then move to the questions of its sources and its implications.

There was a boldness in Roberts's five-decade study of the book and in the fifteen hundred pages he set down about it.

> The Book of Mormon of necessity must submit to
> every test, to literary criticism, as well as to every other
> class of criticism; for our age is above all things critical,
> and especially critical of sacred literature, and we may
> not hope that the Book of Mormon will escape closest
> scrutiny; neither, indeed, is it desirable that it should
> escape.[3]

He came to symbolize a willingness, an almost reckless willingness, to consider the latest learned exegesis. He tried to stay abreast (mainly through biblical commentaries and the pages of the *Hibbert Journal*) of textual analysis and the contextual efforts of higher criticism. Though he tended to feel the contribution of such criticism was highly tenuous—hanging heavy weights on slender threads[4]—the personal implications were that his own roots went deeper. After some four decades of toil, he said: "For many years, after a rather rigid analysis, as I think, of the evidence bearing upon the truth of the Book of Mormon, I have reached, through some stress and struggle, too, an absolute conviction of its truth."[5]

In fact, in the quagmire of the struggle he became almost sanguine. Thus he could write in August 1905, "I do not believe the Book of Mormon can be assailed and overcome."[6] This was not because he assumed the faithful and credulous would refuse to abandon the book. It was because, regardless of the criteria brought to test it, and no matter how one defines evidence, the book would stand up as an authentic historical document.

Fifty years later the efforts of the counter-theorists (including the regalvanized Spaulding theory) have come full circle. All talk of a ghostwriter or ghostwriters has been discredited. And sociologist-historian Thomas O'Dea expresses the "common sense" conclusion that Joseph Smith himself wrote the book.[7] But the marvel of the product requires radical reappraisal of the alleged author. It is frequently said today, "Joseph Smith was a genius." Anyone who could produce (however one defines "produce") such an elaborate document would of course be a master, a multiple-talent genius in creative imagination and literary forms. He would also have to have the power of a "zeitgeist," and subliminal "cultural tendencies," and a superhuman grasp of the whole sweep of Middle Eastern and pre-Columbian American history.

And that is just the point: how could any genius or set of geniuses in the nineteenth century concoct a book that is filled with stunning details, now confirmable, of the ancient cultures it claims to represent? By the use of Occam's razor and David Hume's rule that one only credits a "miraculous" explanation if alternatives are more miraculous, the simplest and least miraculous explanation is Joseph Smith's: he translated an ancient record. It imposes what Roberts called "a greater tax on human credulity" to say Joseph Smith, or anyone in the nineteenth century, created it.[8]

As for the translation itself, Roberts argued that transmission of information through angelic ministrants and the use of the Urim and Thummim in translation is thoroughly biblical. Addressing himself to those who had no confidence whatever in the Bible, he went on to plead for an open mind with respect to man's ingenuity and the marvelous instruments that have come into his hands which make the Book of Mormon claims at least possible.[9]

2. ROBERTS AS HISTORIAN

His study of American antiquities and his tracing of legends and mythology gave B. H. Roberts a disciplined caution. He knew that fallible memory and active imagination and the flux of purpose in telling and retelling could turn any authentic story into palpable fiction. He knew as well that in the midst of such oral traditions and folklore there are often kernels of truth. With the instincts of a courtroom attorney intent on cross-examination, he interviewed those who had firsthand knowledge of the coming forth of the Book of Mormon. He lived in the midst of first-generation witnesses.

During his first mission to Iowa in 1884, he visited David Whitmer, one of the three witnesses, who said among other things, "Young man, if that book is not true nothing on God's earth is true." Then David Whitmer added that he had been cautioned on the revelatory day, "David, blessed is he that endureth to the end." Roberts felt there was hidden warning in these words, for David Whitmer was the only one of the three witnesses who died outside the Church.[10]

Roberts lamented the fact that many encyclopedias claimed that each of the three witnesses later denied his testimony of the Book of Mormon. The constraint of evidence—some of it gathered by Elder Roberts—led many editors to retract and reverse that statement. Late in life Roberts himself made a biographical project out of the life of Oliver Cowdery, planning to present him as the paradigm of a man of "almosts," who came close to destiny but who finally was stripped of his gifts and leadership role. But in response to prayer Roberts became convinced that Oliver Cowdery had completed his mission and that his private estrangement from Joseph Smith added weight to his unrelenting witness of the Book of Mormon. Roberts threw his manuscript of Oliver Cowdery's "almost" achievements into the fire.[11] That the witnesses of the Book of Mormon held to their testimonies, especially in light of the turbulent circumstances of their lives and the many attempts to discredit them, was to Roberts heavy evidence indeed. He himself said their testimonies of the book were "unimpeached and unimpeachable."[12]

Then later in his official capacities as a General Authority and as an assistant Church Historian, B. H. Roberts had many additional interviews with other early participants in the Mormon drama—John Taylor, Wilford Woodruff, Lorenzo Snow, Joseph F. Smith, the Pratt brothers, and others, including Anson Call, Philo Dibble, Nathan Porter, and Edward Stevenson.

3. ROBERTS AS ANALYST OF A "TRANSLATION"

B. H. Roberts was preoccupied with Joseph Smith's role as translator. One reason was that critics turned Joseph's phrase "by the gift and power of God" into a claim he never made, that of verbal inerrancy. Roberts wrote a whole treatise on these issues, concluding that Joseph Smith could not escape his own skin. Joseph's vocabulary and grammar are as clearly imposed on the book as are fingerprints on a coin. When Harold Glen

Clark asked President Roberts if the Book of Mormon would read differently had it been translated by someone else, B. H. Roberts replied, "Of course, not in substance and basic message but in modes of expression."[13] Although Joseph Smith affirmed he used a Urim and Thummim, the instrument did not do everything and the Prophet nothing. Roberts insisted that the translation process was neither so simple nor so easy a thing as has been supposed by both advocates and critics of the Prophet.[14] On the contrary, "brain sweat" was required, and preparation, and labor. Further, as an illustration that exact word-for-word translation of one language into another is impossible, Roberts presented examples from the Greek New Testament showing that the word *Master* used in the authorized version is a translation of six different Greek words all having different shades of meaning. *Judgment* stands for eight different Greek words.[15] He concluded, "Let us rid ourselves of the reproach of charging error, even though it be of forms of expression, unto God."[16] Elder Roberts hoped for the day when the President of the Church would authorize that the Book of Mormon be "made a classic in English . . . without changing the shade of a single idea or statement."[17] He did not live to see it become a classic in other translations.

4. ROBERTS AS ADVOCATE AND DEFENDER

In his systematic analysis of the Book of Mormon, volumes 2 and 3 of *New Witnesses for God* (he called it correctly "the fullest treatise on the Book of Mormon yet published"),[18] B. H. Roberts considered objections to the book and also counter-theories of its origin (including Alexander Campbell's, which Campbell later abandoned). Some of those objections included the following: awkward style and errors in grammar (Roberts answered they could be traced to the translator); passages which reflect King James terminology (the mental framework of young Joseph Smith); linguistic issues such as uniformity versus diversity in style (clearly several styles are demonstrable); variant readings of Isaiah in 2 Nephi (likely from a credible common source); apparent pre-Christian knowledge of the gospel (Paul and New Testament writers presuppose that); the giving of the priesthood to others than the tribe of Levi (why not?); the birth of Jesus "at Jerusalem" (no, "in the land of" Jerusalem); Nephite knowledge of the "call of the Gentiles" (historical and prophetic); the alleged three days of darkness in the Western Hemisphere (not of the whole world); the unoriginality of the book (it should be true to Jewish understanding—but there are many surprises); alleged "modern" astronomy in the book (not really); geographical issues (plausible enough); questions arising from the Anthon transcript and its relationship in hieroglyphics and Mexican picture writing (wait for Egyptologists); alleged plagiarisms of historical and biblical stories (religious experience is not falsified by being repetitive); the absence of Book of Mormon names in native American languages (similar names); the building of the Nephite temple (a small temple built by a small colony); the mention of iron and steel and the horse among the Nephites (iron is defensible from other sources, the horse is problematic); the incredible Jaredite barges (not incredible); the marvels of the Liahona (there are historical analogies in the Bible); the unmanageable weight of the plates (heavy but not debilitating); and the unheard-of antics of a beheaded soldier named Shiz (there are other known cases).[19]

Roberts thought it significant that most of these objections involved a misreading or misrepresentation. Yet he also allowed that his own answers to certain anachronisms in the book were at that time less than satisfactory. That little or no evidence of some of the events or elements of the Book of Mormon could be discovered in 1900-1930 nonscriptural sources is hardly proof that the narrative is mistaken or implausible. In the spirit of a logician, he urged that negative knowledge—that something didn't happen—is much more difficult to prove than what did. Negative theory is less valuable than one trifle of positive evidence, with which the Book of Mormon is replete.

Contemporary scholars, far more specialized and better prepared with linguistic tools, have begun at the other end. By studying the Jewish-Arab cultures of the sixth century B.C. and earlier, and again the meso-American culture of the appropriate later periods, they define "patternistic" themes and traits. The Book of Mormon can now be checked to see where it matches these contemporary findings. Hugh W. Nibley's *Lehi in the Desert and The World of the Jaredites* provides an Old World context, and John L. Sorenson's work concludes that the Book of Mormon is also a "meso-American codex" and pleads that scholars in anthropology and archaeology apply the book to their cultural researches even though they are hesitant about its claim to be a sacred text.[20] Meantime, new discoveries of ancient writings reaching into the same periods provide scholars with tighter controls on the claims of the book. The "coincidences" continue to pile up.

5. ROBERTS AS WISDOM SEEKER

B. H. Roberts saw the Book of Mormon as a well of aphorisms. He listed more trenchant sayings from the Book of Mormon than from any source other than the Bible. These sayings, he believed, were comparable in their edge and insight not only to biblical but also to Hindu and Chinese classics. The following were among those he wrote into his own notebook and memorized:

> Adam fell that men might be; and men are, that they might have joy (2 Nephi 2:25).
> It must needs be, that there is an opposition in all things (2 Nephi 2:11).
> When ye are in the service of your fellow beings ye are only in the service of your God (Mosiah 2:17).
> Wickedness never was happiness (Alma 41:10).
> To be learned is good if they hearken unto the counsels of God (2 Nephi 9:29).
> It is by grace that we are saved, after all we can do (2 Nephi 25:23).
> See that ye bridle all your passions, that ye may be filled with love (Alma 38:12).
> What manner of men ought ye to be? Verily I say unto you, even as I am (3 Nephi 27:27).
> I give unto men weaknesses that they may be humble;
> . . . for if they humble themselves before me, and have

> faith in me, then will I make weak things become strong unto them (Ether 12:27).
> Despair cometh because of iniquity (Moroni 10:22).
> Without faith there cannot be any hope (Moroni 7:42).
> Charity is the pure love of Christ, and it endureth forever; and whoso is found possessed of it at the last day, it shall be well with him (Moroni 7:47).
> The laborer in Zion shall labor for Zion; for if they labor for money they shall perish (2 Nephi 26:31).[21]

Roberts elsewhere warned against a tendency to disparage such phrases which come quickly to the tongue even before their full significance is apparent to the mind—a tendency toward "air-sniffing" contempt for the moral wisdom of the ages. Beauty and value remain even in the most threadbare of such counsels.[22] Who can calculate the power of the repetitive phrase in the Jewish Passover seder, "Next year in Jerusalem"? Or the two words that have grown out of the holocaust of the Jews, "Never again!"? B. H. Roberts felt comparable impact in such phrases as, "Oh remember, remember my son," "wickedness never was happiness."

6. ROBERTS AS CREATIVE WRITER

From college days and in the wake of his duties as an editor and journalist with the *Millennial Star* and the *Salt Lake Herald,* B. H. Roberts aspired to creative writing. He had already demonstrated narrative gifts and a dramatic sense. Short stories, plays, and even a historical novel were on his agenda of things to do. As a start, he wrote stories on Moroni, a sketch of a "Nephite Republic," and a fictionalized and heightened account of the life of Alma's son Corianton, a tale of sneaking indulgence and remorse and renewal.[23] The story was adapted by O. U. Bean into a play. It is not surprising that it enjoyed local acclaim, but it also found its way from the Salt Lake Theater to Broadway. Though it is a moralizing story, the response to it, for Roberts, pointed to the dramatic possibilities of this and a hundred segments of the Book of Mormon. Not only did he feel that Book of Mormon characters have flesh-

and-blood counterparts in our own day and in our own interior lives, but he also thought it utterly inept to speak of the Book of Mormon as "antiquated" or of its idealisms and descriptions of barbarism as "unreal." He saw it as a mine of sinewy spiritual inspiration. He visualized the book of 3 Nephi as a pageant, a magnificent Easter vision which could not be matched anywhere in the world of literature.[24] For Roberts, one might read 3 Nephi from no other motives than those he brings to Homer or Beowulf.

As the Church centennial approached (1930), he dreamed of a major motion picture with a script built upon one or more of the epic civilizations portrayed in the book. It was not to be.

Although he did not live to realize it, B. H. Roberts, as president of the Eastern States Mission, was the "Elias" of the now nationally known Palmyra Pageant. It was he who set up an elaborate celebration on 23 September 1923 on the occasion of the hundredth anniversary of the receiving of the plates from the Hill Cumorah. He had prepared five careful addresses but because of illness delivered only two. The press described his Hill Cumorah address as "like some graphic panorama of the past," like a "Norse saga," and President Roberts wrote home that this one paragraph justified his entire effort.[25] Also through his efforts, the Church acquired the Hill Cumorah, the Joseph Smith Farm, the Sacred Grove, and the Whitmer Farm.[26] "I rejoice that we have these places," he said. He was pleased with the call to New York in the first place because it was the territory of "the early scenes of the Prophet's life, the first vision and the coming forth of the Book of Mormon, the Hill Cumorah, etc.," which "naturally would endear this section of the country to the mind and heart of Elder Roberts."[27] Several articles grew out of the five years he spent there.[28]

7. Roberts as Doctrinal Teacher

B. H. Roberts was more perceptive than many who tend to read traditional concepts into Book of Mormon verses. The absence of many of the traditional religious doctrines impressed him. Convinced that this book grew out of ancient sectaries of

Judaism and from the firsthand contact of a whole community with the resurrected Christ, he felt these absences were significant. For instance, in the Book of Mormon there is no doctrine of ex nihilo creation, nor of original sin, nor of a triune hypostatic God, nor of divine immateriality, nor of faith alone, nor of the all-sufficiency or only-sufficiency of the Bible, nor of the priesthood of all believers, nor of predestination, nor of total depravity. For Roberts, these were later "Christian" doctrines because none of them could be legitimately defended from the Bible itself.

As to the "originality of the Book of Mormon,"[29] Roberts there found doctrines exceeding the native intelligence of Joseph Smith, and his associates, and indeed the combined intelligence and learning of the nineteenth century. Among these truths were the definition of truth itself (Jacob 4:13); the doctrine of opposite existences (2 Nephi 2); the doctrine (with cosmological implications) that the universe splits into two categories, "things to act and things to be acted upon" (2 Nephi 2:14); a foundation for an unqualified affirmation of man's agency (2 Nephi 2:27, 10:23; Alma 61:21); a doctrine of the fall of Adam as instrumental to a higher good (2 Nephi 2:10-11, 15; Alma 42:16-17); a doctrine of the nature of evil as "among the eternal things"—"as eternal as good; as eternal as law; as eternal as the agency of intelligence"[30] (2 Nephi 2:17; Jacob 5:59; Alma 41:13) and thus a "master stroke" in the solution of the classical problem of theodicy[31] (how can a God of power be responsible for evil and the devil?) (2 Nephi 2:15-25); and a doctrine of the purpose of man's existence (2 Nephi 2:25). Here he contrasts the classical catechisms, confessions, and creeds of the major Christian and Jewish faiths. He formulates this doctrine from the words of Lehi as follows: "Earth life became essential to intelligences— Adam fell that this earth life might be realized. The purpose of man's earth life is that he might have joy. The purpose of the gospel is to bring to pass that joy."[32]

In his fourth yearbook of *The Seventy's Course in Theology* on the Atonement, Roberts concluded that the Book of Mormon teaching is unique on the role of Christ, that the balance of justice and mercy is the eternal foundation of the meaning and necessity and power of the atonement of Jesus Christ:

> [This] is a doctrine, in modern times, peculiar to "Mormonism"; or, to speak more accurately, to the New Dispensation of the Gospel revealed to Joseph Smith; and is derived almost wholly from the teachings of the Book of Mormon.[33]

In its account of the free and complete redemption of little children and the redemption of those who die without the law, he wrote, the Book of Mormon is also patently clear. In fact, having compared the Book of Mormon teaching with classical "soteriology" in Anselm, Thomas, Augustine, Calvin, and Luther, B. H. Roberts concluded that nowhere else in all Christian literature is such mighty understanding of the Christ presented. Accepted as a "fifth Gospel" it would "put to silence several great controversies."[34]

Above all, he "rejoiced exceedingly" to show that the Book of Mormon does not simply affirm that Jesus is the Christ but that it clarifies what it means for Jesus to be the Christ. In contrast to those who have held that Mormonism denies or qualifies the deity of Jesus Christ, Roberts held that the Book of Mormon is solid testimony to the contrary. Therein is revealed that Christ is the complete revelation of the one divine nature, the express image of the Father, and that in nature and attributes the Father is exactly like the Son. It is in that sense that Mormons are (and in another sense are not) monotheists. "There is only one God-nature."[35] When intelligences in the universe fulfill the will of God and receive of his fulness, they too become "harmonized" and participate in that God-nature. Christ was the first who by his life and sacrificial death reflected and revealed "all of Him!—God revealed in all His fulness."[36] In the late 1920s Elder Roberts convinced the leadership of the youth organizations of the Church to set up a banner-slogan: "We stand for absolute faith in the eternal God, revealed in Jesus Christ."[37] And in his own sermons he utilized the tract he had written while president of the Eastern States Mission in the series of four tracts, "Why 'Mormonism'?"

Mormonism is here to be, through the Book of Mormon, a witness to the Deity [more than to the divinity] of Jesus Christ: "to the convincing of the Jews and Gentiles that JESUS is the CHRIST, the ETERNAL GOD, manifesting HIMSELF to all nations."[38]

8. ROBERTS AS DEVIL'S ADVOCATE

B. H. Roberts found and in many cases anticipated objections and reductive approaches to the book. He was known to turn the tables on young Mormon missionaries and represent "the case against" with crisp skill, pushing points of vulnerability that tested their mettle. He warned them against superficial response. Most of his colleagues disapproved of such confrontations, but Roberts would say, "You will have a good experience. It will open your eyes and deepen your understanding."[39]

On 4 and 5 January 1922, B. H. Roberts made an oral presentation before the General Authorities concerning what some critics claimed were anachronisms in the Book of Mormon —the mention of horses, of cimeters or swords, and of silk. These were troublesome to him as well as to the critics. He also presented a lengthy analysis of a tougher problem still—the variety of language dialects in Central and South America, more varied than the time period claimed by the Book of Mormon could account for. The meetings lasted for ten hours on the first day and through the whole day and evening of the second. Elder James E. Talmage of the Council of the Twelve Apostles recorded that he and others were asked to help Elder Roberts prepare answers, though none were clearly on the horizon. Elder Talmage, nevertheless, predicted in his journal that the Book of Mormon would be vindicated.[40]

Later, in March of 1922, Roberts prepared a draft of a written report to the First Presidency and the Quorum of the Twelve. It included a further discussion of the linguistic problems and other points as well. The study of such books as those of Josiah Priest, Ethan Smith, and others led him to examine such questions as: What literary and historical speculations were abroad in the nineteenth century? Could Joseph Smith

have absorbed them in his youth and could these influences
have provided the ground plan for such a work as the Book of
Mormon? Did Joseph Smith have a mind "sufficiently creative"
to have written it? And what internal problems and parallels
within the Book of Mormon called for explanation? In confront-
ing such questions Roberts prepared a series of "parallels" with
Ethan Smith's *View of the Hebrews;* a summary of this analysis
excerpted passages from Ethan Smith's work and lined them up
in columns with comparable ideas in the Book of Mormon.[41]
Examination of such questions was contained in a typewritten
manuscript entitled "Book of Mormon Study."[42]

About this particular study, certain points must be kept in
mind if it is not to be gravely misunderstood. First, it was not
intended for general dissemination but was to be presented to
the General Authorities to identify for them certain criticisms
that might be made against the Book of Mormon. In his 1923
letter, Roberts wrote:

> Let me say once and for all, so as to avoid what
> might otherwise call for repeated explanation, that what
> is herein set forth does not represent any conclusions of
> mine. This report [is] . . . for the information of those
> who ought to know everything about it *pro and con,* as
> well that which has been produced against it as that
> which may be produced against it. I am taking the posi-
> tion that our faith is not only unshaken but unshakeable
> in the Book of Mormon, and therefore we can look
> without fear upon all that can be said against it.[43]

It is not clear how much of this typewritten report was actually
submitted to the First Presidency and the Twelve, but it is clear
that it was written for them.

In 1932 Roberts wrote to a missionary who had heard
rumors of his work: "I had written it for presentation to the
Twelve and the Presidency, not for publication. But I suspended
the submission of it until I returned home, but I have not yet
succeeded in making the presentation of it."[44]

Second, the report was not intended to be balanced. A kind
of lawyer's brief of one side of a case written to stimulate discussion in preparation of the defense of a work already accepted

as true, the manuscript was anything but a careful presentation of Roberts's thoughts about the Book of Mormon or of his own convictions.

Third, many of the perceived problems are no longer problems. Roberts himself soon came to realize that the peoples of the Book of Mormon do not represent the only migration that inhabited the Western Hemisphere. So the problem of linguistic variation dissolved. Later scholars would find evidence of cimeters, of silk, and of horses.[45]

Roberts said in 1933 that he had concluded Ethan Smith played no part in the formation of the Book of Mormon.[46] Appreciative of irony, he might well have smiled at the sequel. After his death, ill-wishers published the "parallels" of the book without Elder Roberts's cover-letter disclaimer.[47] Others have gleefully recited other "problems" as he presented them, seemingly unaware that they were reflecting neither Roberts's own considered conclusions nor the current state of research. Fawn Brodie wrote in her biography of Joseph Smith that *View of the Hebrews* "may" have given Joseph Smith the idea of writing the book. While conceding that it "may never be proved" that Joseph ever saw *View of the Hebrews,* she was confident that "the striking parallelisms between the two books hardly leave a case for mere coincidence."[48] So doing, she unwittingly provided the criteria that validates the Book of Mormon. The "striking parallelisms" between the Book of Mormon and its own claimed historical matrix are far more striking, indeed destroying the case for "mere coincidence," while such genuine historical parallels do not exist for Ethan Smith's speculative treatise. Before his death in 1933, Roberts had concluded that the central claims of Joseph Smith and Ethan Smith are not only independent but incompatible.

Roberts felt he had established beyond doubt that there is enough independent evidence for pre-Columbian, Jewish, or Hebraic influence on native American races to make the Book of Mormon claims at least credible. The evidence was accumulating rapidly in the last decade of Elder Roberts's life (it has been an avalanche since), so much so that he told fellow-historian Preston Nibley in 1930 that he wished to call in his

New Witnesses volumes and start over.[49] To missionary associates he confided that he hoped to visit Central and South America and there examine firsthand the remnants of ancient middle-American peoples. Most of his work, he admitted, had been as a "compiler," heavily dependent on secondary sources for his conclusions. Age and declining health dissolved this hope ("How our visions vanish as time rushes upon them," he wrote in the late 1920s).[50]

Teachers who have used the "Devil's Advocate" approach to stimulate thought among their students, lawyers who in preparation of their cases have brought up what they consider the points likely to be made by their worthy opponents—all such people will recognize the unfairness of taking such statements out of context and offering them as their own mature, balanced conclusions. For ill-wishers to resurrect Roberts's similar "Devil's Advocate" probings is not a service to scholarship, for they are manifestly dated. And it is a travesty to take such working papers as a fair statement of B. H. Roberts's own appraisal of the Book of Mormon, for, as this paper abundantly demonstrates, his conviction of its truth was unshaken and frequently expressed down to the time of his death.

9. Roberts as One Spiritually Athirst

In Roberts's mind and heart the Book of Mormon was "precious withal,"[51] and one who began with faith could later be edified by what Elder Roberts called an intellectual testimony of its truths. Or one could begin with the intellect and end with an edifying faith in the personalities behind it. During his mature life he went back and forth between the two, equally excited by the feelings of discovery. To intimates, on more than one occasion, he quoted Brigham Young's statement "that no man had yet so much as heard of the Book of Mormon but what the Spirit of the Lord whispered quietly to his soul that the book was true."[52] Though renowned for his gifts as a speaker, B. H. Roberts agonized over the fact that he could never communicate the intensity, the power, the consuming white light that seemed to him to shine through the book.

In April 1928 on only one of thirty occasions when he used the Tabernacle pulpit on this subject, he said after reading of the ancient Nephites crying "Hosanna" in the presence of Christ:

> Now, tell me in what Church or cathedral in the world, in what sacred grove, in what place among the habitations of men will be found a more glorious Easter vision of the Christ than this? And the world would have lost this if it had not been for the Book of Mormon coming forth and there is a hundred more such glorious things that have come to the world in that book to enlighten the children of men.[53]

He closed with a prayer, for on this level the paralytic influence of analysis gave way to faith and its fulfillment. It was the praise of God that shone in him as he sang his song of praise.

By 1930, Roberts had polished his two major works—the six-volume *Comprehensive History of The Church* and his three-volume manuscript, "The Truth, the Way, the Life." His chapter on the Book of Mormon in the *History* is modified only slightly from the conclusions drawn in his *New Witnesses* books. But two chapters on Christ in the final volume of his doctrinal treatise include a more detailed exegesis of 3 Nephi and especially of the teachings of the Christ in their ethical and social bearing. He provided further insight into his assertion that the Book of Mormon "intensifies" the New Testament sermons of Jesus and demands a higher and richer relationship with Christ as Christ (not just Jesus as teacher). This was the absolute preface to a higher mode of personal and social sanctity and righteousness.[54]

At the 1930 centennial celebration, in summarizing the work of the first century and anticipating the beginning of the second, Roberts spoke in the idiom of revelation:

> Hear, O heavens, and give ear, O earth, for God hath spoken. . . . The Record of Joseph in the hands of Ephraim, the Book of Mormon, has been revealed and translated by the power of God, and supplies the world with a new witness for the Christ, and the truth and the fulness of the Gospel.[55]

10. ROBERTS AS IDEOLOGICAL PROPHET

B. H. Roberts did not enjoy being cast in the role of prophet. But he was confident in the triumph of ideas. "If you regard us from the viewpoint of learning and philosophy, we cut no great figure," he said in his mid-life. Yet Mormonism is "essentially a religion for intellectual men."[56] He believed that it would appeal, once seen clearly, to the highest intelligences of the earth:

> I am convinced that when men of intelligence can be brought to the point of being sufficiently humble to read again the Book of Mormon, and to take into account the high purposes for which it was written . . . and will stop sneering at such human elements as may be in it, and will examine once more its teachings upon the great theme of salvation through the atonement of the Christ, they can indeed find wisdom and philosophy and truth in its doctrines.[57]

The book, he predicted, would have gathering and unifying power, not only for the Jewish and Christian world but for all. It would come to "fix the world's standards of philosophical thought and ethical action in ages yet unborn."[58] "Oh, what the world would have lost, if the Book of Mormon had not been brought forth!" he said in April 1928.[59]

In 1933, in his final discourse—titled "God"—B. H. Roberts said again that Joseph Smith received commandments from God "which inspired him" and gave him power from on high to translate the Book of Mormon which, with subsequent revelations, "brought forth a development of the truth that surpasses all revealed truth of former dispensations."[60] He had earlier said the book would come to be viewed as "the greatest literary event of the world since the writings of the decalogue by the finger of God or the publication of the testimony in the New Testament that Jesus is the Christ."[61]

He also said: "We who accept it as a revelation from God have every reason to believe that it will endure every test; and the more thoroughly it is investigated, the greater shall be its ultimate triumph."[62]

He once pointed out a striking prophecy in the Book of Mormon about itself. Nephi records, "There shall be many which shall believe the words which are written; and they shall carry them forth unto the remnant of our seed" (2 Nephi 30:3). How many is "many"? Roberts knew well that a person can believe the Bible, at least in an attenuated sense, without believing the Book of Mormon. But one cannot believe the Book of Mormon without also believing the Bible. The same Nephi also predicts that "other books" will come forth to convince Jew and Gentile "upon all the face of the earth, that the records of the prophets and of the twelve apostles of the Lamb are true" (1 Nephi 13:39). The Book of Mormon and the other books yet to come will not replace the Bible. But the Bible will be reinstated in a greater fulness of splendor and clarity than it has enjoyed in all prior centuries.

B. H. Roberts's ten approaches to the Book of Mormon assured and reassured him that it was authentic scripture. And he died with this faith: The Book of Mormon will not convert the world to a small and encrusted sect called Mormonism, for Mormonism is to become a world movement. The Book of Mormon will help reconvert Christians, and eventually all the family of man, to Christ.

NOTES

1. B. H. Roberts, author of the *Comprehensive History of The Church of Jesus Christ of Latter-day Saints* and editor of the *History of The Church of Jesus Christ of Latter-day Saints*, was one of the Seven Presidents of the First Quorum of the Seventy from 1888 until his death in 1933.

2. See B. H. Roberts, "'Miracles' Part of the Divine Economy," *The Seventy's Course in Theology* (Salt Lake City: Deseret News, 1911), 4:79.

3. B. H. Roberts, "The Translation of the Book of Mormon," *Improvement Era* 9 (April 1906):435-36.

4. See B. H. Roberts, "Higher Criticism and the Book of Mormon," *Improvement Era* 14 (June 1911):668. A more precise account of the Isaiah problem by B. H. Roberts is printed in the *Improvement Era* 12 (July 1909): 681-89 under the title "An Objection to the Book of Mormon Answered."

5. Roberts, "Higher Criticism and the Book of Mormon," p. 667.

6. B. H. Roberts, "Our Work Review of the New Manual," *Improvement Era* 8 (August 1905):784.

7. Thomas F. O'Dea, *The Mormons* (Chicago: University of Chicago Press, 1957), pp. 24, 30-37.

8. B. H. Roberts, "The Probability of Joseph Smith's Story," *Improvement Era* 7 (March 1904):321-31 and (April 1904):417-32; B. H. Roberts, "The Relative Tax on Human Credulity Between Ancient and Modern Dispensations of the Christian Religion," Salt Lake Tabernacle address, 21 October 1924.

9. Roberts, "The Probability of Joseph Smith's Story," pp. 321-31.

10. Diary of J. Orvall Ellsworth, 23 September 1923. Ellsworth was a Ph.D. student in economics at Cornell University at this time. See also B. H. Roberts's account of his interview with David Whitmer, *Conference Report of The Church of Jesus Christ of Latter-day Saints,* October 1926, p. 126.

11. Recollections of Georgia Roberts Maury, a daughter of B. H. Roberts, in an interview with the author, 1966.

12. B. H. Roberts, *New Witnesses for God,* 3 vols. (Salt Lake City: Deseret News Press, 1909), 2:278. Richard L. Anderson has dealt thoroughly with this subject. See "Oliver Cowdery's Non-Mormon Reputation," *Improvement Era* 71 (August 1968):18-26; "Martin Harris: The Honorable New York Farmer," *Improvement Era* 72 (February 1969):18-21; "David Whitmer: The Independent Missouri Businessman," *Improvement Era* 72 (April 1969):74-81; "Five Who Handled the Plates," *Improvement Era* 72 (July 1969):38-47.

13. Harold Glen Clark to Truman G. Madsen, 25 April 1966, in possession of the author. Harold Glen Clark served under B. H. Roberts in the Eastern States Mission and asked this question during a mission school session in Brooklyn.

14. B. H. Roberts, "Bible Quotations in the Book of Mormon," *Improvement Era* 7 (January 1904):191-96.

15. B. H. Roberts, "The Translation of the Book of Mormon," *Improvement Era* 9 (May 1906):544-53.

16. Ibid., p. 549.

17. See B. H. Roberts, YMMIA Manual, 1903-1904, "The Book of Mormon, Part 1," *New Witnesses for God,* vol. 2 (Salt Lake City: General Board of the YMMIA, 1903), chap. 7, pp. 106-21.

18. B. H. Roberts to Charles W. Nibley, 10 June 1908, Historical Department of The Church of Jesus Christ of Latter-day Saints, Salt Lake City, Utah; hereafter cited as Church Archives.

19. Roberts, *New Witnesses for God,* 3:407-557.

20. Hugh W. Nibley, *Lehi in the Desert and The World of the Jaredites* (Salt Lake City: Bookcraft, [1952]; John L. Sorenson, *The Book of Mormon as a Meso-American Codex* (Provo, Utah: Society for early Historical Archaeology, 1977) see also Hugh W. Nibley, *Since Cumorah: The Book of Mormon in the Modern World* (Salt Lake City: Deseret Book Co., 1976).

21. "Bible Companion" and Miscellaneous Notes compiled by B. H. Roberts during World War I when he was a chaplain, Church Archives. (See also Roberts, *Conference Report*, April 1906, p. 17, and April 1928, p. 108.)

22. B. H. Roberts, "A Nephite's Commandments to His Three Sons: Corianton," part 3, *Improvement Era* 3 (August 1900):760-69, and part 4 (September 1900):835-43.

23. B. H. Roberts, "Corianton, a Nephite Story," *Contributor* 10 (March-July 1889):171, 206, 245, 286, 324. Later published as *Corianton, a Nephite Story* (Salt Lake City: Deseret News Press, 1902).

24. Roberts, *Conference Report*, April 1928, p. 112.

25. The paragraph was in the *Rochester Herald* (New York), 22 September 1923. (See also Roberts, *Conference Report*, October 1923, p. 90, and B. H. Roberts, *Comprehensive History of The Church of Jesus Christ of Latter-day Saints*, 6 vols. [Provo: Brigham Young University Press, 1957], 6:524.)

26. Roberts, *Comprehensive History*, 6:525-26.

27. B. H. Roberts, Biographical Notes, dictated in 1933, typescript, in possession of the author, p. 217.

28. See, for example, B. H. Roberts, "Ramah-Cumorah in the Land of Ripliancum," *Deseret News*, 3 March 1928, and "God the Father's Purposes in Creation," *Improvement Era* 29 (January 1926):230-37.

29. Roberts, "Originality of the Book of Mormon," *New Witnesses for God*, 3:166-219; cf. B. H. Roberts, "Originality of the Book of Mormon," *Improvement Era* 8 (September 1905):801-15 and (October 1905):882-902.

30. "Originality of the Book of Mormon," *Improvement Era* 8 (September 1905):8-10. See also Roberts, *New Witnesses for God*, 3:227.

31. B. H. Roberts, "A Master Stroke of Philosophy in the Book of Mormon," *Deseret News*, 16 June 1928. See reply by J. H. Paul, 23 June 1928. See also B. H. Roberts, "The Immortality of Man," *Improvement Era* 10 (April 1907):401-23; "Opposite Existences," *New Witnesses for God*, 3:219-27; and *The Seventy's Course in Theology*, 4th Yearbook, lessons 6-8, pp. 28-46.

32. Roberts, "Originality of the Book of Mormon," *Improvement Era* 8 (October 1905):900. See also pp. 801-15 and 882-902.

33. Roberts, *The Seventy's Course in Theology*, 4:113-14. He refers to major doctrinal sections of the Book of Mormon—2 Nephi 2; Alma 12, 34, and 42; and Mormon 9.

34. Roberts, *Conference Report*, April 1904, p. 16.

35. His most mature statement is in "God," *Discourses of B. H. Roberts* (Salt Lake City: Deseret Book Company, 1948), pp. 79-105; cf. Roberts, *Conference Report*, April 1924, pp. 76-80. He speaks of the Book of Mormon as an instrument to "stem the tide of unbelief" (p. 79) and establish the deity of Jesus Christ (p. 80).

36. B. H. Roberts, Subject Outline Book, 1924, MS, pp. 1-2, Church Archives.

37. Ibid., p. 8.

38. B. H. Roberts, *Handbook of the Restoration,* 1st ed. (Independence, Mo.: Zions Printing and Publishing Company, 1944), p. 318. See also pp. 318-42.

39. Oral History Recordings of Dr. John T. Emmett, 16 December 1967, p. 5. Elder Emmett was secretary to B. H. Roberts in the Eastern States Mission. Transcript in possession of the author.

40. Journals of James E. Talmage, 4 and 5 January 1922, Archives, Harold B. Lee Library, Brigham Young University, Provo. I am indebted to Sterling Albrecht for these references.

41. Ethan Smith, *View of the Hebrews,* Photomechanical Reprints, and "Parallels by Mormon Historian B. H. Roberts" (Salt Lake City: Modern Microfilms, n.d.).

42. The original is in the possession of the Roberts family. A xerox copy of that original has been placed in the Marriott Library at the University of Utah.

43. B. H. Roberts to the First Presidency and the Quorum of the Twelve, March 1923.

44. B. H. Roberts to Elizabeth Skolfield, 12 March 1932, in possession of John Noble Henchley.

45. Nibley, "Steel, Glass and Silk," *Lehi in the Desert,* pp. 210-16; cf. Nibley, *An Approach to the Book of Mormon* (Salt Lake City: Deseret News Press, 1964), pp. 64-65. See also Milton R. Hunter, "Chichén Itza Horse," *Archaeology and the Book of Mormon* (Salt Lake City: Deseret News Press, 1956), pp. 1-10; and "Archaeology and the Book of Mormon: Horses in Ancient America," part 6, *Improvement Era* 58 (October 1955):724-40, and part 7 (December 1955):898-99, 972-77.

46. As reported to the author in a 1978 conversation with Jack Christensen, who visited Roberts shortly before his death. Christensen had earlier provided Roberts with both the first and second editions of Ethan Smith's *View of the Hebrews.*

47. Ethan Smith, *View of the Hebrews,* Photomechanical Reprints, and "Parallels by Mormon Historian B. H. Roberts." "It would seem to indicate that B. H. Roberts had lost his faith in the Book of Mormon" (Introduction, p. 1).

48. Fawn Brodie, *No Man Knows My History,* rev. ed. (New York: Alfred A. Knopf, 1975), pp. 46-48.

49. Preston Nibley in conversation with the author, 1960.

50. B. H. Roberts to Elizabeth Skolfield, 23 April 1928, in possession of John Noble Henchley.

51. Roberts, *Conference Report,* April 1911, p. 58.

52. See Roberts, *Conference Report,* October 1905, pp. 44-45.

53. Roberts, *Conference Report,* April 1928, p. 112.

54. B. H. Roberts, "The Truth, the Way, the Life," vol. 3, chaps. 50, 51, and 52, MS, Church Archives.

55. Roberts, *Conference Report,* April 1930, p. 47.

56. Ibid., April 1911, pp. 57-59.

57. Ibid., pp. 59-60.

58. Ibid., October 1906, p. 65.

59. Ibid., April 1928, p. 107.

60. B. H. Roberts, *Discourses of B. H. Roberts,* p. 105.

61. Roberts, *Conference Report,* October 1923, p. 91.

62. Roberts, "The Translation of the Book of Mormon," p. 436.

2

John W. Welch

Chiasmus
in the
Book of Mormon

John W. Welch, an attorney specializing in tax matters, joined the faculty of the J. Reuben Clark Law School in 1980. He is the author of several articles on literary structure in the Book of Mormon. President of the Foundation for Ancient Research and Mormon Studies, he has contributed to BYU Studies and is co-author and general editor of the recently published book, Chiasmus in Antiquity. *He received a B.A. in history and an M.A. in classical languages from Brigham Young University, where he was valedictorian and became a Woodrow Wilson Fellow. He went on to study at Oxford University, and received his J.D. from Duke University in 1975. His research into literary forms in ancient scriptures led him to the original discovery in 1967 of chiasmus in the Book of Mormon. Chiasmus, a rhetorical device used prevalently in the Bible and in other ancient literatures, was relegated to the intellectual subconsciousness of modern Western civilization until the mid-*

nineteenth century. Since there is no evidence that anyone in America understood chiasmus in 1830 when the Book of Mormon was published, the remarkable presence of complex chiasms in the Book of Mormon testifies to the ancient origin of the text. It also amplifies the significance of central events and enhances interpretation of many scriptures.

From the day the Book of Mormon rolled off the press in 1830, those who gave it credence asserted that it obviously read like a Hebrew text. Those who were not so convinced insisted that it obviously read like anything but a Hebrew text.[1] Actually, all that became obvious was the failure of both believers and unbelievers to cite much specific evidence. However, numerous Hebrew characteristics of the Book of Mormon have been recognized in recent literature;[2] in addition to these we can now cite many specific passages which bear the distinct stamp of an ancient Hebraic literary form which scholars call *chiasmus.*

WHAT IS CHIASMUS?

Chiasmus appears to have begun as a structural form that later developed into an intriguing rhetorical device which has been used sporadically in prose and poetry for nearly three thousand years. Despite its long usage, awareness of the form in its extended instances remained, except in isolated cases, a part of the intellectual subconsciousness of modern Western Europe until frequent chiastic passages were discovered in the Bible. Since that time in the mid-nineteenth century, several reputable scholars, mostly theologians, have published on the subject. Their works indicate that, although chiasms appear in Greek, Latin, English, and other languages, the form was much more highly developed in Hebrew and dates to the oldest sections of the Hebrew Bible and beyond.

Chiasmus can be defined most simply as an inverted type of parallelism. Two lines of poetry are said to be parallel if the component elements of one line correspond directly to those of the other in a one-to-one relationship. There are numerous examples of direct parallelism in Proverbs, e.g.,

A soft answer turneth away wrath:
But grievous words stir up anger.
(Proverbs 15:1)

If the second line of a parallelism is inverted, that is to say, if its last element is placed first and the first, last, then a chiasm is created, as, for example, in the following verse:

For *my* thoughts are not *your* thoughts,
Neither are *your* ways *my* ways, saith the Lord.
(Isaiah 55:8)

And from the New Testament:

He that *findeth* his life shall *lose* it:
And he that *loseth* his life for my sake shall *find* it.
(Matthew 10:39)

Formulating this graphically, the simple chiasm takes on the form of a χ:

The name *chiasmus,* derived from chi (χ), the twenty-second letter in the Greek alphabet, and the Greek *chiazein* ("to mark with a χ"), is thus descriptive of the form itself.

As a literary device, chiasmus has proved durable and useful because of its many applications. For example, Heraclitus, one of the earliest Greek philosophers, used chiasmus to accentuate his notion of eternal flux and opposition:

Cold things grow warm,
What is warm cools;

the moist dries,
the dry dampens. (Fragment 39)

Immortals are mortal,
mortals are immortal,

each living the others' death
and dying the others' life. (Fragment 67)

Several centuries later, Cicero effectively used chiastic lines as a rhetorical device for placing emphasis:

Matrem habemus, ignoramus patrem. (*Republic* 2:33)

Some English authors, perhaps influenced by their training in the classics, used chiasmus in poetry. In Pope's "Essay on Man" this short chiasm appears:

. . . flame lawless through the void,
Destroying others, by himself destroyed.
                    (2.65-66)

Even in our modern nursery rhymes and maxims, the natural rhythm and immediate appeal of chiastic lines is apparent. Thus, "Old King Cole was a merry old soul, and a merry old soul was he" is charming; and "He who fails to prepare, prepares to fail" sounds solid and convincing.

The reader, however, will notice that all these chiasms contain only two elements, whose order is then reversed. This is significant in differentiating the relatively simple chiasmus known for some time in the West from the much more complex chiasmus characteristic of Hebrew and other such ancient languages. Whereas in languages such as Greek, Latin, and English, chiasms are most often composed of two elements, in Hebrew there appears to be no limit to the number of terms or ideas that may commonly be employed. A chiasm may be expanded to include any number of terms written first in one order and then exactly in the reverse order, i.e.,

a-b-c-d- . . . -x-x- . . . -d-c-b-a.

Such structures might be several verses or even several chapters long. A simple illustration of this, with five elements in an inverted parallelism, is found in Psalm 3:7-8:[3]

Save me
  O my God,
    For thou hast smitten
     All my enemies
      On the cheek-bone
      The teeth
     Of the wicked
    Thou hast broken.
  To Yahweh
The salvation.

A second example comes from Isaiah 60:1-3:

Arise,
  Shine,
    For thy light is come,
     And the glory
      Of Yahweh
       Upon thee is risen.
        For behold, dimness shall cover the earth
        And gross darkness the peoples.
       But upon thee will arise
      Yahweh
     And his glory shall upon thee be seen
    And nations shall come to thy light
   And kings to the brightness
Of thy rising.

There are several good reasons why a literary form of this peculiar type was particularly attractive to the ancient Hebrews. First, chiasms are easy to memorize. The Hebrew tradition, unlike the written Greek tradition, was oral. Not only were manuscripts and scrolls scarce, but there were also few who could read them. Therefore, the tales of early Israel and the songs of her prophets were handed down through generations by word of mouth, and long passages of the Torah were committed to memory.[4] In their memorization and recitation, the ancients were surely aided by chiastic groupings and repetitions. Second, chiasmus was simply a vogue. Just as sixteenth-century English poets were fond of the sonnet, chiasmus seems to have been preferred by many of the ancient Hebrew writers of the Old Testament. Third, the form can be very pleasing aesthetically because of its vast potential to coordinate abrupt juxta-positions within a single unified literary system while focusing simultaneously on a point of central concern. Furthermore, and perhaps most significantly, chiasmus afforded a seriously needed element of internal organization in ancient writing, which did not have paragraphs, punctuation, capitalization, and other such synthetic devices to demarcate the conclusion of one idea and the commencement of the next. Ancient texts were written in a steady stream of letters from the beginning of a book to the end, sometimes even without spaces between the words. Chiastic or other parallel forms, therefore, could serve an important organizational function by indicating units of thought or sections of text. Finally, ancient religious literature frequently served liturgical purposes, and the structure of chiastic writing may have made it suitable for use in certain ritual settings requiring alternate recitations.

Chiasmus remained a common literary device in much of ancient literature and was one which was expressly recognized, for example, by the scholiasts in Alexandria in the second century B.C. But the form, especially in its more elaborate mani-festations, appears to have fallen into disuse and obscurity in the first centuries after Christ, when many ancient institutions from Greek, Roman, Jewish, and other civilizations underwent great change, if not destruction, and when more familiar modern manners of writing began to develop.

The rediscovery of chiasmus in the Bible can be credited to three theologians of the nineteenth century: Robert Lowth, John Jebb, and John Forbes. Lowth, the Bishop of London, and Jebb, the Bishop of Limerick, both wrote 300-page volumes describing Hebraisms in the holy scriptures.[5] Although both made initial observations of the chiastic form, their emphasis was placed almost entirely on poetic imagery and direct paral-lelism, and only Jebb paid much attention to *epanodos* (the Greek term he used to describe inverted parallelism). In 1854, however, John Forbes completed a much more extensive study, *The Symmetrical Structures of Scripture.*[6] With the publication of Forbes's book, it is possible to begin speaking of relatively well-developed appreciation of chiastic forms in the Bible. Since then numerous other writers have utilized a knowledge of the form in critical studies of the holy scriptures, indicating that it has been recognized as genuine and significant.[7]

CHIASMUS IN THE OLD AND NEW TESTAMENTS

As the Old Testament represents the earliest extant Hebrew writings, it is the best evidence of the antiquity and general nature of chiasmus as developed by the Hebrews. Based on his detailed modern analysis of biblical chiasmus, Nils Lund has formulated seven rules of chiastic passages, three of which are most interesting for this study.[8] The first states that the center of the passage is always the turning point. The third notes that identical ideas will often be distributed so as to occur at the beginning, middle, and end of a chiasm, but nowhere else. The seventh claims that there is often a mixture of directly parallel and inverted parallel lines in the same unit. These characteristics are readily apparent in the following biblical passages:

Example 1

And all flesh *died* that moved upon the *earth,*
  Both birds,
    And cattle,
    And beasts,
      And every creeping thing that creepeth upon
        the earth,
      And every man:
        All in whose nostrils was the breath of the
          spirit of *life*
        Of all that was on the *dry land*
        Died;
        And was destroyed
        Every *living* thing
      That was upon the face of the *ground*
      Both man,
    And creeping things,
   (And beasts),
    And cattle,
  And birds of the heavens,
And they were *destroyed* from the *earth.*
        (Genesis 7:21-23)

Example 2

Seek ye me, and ye shall *live.*
  But seek not after *Bethel,*
    Nor enter into *Gilgal,*
      And pass not to Beer-sheba:
      For *Gilgal shall* shall surely go into captivity,
  And *Bethel* shall come to naught.
Seek Yahweh, and ye shall *live.* (Amos 5:4b-6a)

Example 3

Do ye indeed, O *gods,* speak *righteousness*?
Do ye *judge* uprightly, O ye sons of men?

  Nay, in the heart ye work *wickedness*
  Ye weigh out the *violence* of your hands in the earth.

    The wicked are estranged from the *womb*
    They go astray as soon as they are born, speaking
        lies.

      Their poison is like the poison of a *serpent*
      Like the deaf adder that stoppeth her ear
      Which hearkeneth not to the voice of charmers,
      The most cunning binder of spells.

      O God,
        Break
          Their teeth in their mouth;
          The great teeth of the young lions
        Break out
      O Yahweh.

      They shall melt away like waters,
      They shall go away for them,
      Like tender grass which wilts away.
      Like a *snail* will melt as it goes along.

    Abortions of a *woman*
    That have not beheld the sun!

  The righteous shall rejoice when he seeth the
        vengeance
  He shall wash his feet in the blood of the *wicked.*

And men shall say, surely there is a reward for the
      righteous
Surely there is a *God* that *judgeth* the earth. (Psalm 58)

Example 4

Therefore I speak to them in *parables:*
   Because they seeing *see* not; and hearing they *hear* not.
    In them is fulfilled the *prophecy* of Esaias which
         sayeth
     By hearing ye shall *hear* not; and seeing ye shall
        see not
      For this people's *heart* is waxed gross
      And their *ears* are dull of *hearing*
       And their *eyes* they have closed
        lest at any time they should *see*
       With their *eyes*
      And *hear* with their *ears,*
     And should understand with their *heart* and be
        converted.
    Blessed are your eyes, for they *see* and your ears,
      for they *hear*
   Many *prophets* and righteous men
   Have longed to *see* what you see and *hear* what you
      hear and have not.
Hear ye therefore the *parable* of the sower.
                 (Matthew 13:13-18)

CHIASMUS IN THE BOOK OF MORMON

We now turn to the question of chiasmus in the Book of Mormon. The first chapter of the book claims that it was written in "the language of the Egyptians" but according to "the learning of the Jews" (1 Nephi 1:2); that is, it was written with Egyptian characters and elements but in Hebraic style. If the Book of Mormon truly is a direct translation of a text formulated in accordance with ancient Hebrew learning, chiasmus might well be present as an integral part of its literary style. If so, an understanding of chiasmus should be helpful in interpreting and understanding the design of the total book.

If chiasmus can be convincingly identified in the Book of Mormon, it will testify of the book's ancient origin. No one in America, let alone in western New York, fully understood chiasmus in 1830. Joseph Smith had been dead ten full years before John Forbes's book was published in Scotland. Even many prominent Bible scholars today know little about chiastic forms beyond the name and a few passages where they might be found. The possibility of Joseph Smith's noticing the form accidentally is also remote, since most biblical passages containing inverted word orders have been rearranged into natural word orders in the King James translation. Even had he known of the form, he would still have had the overwhelming task of writing original, artistic chiastic sentences. Try writing a sonnet or a multi-termed chiasm yourself: your appreciation of these forms will turn to awe. If the Book of Mormon is found to contain true chiastic forms in an ancient style, then is not the book's own repeated claim to be the product of an ancient culture veritably substantiated?

An understanding of chiasmus will also greatly enhance interpretation of Book of Mormon scriptures. If the ancient authors of the Book of Mormon consciously set particular elements parallel to each other, then these elements must be considered together in order to be fully understood in their complete context. Moreover, the thoughts which appear at the center of a chiastic passage must always be given special attention, and any antithetical ideas introduced at the turning point must be contrasted with their properly corresponding ideas. Knowledge of chiasmus will clarify questions of structure within shorter passages and of unity within whole books.[9] For example, why Nephi divided his writings into two books, instead of leaving them all in one, will be explained by chiasmus. Stylistic devices, especially the frequent repetitions which have often been seen as ignorant and redundant, will be appreciated in the light in which they originally shone.

Chiasms may appear anywhere in the Book of Mormon, although they primarily typify the style of only three of the numerous authors—Nephi, Benjamin, and Alma the Younger. These writers use chiasms in practically every possible context, from passages of straight narration or argumentation to others of beautiful poetic eloquence. The following examples speak for themselves and require little further explanation.

Example 1

The *Jews*
  shall have the *words*
    of the *Nephites,*
    and the *Nephites*
  shall have the *words*
of the *Jews;*

and the *Nephites* and the *Jews*
  shall have the *words*
    of the lost tribes of *Israel;*
    and the lost tribes of *Israel*
  shall have the *words* of
the *Nephites* and the *Jews.*

(2 Nephi 29:13)

Example 2

But men drink damnation to their own souls except
  they *humble* themselves
    and become as little *children,*
      and believe that salvation . . . is . . . in and through
        the *atoning blood of Christ, the*
        Lord . . .
    For the *natural man*
      is an enemy to *God,*
        and *has been* from the fall of Adam,
        and *will be,* forever and ever,
        unless he yields to the enticings of the *Holy*
        Spirit,
    and putteth off the *natural man*
    and becometh a saint through the *atonement of*
      Christ the Lord,
  and becometh as a *child,*
submissive, meek, *humble* . . .

(Mosiah 3:18-19)

Example 3

Whosoever shall not take upon him the *name of Christ*
    must be *called* by some other name;
        therefore, he findeth himself on the *left hand of*
            God.
    And I would that ye should *remember* also, that
            this is the name . . .
        that never should be *blotted out,*
            except it be through *transgression;*
                therefore,
            take heed that ye do not *transgress,*
        that the name be not *blotted out* of your
            hearts. . . .
    I would that ye should *remember* to retain the
            name . . .
        that ye are not found on the *left hand of God,*
    but that ye hear and know the voice by which ye shall
            be *called,*
and also, the *name* by which he shall call you.
                (Mosiah 5:10-12)

Needless to say, the word order in these last two examples is
especially striking. These passages are just two small parts of the
very complex chiastic structure of King Benjamin's entire
speech.[10] His use of chiasmus is not illogical: at the time that he
delivered this famous speech, he was acting in a traditional
coronation and would naturally be using the most traditional
and convincing rhetoric at his command. Benjamin's thoughts
had been carefully prepared beforehand and had even been
"written and sent forth among those that were not under the
sound of his voice" (Mosiah 2:8). This degree of painstaking
deliberation in writing was the rule, rather than the exception,
among the Book of Mormon prophets. In cases such as these,
chiasmus is used to give emphasis to points of special
importance.

Example 4

And they said unto me: We have not; for the Lord
                maketh no such thing *known unto us.*
    Behold, I said unto them: How is it that ye do not
            keep the *commandments* of the Lord?

How is it that ye will *perish,*
　because of the *hardness of your hearts?*
　　Do ye not remember the things which the *Lord*
　　　hath said?
—If ye will not *harden your hearts,*
and ask me in *faith,* believing that ye shall receive,
with diligence in keeping my *commandments,*
surely these things shall be *made known unto you.*
(1 Nephi 15:9-11)

A chiasm may also appear as a logical device, for its completeness rounds out a thought forcefully and ties in all loose ends tightly. Nephi so successfully used the foregoing line of reasoning against his rebellious brothers that, as he later recorded the events of his family's lengthy journey to the New World, he could still recall his unanswerable rebuttal. The turning point of the argument is a piercing question: "Do ye not remember the things which the Lord hath said?" The same thought, concerning that which the Lord has said or will say, appropriately appears at the extremes as well as in the middle of this chiasm. Notice also that the first half of the chiasm contains the words of Nephi, while the second half is built from the words of the Lord, comprising a deft shift at the center. What better debate partner could Nephi have in his parallelism than the Lord? The only key terms in the passage which are parallel but not identical are *perish* and *ask in faith.* Perhaps Nephi uses them to contrast the living strength of true faith with the fear of death which accompanies any traveler through the wilderness.

Example 5

A　Behold, the Lord hath created the *earth* that it
　　　　should be inhabited;
　　and he hath created his children that they should
　　　　possess it.

　　B　And he raiseth up
　　　　　　　　　　a righteous
　　　　　　　　　　nation,
　　　　and destroyeth
　　　　　　　　　　the nations
　　　　　　　　　　of the wicked.

B '   And he leadeth away
        the righteous
                  into precious lands,
        and the wicked
    he destroyeth,
                  and curseth the land
                  unto them for their
                  sakes.

A '   He ruleth high in the heavens,
       for it is his throne,
    and this *earth*
       is his footstool.
            (1 Nephi 17:36-39)

This passage is an intricate gem. It masterfully combines direct parallelisms with inverted parallelisms. Parts A and A ' each contain two directly parallel thoughts, in A the Lord's creation of the earth and the creation of his children, and in A ' the Lord's throne and his footstool. It is interesting that the word *earth* appears in both A and A '. Parts B and B ' are built of four poetical lines, each containing three parts. In both B and B ', two of the three parts are inverted when they reappear the second time, i.e.,

    righteous / nation
    nations / of the wicked

    he leadeth away / the righteous
    the wicked / he destroyeth

Furthermore, these inverted parts come at the end of the lines in B but at the beginning of the lines in B '. This leaves the words *raiseth up* and *destroyeth* at the beginning of B and *precious lands* and *curseth the land* at the end of B' in direct parallel form. Thus another chiasm is formed between the directly parallel portions of B and B ' and the inverted portions of B and B ', i.e.,

         B   inverted   direct
         B '   direct   inverted

For extra measure the first line in B and the first line in B′ express the same idea, the blessing of the righteous, while the second line in B and the second line in B′ both express the idea of being punished. So in the midst of inverted parallelisms, the direct parallelism is also skillfully maintained.

Example 6

A   1 And, notwithstanding we believe in Christ, we keep the *law of Moses,*
        2 and look forward with *steadfastness unto Christ,*
        3 until the *law* shall be *fulfilled.*
        4 For, for this *end was the law given;*

B   wherefore the *law* hath become *dead unto us,* and we are made *alive in Christ* because of our faith;
        yet we keep the *law* because of the commandments.

    C And we talk of Christ,
        we rejoice in Christ,
        we preach of Christ,
        we *prophesy* of Christ,

    C′ and we write according to our *prophecies,*
        that our children may know
        to what source they may look
        for a remission of their sins.

B′   Wherefore, we speak concerning the *law* that our children may know the *deadness of the law;*
        and . . . may look forward unto that *life* which is *in Christ,*

A′   4 and know for what *end the law was given.*
        3 And after the *law* is *fulfilled*
      2 *in Christ,* that they need not *harden* their hearts against him
    1 when the *law* ought to be done away.
        (2 Nephi 25:24-27)

Example 7

A   The meaning of the *word restoration* is to bring
     back again

    B   evil for evil,
       or carnal for carnal,
       or devilish for devilish—

w_1w_2 *good* for that which is *good;*

    x_1x_2 *righteous* for that which is *righteous*

       y_1y_2 *just* for that which is *just;*

          z_1z_2 *merciful* for that which is *merciful.*
                Therefore, my son, see that you
                are

          z'_2 *merciful* unto your brethren;

       y'_2 deal *justly,*

    x'_2 judge *righteously,*

w'_2 and do *good* continually;

                and if ye do all these things then
                shall ye receive your reward; yea,

          z'_1 ye shall have *mercy* restored unto
              you again;

       y'_1 ye shall have *justice* restored unto you
           again;

    x'_1 ye shall have a *righteous* judgement
        restored unto you again;

w'_1 and ye shall have *good* rewarded unto you
        again.

    B′   For that which ye do send out
       shall return unto you again,
       and be restored;

A′   therefore, the *word restoration* more fully
    condemneth the sinner, and justifieth him not at all.
               (Alma 41:13-15)

The twist here is clever: after listing four pairs of terms, Alma pairs two lists of four terms and reverses their order at the same time. Or to use a chiasm to describe this chiasm: Alma writes a list of pairs and then a pair of lists. The chiasmus here reaches yet a further level, since the first nominatives in the list of pairs (w_1, x_1, y_1, and z_1) and the last list in the pair of lists (w'_1, x'_1, y'_1 and z'_1) both describe the reward to be received, while the second nominatives (w_2, x_2, y_2 and z_2) and the first of the separate lists (w'_2, x'_2, y'_2, and z'_2) describe the attributes necessary to obtain those rewards. In all seriousness, a great play on words.

By far the most subtle use of chiasmus is its role in the structural design of longer passages and books. The book of Mosiah, for example, utilizes a chiastic structure in its underlying organization, at the expense of chronological order.[11] Like the book of Mosiah, the book of 1 Nephi, King Benjamin's speech, and Alma chapter 36 also use a chiastic framework as a foundation. Of this group, only Alma 36 is sufficiently brief for effective illustration here of the way in which complex chiasmus can be employed in a longer passage to emphasize a central theme.[12] In this chapter Alma recounts to his son Helaman the story of his conversion. Contrary to what one might be led to believe from Alma's earlier account of his conversion (Mosiah 27:10-31), the supernatural events associated with his conversion were not of primary importance to him as he remembered them in his more mature years. The structure of the chapter shows that Alma's conversion centered instead upon a spiritual confrontation in which Alma turned to Jesus Christ for deliverance from his sins:

Example 8

My son, give ear to my words (1)
  Keep the commandments and ye shall prosper in the
      land (1)
    Do as I have done (2)
      Captivity of our fathers—their bondage (2)
      He surely did deliver them (2)
        Trust in God (3)

Support in trials, troubles and afflictions (3)
I know this not of myself but of God (4)
Born of God (5)

Alma seeks to harm the church (6)
Limbs paralyzed (10)
Fear of the presence of God (14)
Pains of a damned soul (16)
Alma remembers one Jesus Christ (17)
Christ will atone for the sins of the
world (17)
Alma calls upon Jesus Christ (18)
Joy as exceeding as the pain (20)
Longing to be with God (22)
Use of limbs returns (23)
Alma seeks to bring souls unto God (24)

Born of God (26)
My knowledge is of God (26)
Supported under trials, troubles, and
afflictions (27)
Trust in him (27)
He will deliver me (27)
Egypt—captivity (28-29)
Know as I do know (30)
Keep the commandments and ye shall prosper in the
land (30)
This is according to his word (30)
(Alma 36)

Given our twentieth-century understanding of chiastic writings
and their historical occurrences, this one chapter is strong evidence that the Book of Mormon was not written in the nineteenth century.

This chapter is as extensive and precise as any chiastic
passage I am aware of in ancient literature. Besides having
practical structural value, chiasmus has a distinct charm and
beauty in a passage such as this. The first ten verses and the last
eight form an artistic frame around the central motif which
contrasts the agony of conversion with the joy of conversion. In
the center Alma makes this contrast explicit, when he says in
verse 20, "my soul was filled with joy as exceeding as was my
pain." No literary device could make this contrast more force-

fully than chiasmus. Moreover, chiasmus allows Alma to place the very turning point of his entire life exactly at the turning point of this chapter: Christ, because of the effects of the future atonement, belongs at the center of both. Compared with the abrupt antithetic parallelisms found in the recounting of this incident recorded in Mosiah 27, the chiasmus in Alma 36 is monumental and meaningful. The chiastic structure amplifies the significance of Alma's conversion and the centrality of spiritual realities around which it turned.

Conclusion

The intent of this article is to introduce one concept of formal analysis into Book of Mormon studies. The form which has been examined is chiasmus, a basic element of ancient literature, particularly that of the ancient Hebrews. Although all knowledge of this form lay dormant for centuries, it was rediscovered and reexplored in the nineteenth century when formal criticism began to emerge. But by the time the concept of chiasmus received currency or recognition, the Book of Mormon had long been in print. Since the Book of Mormon contains numerous chiasms, it thus becomes logical to consider the book a product of the ancient world and to judge its literary qualities accordingly. The book reviewed in this way is moving; it deserves to be read more carefully.

NOTES

1. See Parley P. Pratt, *A Voice of Warning* (Salt Lake City: Deseret Book, 1920), p. 105 (the first edition of this book was published in 1837); and Bruce Kinney, *Mormonism, the Islam of America* (New York: F. H. Revell, 1912), p. 60.

2. Hugh Nibley has researched Hebrew and Near Eastern aspects of the Book of Mormon in detail; his previous works dealing with the subject include *Lehi in the Desert and The World of the Jaredites* (Salt Lake City: Bookcraft, 1952), *An Approach to the Book of Mormon,* 2d ed. (Salt Lake City: Deseret Book Co., 1964), and *Since Cumorah: The Book of Mormon in the Modern World* (Salt Lake City: Deseret Book Co., 1967).

3. Many chiasms have not survived the King James translation although they may be crystal clear in the Hebrew. To the extent the following examples

vary from the King James Version, they are verbatim translations from the Hebrew or Greek.

4. Paul Gaechter, *Die literarische Kunst im Matthäus-Evangelium* (Stuttgart: Verlag Katholisches Bibelwerk, 1965), p. 6.

5. Robert Lowth, *De Sacra Poesi Hebraeorum Praelectiones Academicae,* translated by G. Gregory, new edition with notes by Calvin E. Stowe (Andover, Mass., 1829); and John Jebb, *Sacred Literature* (London, 1820). See also Thomas Boys, *Tactica Sacra* (London, 1824) and *Key to the Book of Psalms* (London, 1825).

6. John Forbes, *The Symmetrical Structure of Scripture* (Edinburgh: T. & T. Clark, 1854).

7. An extensive bibliography of scholarly works utilizing chiasmus can be found in John W. Welch, ed., *Chiasmus in Antiquity* (Hildesheim: Gerstenberg Verlag, 1981).

8. Nils Lund, *Chiasmus in the New Testament* (Chapel Hill: University of North Carolina Press, 1942), pp. 40-41. To these rules, I would add the following principles for use in testing for chiasmus: (1) chiasmus should be relatively self-evident, encompassing a complete literary unit within the text, and not forced upon a partial passage artificially; (2) it generally does not occur where other organizing schemes are primary (i.e., "Hickory, Dickory, Dock" is not chiastic because it is a limerick); (3) it should take into account every predominant word or thought in the unit, and similarly should not rely upon insignificant or dispensable parts of speech; and (4) in the absence of a very well-defined crossing effect or inversion at a center point which is also the central or turning point in the meaning of the passage, only the most obvious patterns should be called chiastic.

9. The first edition of the Book of Mormon was printed in standard paragraph form without verses. Arbitrary chapter divisions appear in the 1830 edition (1 Nephi with seven, 2 Nephi with fifteen, etc.). The current chapter divisions and separation into verses were made by Orson Pratt in 1879. Therefore, one need not be concerned to take chapter and verse into account when studying the structure of a passage.

10. Discussed in detail in my thesis, "A Study Relating Chiasmus in the Book of Mormon to Chiasmus in the Old Testament, Ugaritic Epics, Homer and Selected Greek and Latin Authors" (M.A. thesis, Brigham Young University, 1970), pp. 135-50.

11. Ibid., pp. 150-51, 170.

12. Such a detailed analysis of a twenty-two-chapter book, 1 Nephi, is attempted by Noel B. Reynolds in chapter 3 of this volume.

3

Noel B. Reynolds

Nephi's Outline

Noel B. Reynolds is Associate Academic Vice-President and Professor of Philosophy and Government at Brigham Young University. He was a college valedictorian at Brigham Young, and went on to receive his M.A. and Ph.D. from Harvard University in political theory and philosophy, where he received numerous awards, including the Richard M. Weaver and the Harvard Graduate Prize fellowships. He has more recently completed postdoctoral work at Harvard as a Fellow in Law and Philosophy. He has also served as chairman of the BYU Department of Philosophy and has taught at the J. Reuben Clark Law School. He has published articles on legal philosophy and related topics and is currently completing a volume on Plato's politics. In this article, Reynolds departs from his philosophical studies and explores the "wealth of exactly ordered detail" in 1 Nephi of the Book of Mormon. He describes a com-

plex chiastic structure based on both standard and inverted parallelism throughout the book. These rhetorical patterns, Reynolds argues, have specific purpose—they develop and prove "Nephi's thesis" of 1 Nephi 1:20, and distinguish 1 Nephi from 2 Nephi. Further, as Joseph Smith had no way to be aware of such elaborate literary structures, it seems evident that their presence in the Book of Mormon testifies of truly ancient origins.

There are at least two distinct reasons to examine the literary structure of the Book of Mormon. For those who recognize the Book of Mormon as sacred scripture, such a study can enhance their appreciation of its teachings. For others, a literary analysis provides a subtle test of the skeptical hypothesis that this book is a unique product of early nineteenth-century American folk culture. Although the Book of Mormon has been of central importance to both of these groups for a century and a half, it is surprising to discover that very few members of either group have examined it from literary or cultural perspectives. Hugh Nibley's invaluable comparison of the Book of Mormon with ancient Near Eastern culture and John Welch's ground-breaking discovery of ancient literary patterns in the Book of Mormon are among the few such analyses, as is Richard Bushman's insightful and sensitive comparison of Nephite political assumptions with those of early nineteenth-century Americans.[1]

The scriptural text which we refer to as the small plates of Nephi was apparently known to the ancient Nephites first as the plates of Nephi and later as the plates of Jacob, a name which distinguished it from the plates of Nephi or the large plates.[2] Although Nephi refers frequently to the commandment to write the small plates, it becomes apparent only late in his narrative that this commandment was not received until some thirty years after the departure from Jerusalem. Furthermore, it also appears that it took him approximately ten years to write the first twenty-five chapters.[3] This ten-year writing period, based on a perspective of thirty years, gave Nephi both the distance and the time he needed to devise a highly complex account with a carefully fashioned rhetorical structure.

As I undertook an analysis of Nephi's writings, I was first impressed with their episodic character. Nephi's story reports a number of diverse, selected events which, on first impression, seemed loosely structured and plagued with the author's repetitious moralizing. There seemed to be no clear reason for dividing 1 Nephi from the first several chapters of 2 Nephi, as the latter book continues the same story.

Renewed analysis, however, reveals that 1 Nephi is an extended argument based on a thesis which the author announces near the beginning of his narrative and repeats in many forms throughout the book: "Behold, I, Nephi, *will show unto you* that the tender mercies of the Lord are over all those whom he hath chosen, because of their faith, to make them mighty even unto the power of deliverance" (1 Nephi 1:20).[4] Taking this thesis for a guide and rereading 1 Nephi, we discover that the entire book is a compilation of approximately thirty proofs of this idea that the Lord will deliver those who obey him and endure in faith.[5]

Nephi supports his thesis with a wide variety of evidence designed to appeal especially to the "stiffnecked" and "hard-hearted," such as his own brothers, as well as to the righteous. He reports six incidents during his family's journey to the promised land in which the Lord interposes himself: by the power of his Spirit, by the appearance and speech of an angel, by his voice, by shock, and also by his power in a tempest at sea. Each of these stories demonstrates that victory does finally come to the faithful in even the most difficult assignments.

An additional range of evidence is drawn from similar stories and experiences from the history of Israel as recorded on the brass plates. Prophecies from the brass plates constitute a further series of proofs for Nephi's thesis, as do the visions and prophecies received by him and his father. Most significant of these proofs is the atonement of Jesus Christ, as revealed to the prophets. For, ultimately, it is by the power of the Atonement that men can be delivered from their greatest enemy, if they will be faithful.

Nephi's faith, as manifest in his writing, is consistently poised against the murmurings and doubtings of his faithless brothers. His primary purpose is to persuade those whose faith might be weak but who may be receptive. Laman and Lemuel must be persuaded many times; Sariah only once. Nephi repeats his thesis frequently in one form or another so that we cannot fail to see how each of his proofs constitutes independent evidence of the mercy shown by the Lord to the faithful. Finally, the seriousness and the importance of the thesis are dramatically emphasized because both Lehi and Nephi consciously stake their lives on the thesis—with wonderful results.

The recognition that 1 Nephi is a carefully developed argument reveals Nephi as a great champion of the teaching that men must rely on the arm of the Lord and that the Lord will always prepare the way for the faithful to fulfill the commandments given to them, regardless of the opposition they face.

Yet further analysis reveals a far more complex structure. At the beginning of the book, Nephi explains that he will first make an abridgment of his father's record, then an account of his own doings. Beginning at chapter 10, he states that he will now commence with an account of his own proceedings, reign, and ministry. At the end of chapter 9, as at the end of chapter 22 (the last chapter in 1 Nephi), Nephi concludes with a restatement of his thesis, punctuated by the formal ending, "And thus it is. Amen."[6] The suggestion seems to be that there are two records, an abridgment of Lehi's record followed by an account of Nephi's proceedings, but if those few verses were removed, we would never suspect two records. The story is continuous; Nephi is the narrator of the entire book from beginning to end. And the very next verse continues the speech of Lehi that was interrupted to end chapter 9. We know of Lehi's teachings through Nephi's report, not through a condensation of Lehi's own record. So why does Nephi divide the book in this seemingly arbitrary manner? He even mentions parenthetically that "it mattereth not" to him that he be particular to give a full account of all of the doings of his father . . . "for the fulness of mine intent is that I [Nephi] may persuade men to come unto the God of Abraham, and the God of Isaac, and the God of Jacob, and be saved" (1 Nephi 6:3-4).

The answer seems to be not that there are two distinct records in 1 Nephi, but rather that the book is divided into two parallel structures. The verses previously referred to serve primarily to call our attention to that structural division. A comparison of these two structural halves reveals that the major elements of each portion are directly parallel to each other (see Table 1).[7]

This table raises two questions: First, are the similarities as real as they appear to be, and were they intentionally designed by Nephi? Second, why are elements 3, 5, 9, and 11 rearranged in Nephi's account? The answers that emerge to these questions are very helpful in understanding Nephi's overall intent.

One way to answer the first question is simply to read through the entire book, making a detailed comparison. The more obvious parallels appearing in the same order in both accounts are: the statements that Nephi will make a record of his proceedings, the record of the visions and prophecies of Lehi, the discussions of Nephi's desire to know the mysteries of God and his subsequent prophecies and visions, the mention of seeds gathered for use in the promised land, Nephi's discussion of the distinctions between the two sets of plates he is making, the preaching and prophesying to Laman and Lemuel, and the formal endings conjoined with restatements of Nephi's thesis.

The other elements of the comparison are not so obviously parallel. These include the six stories of experiences from the journey of Lehi's family, comprising the three longest elements in both Nephi's and Lehi's accounts (see Table 2 below). As we begin to compare the three stories which appear in Lehi's account with the three appearing in Nephi's, it becomes evident that there are conscious pairings between the two groups. There are too many points of direct resemblance on each side for coincidence.

TABLE 1

Lehi's Account Compared to Nephi's Account

(A) 1 Nephi 1-9 (Lehi's Account)	(B) 1 Nephi 10-22 (Nephi's Account)
1. Nephi makes a record (or account) of his proceedings but first gives an abridgment of Lehi's record (1:1-3, 16-17).	1. Nephi now commences to give an account of his proceedings, reign, and ministry but first "must speak somewhat of the things of [his] father, and . . . brethren" (10:1).
2. Nephi gives a brief account of Lehi's prophecies to the Jews, based on visions he received in Jerusalem (1:5-15, 19).	2. Nephi reports Lehi's prophecies about the Jews, as given to Laman and Lemuel in the wilderness (10:2-15).
3. Lehi is commanded to journey into the wilderness, and he pitches his tent in the valley he names Lemuel (2:1-7).	3. Nephi desires to see, hear, and know these mysteries; he is shown a great vision by the Spirit of the Lord and by an angel (10:17-14:30).
4. Lehi teaches and exhorts his sons, and they are confounded (2:8-15).	4. Nephi instructs and exhorts his brothers, and they are confounded (15:6-16:6).
5. Nephi desires to know the mysteries of God; he is visited by the Holy Spirit and is spoken to by the Lord (2:16-3:1	5. Lehi is commanded to journey further into the wilderness, and he pitches his tent in the land he names Bountiful (16:9-17:6).
6. Lehi is commanded in a dream to send his sons for the brass plates of Laban; this he does (3:2-5:22).	6. Nephi is commanded by the voice of the Lord to construct a ship; this he does (17:7-18:4).
7. In response to a command from the Lord, Lehi sends for Ishmael's family (7:1-22).	7. In response to a command from the Lord, Lehi enters the ship and then sails (18:5-23).
8. They gather seeds of every kind (8:1).	8. Lehi's family plants the seeds and reaps in abundance (18:24).
9. Lehi reports to his sons details of the great vision received in the wilderness (8:2-35).	9. Nephi details the distinctions between the two sets of plates (19:1-7).
10. Lehi exhorts Laman and Lemuel, preaching and prophesying to them (8:36-38).	10. Nephi preaches and prophesies to Laman and Lemuel, his descendants, and all Israel (19:7-21:26).
11. Nephi makes a distinction between the two sets of plates (9:1-5).	11. To explain Isaiah's prophecies to his brothers, Nephi draws on the great vision given to him and Lehi (22:1-28).
12. Nephi ends with a general formulation of his thesis and the formal punctuation: "And thus it is. Amen" (9:6).	12. Nephi ends with the highest formulation of his thesis, focusing on the salvation of man, and with the formal punctuation: "And thus it is. Amen" (22:29-31).

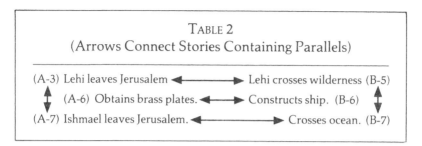

TABLE 2
(Arrows Connect Stories Containing Parallels)

(A-3) Lehi leaves Jerusalem ◄─────► Lehi crosses wilderness (B-5)

    (A-6) Obtains brass plates. ◄───► Constructs ship. (B-6)

(A-7) Ishmael leaves Jerusalem. ◄─────► Crosses ocean. (B-7)

Compare, for example, the story of the trip to bring back Ishmael and his family (A-7) with the story of the journey to the ship (B-7):

1. Both accounts are prefaced in the usual way by a command given to Lehi.

2. In each case Nephi's brothers first became rebellious because of their afflictions and lack of faith.

3. After Nephi's exhortations, they rebel against him and bind him with cords.

4. In the first story Nephi is given power from God to burst his bonds, but in the second he specifies that the Lord permitted him to be bound for a purpose.

5. In both instances one of Ishmael's daughters and others plead with Laman and Lemuel to reconcile themselves with Nephi.

6. In the first story they are successful, but in the second these pleas fail and the older brothers are persuaded to relent only when the power of God threatens them with destruction by a storm.

7. In each case relief comes as Nephi prays.

8. Both times Laman and Lemuel repent of their actions.

This analysis shows eight analogous items in the same order in two completely different stories which occupy parallel positions in the structural halves of 1 Nephi. The strength of the claim of parallelism between these two stories does not rest primarily on the uniqueness of the matched items, as only two elements in the series of eight are unique to these two stories. Rather, as in examples which will follow, the strength of the claim rests on the precise order of the parallel elements within each episode.

Analysis reveals this same parallel of details in each of the sets of stories listed in Table 2. Combined with the obvious parallels mentioned earlier, this provides very strong support for dividing 1 Nephi into two parallel accounts, the first labeled "Lehi's account" and the second "Nephi's account." Nephi did not rigorously divide the two accounts[8] but rather created the appearance of a division primarily to provide us with a guide to the formal structure of the book.

The answer to the second question, concerning the switched ordering of some of the parallel elements, is more complex. Nephi's desire to know the mysteries of God and his experience with the Spirit is reported in Lehi's account (A-5) as part of the story of Lehi's departure into the wilderness. But in Nephi's account (B-3), the discussion of his desire to know the mysteries of God and the recounting of his vision occur as an appendage to Lehi's report of the tree of life, not as part of the parallel story

			TABLE 3
LEHI'S ACCOUNT	(A-3)		Lehi is commanded to journey into the wilderness, and he pitches his tent in the valley he names Lemuel.
	(A-4)		Lehi teaches and exhorts his sons, and they are confounded.
		(A-5)	Nephi desires to know the mysteries of God; he is visited by the Holy Spirit and is spoken to by the Lord.
NEPHI'S ACCOUNT		(B-3)	Nephi desires to see, hear, and know these mysteries; he is shown a great vision by the Spirit of the Lord and by an angel.
	(B-4)		Nephi instructs and exhorts his brothers, and they are confounded.
(B-5)			Lehi is commanded to journey further into the wilderness, and he pitches his tent in the land he names Bountiful.

of the journey to the land of Bountiful (B-5). The question remains: if a parallel were intended, why did Nephi allow the reversal of parallel elements to occur twice? One observation which may provide an answer is that these reversals suggest the pattern of chiasmus.

TABLE 4				
LEHI'S ACCOUNT	(A-9)	Lehi reports to his sons details of the great vision received in the wilderness.		
		(A-10)	Lehi exhorts Laman and Lemuel, preaching and prophesying to them.	
			(A-11)	Nephi makes a distinction between the two sets of plates.
NEPHI'S ACCOUNT			(B-9)	Nephi details the distinctions between the two sets of plates.
		(B-10)	Nephi preaches and prophesies to Laman and Lemuel, his descendants, and all Israel.	
	(B-11)	To explain Isaiah's prophecies to his brothers, Nephi draws on the great vision given to him and Lehi.		

Briefly stated, chiasmus is a peculiar and long-forgotten literary form present in the very earliest Hebrew writing as well as in other ancient Near Eastern works.[9] In the Hebrew tradition it developed into a rhetorical device in which two sets of parallel elements are presented. The first set is presented 1, 2, 3, etc., but order of presentation is inverted in the second set, 3, 2, 1. An element is often centered between the two sets, usually placed there for emphasis. When the apparently disordered elements of 1 Nephi (Table 1) are abstracted and placed together, two chiasms result, as shown in Tables 3 and 4.

As this suggestion of chiastic structure is explored, a further parallel emerges between the halves of 1 Nephi. Each forms a separate chiasm centering on its most important story, the expedition to obtain the brass plates in the first half (A) and the construction of the ship in the second (B).[10] Table 5 outlines this chiastic structure in the first nine chapters of 1 Nephi.

Again the question arises: are such general parallels as Lehi's taking his family into the wilderness and Ishmael's taking his family into the wilderness really sufficiently similar to give them a coordinate location in the formal structure of a chiasm? As in the preceding analysis, a detailed comparison makes the parallels even more evident. There are eight elements in these two stories which occur in the same order:

1. Both open with a family going into the wilderness because of the Lord's command to Lehi.

2. This departure is followed in both instances by the murmuring and rebellion of Laman and Lemuel, who desire to return to Jerusalem.

3. In each case, Laman and Lemuel are then admonished—in the first episode by Lehi, in the second by Nephi.

TABLE 5
Chiasmus in 1 Nephi 1-9 (Lehi's Account)

1.   Nephi discusses his record, and he testifies it is true (1:1-3).

　　2.   Lehi's early visions are reported, followed by his preaching and prophesying to the Jews (1:6-15, 18-20).

　　　　3.   Lehi takes his family into the wilderness (2:2-15).

　　　　　　4.   The Lord speaks prophecies to Nephi about Lehi's seed (2:19-24).

　　　　　　　　5.   Lehi's sons obtain the brass plates, and Nephi records the most striking example of the murmuring of his faithless brothers (3:2-5:16).

　　　　　　4'.   Lehi, filled with the Spirit, prophesies about his seed (5:17-19; 7:1).

　　　　3'.   Ishmael takes his family into the wilderness (7:2-22).

　　2'.   Lehi's tree of life vision is reported, followed by his prophecies and preaching to Laman and Lemuel (8:2-38).

1'.   Nephi again discusses his record, and he records his testimony (9:1-6).

4. Lehi testifies in the first story that Jerusalem will be destroyed, and in the second story Nephi testifies of the same.

5. In the first episode Laman and Lemuel seek to kill their father, and at the same point in the second they seek to kill Nephi.

6. In the first story Lehi is spared as he confounds Laman and Lemuel by the power of the Spirit, and in the second story Nephi is spared as he bursts his bonds through the power of God.

7. Both stories then report the submission of the rebellious brothers: in the first case they obey their father and in the second as they seek their brother's forgiveness.

8. Each story ends at Lehi's tent.

Again we have such a wealth of exactly ordered detail that the intended parallelism is hard to deny. Yet here we have compared the Ishmael story to a different story than the one to which it was compared earlier. It is striking that Nephi was able to write each of these stories so that he could use them in parallel construction with two other stories which themselves do not occur as parallels.

This parallel construction is largely facilitated by the single overall pattern in which all six stories are cast. Each begins with a divine command to the prophet Lehi which leads to a conflict between his rebellious, faithless sons and the obedient, faithful Nephi. In each case the resolution of the conflict is facilitated by some demonstration of divine power, and the command of God is fulfilled by the faithful. In most cases the rebellion of Laman and Lemuel ends in a measure of submission or repentance as Lehi or Nephi forgives them. The lesser details of each story and the variations in the order of the elements are the marks which identify parallel accounts.

The reader will find a similar system of parallels in all four lesser stories of 1 Nephi (see Table 2). To show this we must first examine the chiastic structure of 1 Nephi 10-22, as it is outlined in Table 6. Many of the parallels of this chiasm are self-explanatory. The structural requirements of this chiasm explain why Lehi's exposition of his own vision of the tree of life and the prophecies of the Jews and Gentiles must be left out in the first report and inserted at this later point. Furthermore, we can now see why Nephi's discussion of how one can come to know the mysteries of God is in a slightly different order in the second half of 1 Nephi as compared to its occurrence in the first half. Its position in the chiasm of the second half apparently has priority.

TABLE 6
Chiasmus in 1 Nephi 10-22 (Nephi's Account)

---

1. Lehi expands on his great vision, detailing prophecies about the Jews and Gentiles (10:1-16).

    2. Nephi explains that all men can know the mysteries of God by the power of the Holy Ghost (10:17-22).

        3. Nephi reports the great visions and prophecies given to him (11-14).

            4. Overcome by the hardness of his brethren, Nephi interprets the great vision to his family, rehearsing one of Isaiah's prophecies as support (15:2-16:5).

                5. Lehi takes his family further into the wilderness (16:9-17:6).

                    6. Nephi builds a ship and records his most complete reply to the murmuring of his brothers (17:7-18:4).

                5'. Lehi takes his family across the ocean in the ship (18:5-25).

            4'. Concerned for those at Jerusalem, Nephi writes for his descendants and all the house of Israel and explains the ancient prophecies of a Redeemer (19:3-23).

        3'. Nephi quotes chapters of a prophecy from Isaiah which parallels portions of his own great vision (20-21).

    2'. Nephi explains to his brethren that prophecies are only to be understood by the same Spirit that also manifested these things to the prophets (22:1-3).

1'. Nephi offers a final summary of the prophecies about the Jews and the Gentiles, drawing primarily from the language of the great vision but also from the brass plates (22:3-28).

Again the cautious reader may doubt that all of these chiasms are intentional. But detailed analysis of two stories—the story of Lehi and his family traveling in the wilderness between the valley of Lemuel and the land of Bountiful (B-5) and the story of their journey by ship to the promised land (B-7)—will provide initial grounds for taking these parallels seriously.

1. Each story begins as the voice of the Lord commands Lehi to depart on a journey.

2. In both instances the group gathers all their provisions and their seeds. (It is noteworthy that the only three references to these seeds occur exactly in the parallels that have been mentioned.)

3. In the first they depart across the river; in the second they put forth into the sea.

4. The journey has barely begun before Nephi's brothers begin murmuring—in the first case because of the difficulties resulting from the loss of Nephi's bow, and in the second because they have forgotten the divine power that has brought them there.

5. In the first story Nephi successfully rebukes the murmurers, but in the second he has no such success.

6. Because of his success in the first story, the families receive instructions from the Liahona or "director," which, Nephi explains, works only by faith. At the corresponding point in the second story, the same director ceases functioning. The parallel statement in the first story gives the explanation for the failure of the compass in the second story.

7. The death of Ishmael, the afflictions of his daughters, and the attempts of Laman and Lemuel to kill Lehi and Nephi are paralleled in the second story by the report of Lehi and Sariah's grief (almost unto death) and suffering due to the sins of Laman and Lemuel.

8. In the first story the voice of the Lord chastens Laman and Lemuel, thus sparing the lives of Lehi and Nephi. In the second only the Lord's power in the storm can soften Laman and Lemuel's hearts.

9. In each case, the chastening is followed by a period of travel. In the first story, the Lord nourishes the group for eight

years in the wilderness. In the second, Nephi guides the ship for many days by following the compass (which now functions perfectly).

10. The first story concludes as the families arrive in the land Bountiful, pitch their tents, and find much fruit and honey. The second story ends as they arrive in the promised land, pitch their tents, find beasts in the forest and a variety of ores.

A first reading of these two stories reveals a certain dissimilarity. During the march through the wilderness (B-5) two separate crises occur: the incident with Nephi's bow and the death of Ishmael; each is followed by rebellion and resolution. However, the list of parallel elements between the stories holds true because Nephi, in effect, makes two crises out of the episode on the ship by excluding part of it on first telling and then going on to a detailed account of the omitted section, treating it structurally as a second episode. This skillful construction orders the events of the second story so that they correspond neatly to those of the first story, confirming that Nephi intended the parallelism.

The combination of ordinary and inverted parallels presented in Tables 1, 5, and 6 suggests a complex set of relationships among the six stories of 1 Nephi (see Table 2). Stories A-6 and B-6 parallel each other as center points on Tables 1, 5, and 6. The parallel functions of A-6 and B-6 are emphasized by the facts that (1) these are the only two stories that are given chiastic structures and (2) taken together these stories raise and answer the central issue of 1 Nephi, as will be explained. But the chiastic structures in each half of 1 Nephi (Tables 5 and 6) combined with the direct parallels between the halves (Table 1) indicate that each of the other four stories (A-3, A-7, B-5, and B-7) should have important parallels with *two* other stories to form a second set of parallel narrations. We have shown that A-7 is designed as a parallel for both A-3 and B-7 and that B-7 also parallels B-5. It remains to be seen whether A-3 and B-5 also fit the suggested pattern. Again we note that two stories may be parallel to a third story without being parallel to each other (A-3 is not parallel to B-7; B-5 is not parallel to A-7).

The strongest parallel is the most obvious one: both stories (A-3 and B-5) recount Lehi's journey in the wilderness. The balanced and ingenious symmetry of the other pairs of stories does not exist here, because A-3 relates the events preceding and following one three-day march, while B-5 relates the events of two short marches plus a summary of the following eight years in the wilderness. Some further evidences of intended parallelism, although not as strong, include the following:

1. Both stories are preceded by verses which state that Lehi had kept all of the commandments he had received from God and that he (A-3) and Nephi (B-5) had been greatly blessed by God.

2. Each story begins with the same elements: the Lord commands Lehi to take his family into the wilderness, they gather provisions, and they depart.

3. In both accounts they pitch their tents after a three- or four-day journey and Lehi names the campsite.

4. When Laman and Lemuel rebel, they are confounded: in the first story by Lehi "filled with the Spirit" and in the second by Nephi speaking "with all the energies" of his soul.

5. Finally, Nephi breaks B-5 into two parts; in both accounts he details the rebellion and chastening of his brothers as a postscript to the stories of the journey. (Although this device adequately establishes the parallel elements in stories B-5 and B-7, it does not have the same effect with A-3.)

Stories A-3 and B-5 have almost as many matched elements as do the other pairs of stories. Even though the elements are not identically ordered, the combination of several parallel elements with some ordered elements, plus the fact that these two stories contain all the wilderness travels, confirms the overall parallelism suggested in the charts.

I have shown that 1 Nephi has a complex structure based on both standard and inverted parallelism, but I have not yet explored the reasons for parallels. Significant ideas can be emphasized by their placement in a chiasm. Alma does this in Alma 36 (see chapter 2 in this volume) to call attention to the brief yet crucial central message of his account, "the coming of one Jesus

Christ . . . to atone for the sins of the world" (Alma 36:17). This statement is both the turning point in his dramatic story and an explanation for the important changes in his life which he details in the remainder of the chiasm.[11]

Analysis of 1 Nephi shows that, not only are A-6 and B-6 related by their central locations in parts A and B respectively, but these are also the only two stories written in chiastic form,[12] as is shown in Tables 7 and 8.

Several important insights are revealed by the chiastic structure of the story of obtaining the brass plates of Laban. The most frequently quoted version of Nephi's thesis—

> I will go and do the things which the Lord hath commanded, for I know that the Lord giveth no commandments unto the children of men, save he shall prepare a way for them that they may accomplish the thing which he commandeth them (1 Nephi 3:7)—

is emphasized by the chiastically parallel testimony of Sariah, stated in almost identical phrases. It is important that each of these testimonies is underscored by the rejoicing of Lehi, who first announced the thesis and who now finds it firmly rooted in the hearts of his wife and son. This may be one reason why Nephi saw the first half of the book as his father's record.

Other interesting details include the parallel between Laban's attempt to slay Laman and Nephi's desire to spare the life of Zoram, Laban's servant. The character comparison between the wicked Laban and the faithful Nephi is very important in helping us to understand the justification for Nephi's midnight execution of Laban. Also, the failure of Lehi's sons to obtain the brass plates through the wordly power of riches is paralleled dramatically by Nephi's miraculous success in obtaining the plates as he is led by the Spirit "not knowing beforehand the things which [he] should do" (1 Nephi 4:6). These comparisons strongly support Nephi's thesis that the Lord protects and aids the faithful.

The central point of this chiasm is but another of the oft-repeated reports that Laman and Lemuel murmured. But in this case they are murmuring not only because of their real or

---

TABLE 7
Obtaining the Brass Plates

---

1. Lehi summarizes the contents of the brass plates, mentioning his genealogy (3:3).

   2. Nephi testifies to his thesis—Lehi is glad (3:7-8).

      3. Laban attempts to slay Laman (3:9-14).

         4. Lehi's sons are sorrowful, but Nephi exhorts them (3:14-21).

            5. Nephi fails to obtain the brass plates by using gold and silver (3:22-27).

               6. Laman and Lemuel murmur, and they beat Nephi and Sam (3:28).

                  7. An angel intervenes, saying that the Lord will help them obtain the plates (3:29-30).

                     8. Laman and Lemuel murmur again. (3:31).

                  7'. Nephi elaborates the angel's message and refers to Moses and the Israelites (4:1-3).

               6'. Laman and Lemuel continue to murmur, but they follow Nephi reluctantly (4:4-5).

            5'. The Spirit leads Nephi to obtain the plates (4:6-38).

         4'. Sariah is sorrowful, and Lehi exhorts her (5:1-6).

      3'. Nephi spares Zoram's life (4:30-37).[13]

   2'. Sariah testifies to Nephi's thesis—Lehi is glad (5:7-9).

1'. Lehi reviews the contents of the brass plates, with special reference to his genealogy (5:10-19).

---

imagined afflictions but also in direct response to an angelic visitation and to reassurance that the Lord will bless them. This is indeed murmuring par excellence! But why does Nephi choose their murmuring as the central point of both this story and Lehi's entire account (the first nine chapters of the book)? This

TABLE 8
Constructing the Ship

1. Nephi is commanded to construct a ship (17:8).

   2. The Lord tells Nephi where to find ore for tools (17:9-10).

      3. The Lord blesses them miraculously in the wilderness, that they might know they are led by him (17:11-15).

         4. Laman and Lemuel murmur and complain, not believing that Nephi can build a ship (17:17-19).

            5. Laman and Lemuel repeat the elements of their standing complaint against Nephi and Lehi, denying both that they have been led or supported by God and that the Jews are wicked or can be destroyed (17:17-22).

               6. Nephi responds to the murmuring of Laman and Lemuel in unprecedented detail of his thesis, invoking the ancient history of Israel as the evidence that they would be most likely to accept (17:23-43).

            5'. Nephi summarizes the great errors and sins of Laman and Lemuel, comparing them to the wicked Jews, and testifies to the power and goodness of God (17:44-47).

         4'. Nephi, in the power of the Spirit, testifies that if God commanded he could not only build a ship but could even make water earth (17:48-52).

      3'. Laman and Lemuel are shaken by the power of the Lord in Nephi, and they testify thereof (17:53-55).

   2'. The Lord shows Nephi how to build the ship (18:1-3).

1'. The ship is finished, the workmanship "exceeding fine" (18:4).

story alone does not answer the question fully; we must compare it with its counterpart in Nephi's record (the second half of the book). The second of these two great stories in 1 Nephi—the building of the ship—is also a chiasm, but it has a sharply contrasting central point (see Table 8).[14]

The story of obtaining the brass plates (Table 7) focuses on the most remarkable instance of Laman and Lemuel's murmuring and is followed immediately by a highly abbreviated account of Nephi's response to them, which includes references to the exodus from Egypt under Moses' inspired leadership. It is significant that the central point of this last chiasm (Table 8) is the longest verbatim account of Nephi's response to the murmuring of his brothers, and that it is the only other response in which he specifically cites as primary evidence for his thesis the interventions of God on behalf of his faithful servants during the Exodus.

Lehi's account focuses on the murmuring; Nephi's account centers on his own response to that murmuring. Together these focal points give in microcosm the story of 1 Nephi and, simultaneously, explain the distinction between 1 and 2 Nephi. The book of 1 Nephi is addressed to Laman and Lemuel—to an audience which seems to accept the powerful interventions of God in ancient times, as recorded in the history of Israel, but which cannot accept and live the teachings of God's prophet, Spirit, or angel, though the message is the same. It contains Nephi's tireless, ingenious, and inspired effort to appeal to that audience, which included many of his own descendants, and to convince them that Jesus would be the Christ and that through the power of the Atonement he could overcome the effects of all the evil in the world. The transition between the two books is effected by Nephi's growing emphasis on the importance of the coming Redeemer, seen in his exhortations to Laman and Lemuel in chapter 19 and in the final reiteration of his thesis, in which he testifies that those who obey God and endure to the end shall be saved at the last day.

In his second book Nephi addresses a much narrower audience: those who embrace the thesis of the first book. Here he emphasizes a selection of prophecies and speeches on redemption and supports these teachings with the fact that he, his father, his brother Jacob, and many ancient prophets such as Isaiah had been redeemed of God. He documents what it means to be redeemed and spells out in a powerful conclusion how we might take advantage of the great blessing of redemption, which is made available to all men through the Atonement.

Because of Nephi's persistent concern in the first book to advance his thesis that God preserves the faithful, and because of his focus on a marginal audience, Nephi chose not to include several important items: Lehi's last instructions and blessings for his sons; the Song of Nephi; the teachings of Jacob, Lehi, and Nephi on the redemption; the teachings and prophecies of Isaiah on the Atonement; and Nephi's detailed discussion of the doctrine of Christ. He incorporates these passages in 2 Nephi, which appears to be a collection of odds and ends, its only unifying features being the thematic emphasis on redemption and the general aim at a higher or more spiritually receptive audience than Laman and Lemuel.[15] It is interesting that the cursing of Laman and Lemuel, who were "cut off from the presence of God" (the antithesis of redemption), is mentioned frequently in 2 Nephi.

We do not have direct access to Nephi's ideas about the rules governing the use of literary structures. Modern studies of the Bible and other ancient literature have produced a variety of inductive reconstructions of stylistic rules the ancients may have used. The rules for chiasmus were obviously very broad, and they varied considerably from one culture and period to another; a combination of short precise chiasms and long general chiastic structures characterizes the ancient Hebrew authors[16] and some of the writers in the Book of Mormon. Without direct access to their rules it is difficult to analyze fully the structure of their writings. In constructing hypothetical outlines we are not certain how to handle sections of text that do not fall neatly into a pattern or that fit a pattern in an obviously unbalanced way.

This analysis leaves some unanswered questions. Several suggested parallel sections of the text are not the same length. Usually the second member of each pair is longer than the first, and in a few cases it is many times as long. There are a few scattered verses, usually repetitive or parenthetical, that are simply left over; I have not attempted to force them into the pattern. The patterns outlined above provide no extraordinary emphasis for the great dreams or visions of Lehi and Nephi, though they do seem to explain why some of the accounts are so brief and others are interrupted. Also, the specific thesis of 1 Nephi may explain why the message of those dreams is not emphasized until 2 Nephi.

There are undoubtedly other aspects of my hypothesis which may raise doubts in the minds of readers. Whether or not the patterns outlined above are exactly right, there is ample evidence that Nephi was consciously working with rhetorical patterns and devices. In this article I have attempted to identify only a few such elements. As others are identified, the patterns suggested here will undoubtedly be revised or even replaced. The more such creative response there is to the hypothesis of this article, the more my objectives in writing it will be fulfilled.

This essay is not an attempt to detail the insights we can glean from the observation of an elaborate rhetorical structure in 1 Nephi. There are several reasons why I feel such an attempt would not have been appropriate. Rather, I have chosen simply to gesture in the direction of the central teachings I see emphasized.

My primary objective is twofold. On the one hand, I am hopeful that this initial effort will prove helpful to others who share my own convictions that this book was written and translated by prophets of God. I hope that it may not only help someone to understand the prophets better but also that it will encourage others to improve on these structural analyses. On the other hand, I hope to draw the attention of those who do not yet share my convictions to certain features of the Book of Mormon which simply cannot be explained away as products of nineteenth-century culture. As chiastic literary structures were not recognized in Hebrew literature until the middle of the century, it seems impossible that *any* modern man could have written the Book of Mormon. The only plausible explanation is the one Joseph Smith gave—the book is an accurate translation of an ancient work.

NOTES

1. Hugh Nibley, *An Approach to the Book of Mormon,* 2nd ed. (Salt Lake City, Utah: Deseret Book Co., 1976); John W. Welch, "Chiasmus in the Book of Mormon," *Brigham Young University Studies* 10 (Autumn 1969): 69-84; and Richard L. Bushman, "The Book of Mormon and the American Revolution," *BYU Studies* 17 (Autumn 1976): 3-20. The Welch and Bushman articles are now contained in this volume, chapters 2 and 8 respectively.

2. Jacob 3:13-14 (cf. 1 Nephi 9:2).

3. 2 Nephi 5:30 (cf. 1 Nephi 19:1-5); 2 Nephi 5:34. Certainly part of the reason it took Nephi so long to write these chapters was the difficulty of making and engraving gold plates; see Jacob 4:1.

4. Italics added.

5. Nephi's father, Lehi, is the first in the Book of Mormon to affirm this; see 1 Nephi 1:14.

6. 1 Nephi 1:11-17 (cf. 1:1-3); 10:1; 9:6; 22:31.

7. The numbering system used in this table is used throughout the article to identify and discuss the various stories in 1 Nephi.

8. The first nine chapters obviously contain several autobiographical sections which appear to be Nephi's substitutes for Lehi's secondhand accounts of Nephi's experiences.

9. For a more thorough explanation of chiasmus, see John W. Welch, "A Study Relating Chiasmus in the Book of Mormon to Chiasmus in the Old Testament, Ugaritic Epics, Homer, and Selected Greek and Latin Authors" (M.A. thesis, Brigham Young University, 1970).

10. These chiasms emerge when major adjacent items in Table 1 are combined. Welch proposes a different chiastic analysis of 1 Nephi which also recognizes the parallel between these key stories; ibid., p. 152.

11. Welch discusses Alma 36 in detail (see chapter 2 in this volume).

12. Welch finds numerous chiastic details in this long passage (1 Nephi 3-5), but there seems to be no inconsistency between his findings and the full chiastic structure proposed here (see "A Study Relating Chiasmus," pp. 124-25, 159-60).

13. In Table 7, elements 3' and 4' are reversed from the order in which Nephi reports them. He could have avoided this reversal only by having Laman and Lemuel sorrowing before Laban tried to slay Laman or by alternating between the events at Jerusalem and Sariah's sorrowing in the camp. Neither of these options would have been acceptable from a narrative viewpoint; and certainly the reversal does not flaw the literary structure, as chiasmus requires careful, distinct order but not mathematical precision.

14. Cf. Welch's analysis of the chiastic arrangement of the words and phrases in the first half of the passage which I have outlined as a single chiasm (see "A Study Relating Chiasmus," pp. 162-64). This chiasm finally emerges with clarity, although it is more problematic. The major reason for this obscurity is the very long central section which must be treated as one item in the chiastic structure.

15. Welch does find one very general chiasm which provides at least a semblance of overall unity in 2 Nephi (see chapter 2 in this volume).

16. Nils W. Lund, *Chiasmus in the New Testament* (Chapel Hill: University of North Carolina Press, 1942), pp. 30-47.

4

C. Wilfred Griggs

The Book of Mormon as an Ancient Book

An Associate Professor of Classics, History, and Ancient Scriptures and Director of Ancient Studies at Brigham Young University, C. Wilfred Griggs has published numerous articles on the New Testament and early Christianity. A frequent contributor to BYU Studies and the Ensign, he has also delivered papers at various colloquia throughout the United States. He earned degrees in history, ancient history, and Greek literature at Brigham Young University, and received his Ph.D. from the University of California at Berkeley. He has worked at archaeological sites in Egypt, Greece, and Italy, and has taught history, religion, and ancient scriptures at BYU for many years. Griggs advances in this article the thesis that the Book of Mormon is indeed an ancient book. He focuses on one passage —the story of the Tree of Life—to demonstrate its striking similarity to other sixth- or seventh-century B.C. texts. Various plates of precious metal inscribed with religious texts have been

found in burial sites around the Mediterranean. Griggs reviews
these writings and notes the Near Eastern, or more particularly
Egyptian, origin of the texts. He then compares Lehi's dream
with these ancient texts and concludes that the Book of Mormon
account is highly similar both to the writings on the metal
tablets and to the related Egyptian literature.

Typical of attempts to discredit the authenticity of the Book
of Mormon are an as yet unpublished manuscript recently sent
to the author by a professional journal for evaluation and an
earlier work by Hal Hougey entitled *The Truth About the "Lehi
Tree-of-Life" Stone.*[1] Both authors list parallels between Lucy
Mack Smith's account of a dream which Joseph Smith, Sr.,
experienced in c. 1811 and the account of the Tree of Life dream
in 1 Nephi 8 through 15.[2] Their purpose is to show that Joseph
Smith, Jr., got the inspiration from his father (either directly or
perhaps indirectly through his mother) for including the dream
and most of the symbols in the dream in the Book of Mormon
narrative. Hougey avers that "arbitrary or unexpected similarities" exist in the two accounts "which rule out the possibility of
independent development," although he does not give criteria
for determining when similarities can be considered "arbitrary
or unexpected."[3] Within the framework of his own skepticism,
Hougey is unwilling or unable to see any alternative to his
hypothesis that Joseph Smith simply borrowed the dream
account from the Smith family traditions.[4]

DETERMINING THE METHOD

The major weakness of works such as those mentioned
above is their one-dimensional approach to the problems which
the Book of Mormon presents to its critics. The assumption that
any parallels from the world of Joseph Smith, real or imagined,
are sufficient to discredit the authenticity of the work is naive.

The challenge of the Book of Mormon lies elsewhere. It claims to be an ancient book, and it must be examined and criticized in terms of its claim.[5] Before he can disprove the antiquity of the book, the critic must analyze the historical, cultural, and social elements which are found throughout the narrative of the Book of Mormon and must show that they cannot represent the ancient world origin claimed for them. Since nobody could feasibly invent a work the length of the Book of Mormon which represented ancient Near Eastern society accurately (even a transplanted segment of that society would retain many characteristics which could be checked for accuracy), subjecting the book to the test of historical integrity would be a rather easy task for any specialist to undertake. The number of fraudulent texts which use Christ as the subject (e.g. the *Archko Volume* or the *Infancy Gospels*) as well as numerous other non-Christian forgeries attest to the ease with which scholars discredit such attempts.

The Book of Mormon deserves the same kind of test, especially in view of the tremendous amount of material relating to the ancient Near East which was recovered during the last century. Because such materials were unknown in the early nineteenth century, they provide a superb control with which to measure the Book of Mormon, for Joseph Smith obviously could not have had access to them in writing the book. It is precisely this dimension of historical criticism, however, which has been almost totally neglected in attempts to establish the book as a fraud. Professor Hugh Nibley, the leading Mormon scholar in the field of antiquity, is at present the only specialist who has applied the test of historical compatibility to the Book of Mormon,[6] and this paper continues in the methodology, if not the erudition, used by Nibley and accepted generally in disciplines related to ancient studies.

An instructive example of how to treat a text such as the Book of Mormon has recently been provided through the providence of manuscript preservation and recovery. In 1958, Professor Morton Smith of Columbia University was examining manuscripts in a monastery near Jerusalem when he happened upon a two-and-a-half-page text purporting to be a letter of

Clement of Alexandria (c. 150-c. 215) to a certain Theodore.[7]
The letter does not correspond to any previously known texts of
Clement and there is no known Theodore who associated with
the Alexandrian theologian. The paper on which the text was
found is a heavy white binder's paper commonly found on
books in Venice during the seventeenth and eighteenth
centuries, and the handwriting on the paper is dated variously
from the late seventeenth century to the early nineteenth century.[8] By scholarly consensus, Smith was able to establish 1750,
plus or minus fifty years, as the date of the writing of the
manuscript. Although the scribe is acknowledged to be experienced, as noted by good spelling and correct use of accents (the
language is Greek), the nature of the writing indicates he was in
a hurry. It is therefore impossible to tell whether he is responsible for the high quality of the text or is simply copying a work
of unusually good literary and grammatical attributes.[9]

The material in the letter was totally unexpected, especially
since it speaks favorably of a *Secret Gospel of Mark* which was
essentially sacramental or ordinance-oriented and which depicted Jesus as a mystagogue for Christians who wished to
become perfect[10] by being led as "hearers into the innermost
sanctuary of the truth hidden by seven veils."[11] With the
modern paper, modern handwriting, and unfamiliar and unexpected contents one would expect to have all the ingredients
for a first-class forgery, but Smith moves on to what he considers "the primary test for authenticity," namely, the examination of the text in terms of its claimed historical and literary
context.[12] After nearly 450 pages of comparing the style,
language, and contents of the short text with already known
ancient sources, Smith concludes that he had found a copy of an
authentic letter of Clement, and "the consequences for the
history of the early Christian church and for New Testament
criticism are revolutionary."[13]

If a two-and-a-half-page text can elicit 450 pages of analysis
and commentary in an attempt to determine its authenticity,
one would not expect less from the scholarly world in the case
of the Book of Mormon.

Given the limitations of time and space, this paper can discuss only two specific instances of recently recovered materials which relate to the original world of the Book of Mormon: the Orphic gold plates, and Egyptian funerary texts. They are worth considering here as a minuscule and partial approach to the larger and complete question of historical compatibility.

THE GOLD PLATES, RIVERS, AND THE TREE OF LIFE

A major religious movement which swept through the Greek world in the sixth century B.C. later became known as Orphism.[14] Due to the paucity of extant sources,[15] little is known concerning early Orphism, although there is consensus that after originating perhaps in Thrace, the religious beliefs spread rapidly via the Greeks throughout the Mediterranean world.[16] The popularity of the movement can be inferred from a fragment of the sixth-century poet Ibykos, which speaks of "well-known" or "famous Orpheus."[17] That Greeks were familiar with and probably were bearing this religious philosophy throughout the eastern Mediterranean, including Egypt, from the seventh century B.C. can be assumed, for it is well known that the Greeks had good trade relations with non-Greek countries of the Near East throughout that century.[18]

W. K. C. Guthrie implies that one may have come into contact with *Orphica* through writings rather than through people, because "Orphism always was a literature, first and foremost."[19] Rather than being a collection of *dogmata* within a narrow tradition, Orphism has been described as a way of life which may not require worship of a new god or a change in established worship patterns,[20] and the movement was influenced by other religions, both Greek and non-Greek.[21] Indeed, the later collection of Orphic literature has been characterized as "a collection of writing of different periods and varying outlook, something like that of the Bible."[22]

Besides the many divergent texts and ideas which became part of the *Orphica,* there appears to have been a special body of material collected into hexametric poems which were considered authoritative in Orphic circles.[23] The earliest preserved tradition concerns this Orphic poetry and states that it was engraved on tablets which were to be found in Thrace.[24] These tablets were made of bronze, according to the pseudo-Platonic dialogue *Axiochos,* and the message engraved upon them concerned the fate of the soul in the spirit world (Hades). The plates were said to have been brought to Delos by two seers from the land of the Hyperboreans (Far North), indicating that it was the religious significance and divine source of the material which justified engraving it upon metal plates.[25]

Günther Zuntz observes that although metals were not used as writing materials as often as papyrus, animal skins, wood, or stone, "they were so used, and that by no means rarely."[26] Among the many examples which could be cited, one notes an inscribed fifth-century bronze disc from Lusoi in Arkadia,[27] and a number of bronze plaques inscribed with legal texts or dedications[28] (need one remind the reader of the contents of the brass plates of Laban at this point for comparison?). Of quite a different nature are the *Defixionum Tabellae* (tablets of enchantments or curses), written on tablets of lead and buried in graves and chthonic sanctuaries. The purpose of burying such texts was to bring to the attention of the deities of the next life the curses invoked by the writers on their enemies. These lead plates date from the fifth century B.C. onward and are found throughout the Greek world, from Sicily to Syria. Zuntz suggests that lead was used because it changes from a shiny silver color when fresh to a "dark color and dead heaviness" in time, an appropriate combination for the pernicious purposes of the texts.[29]

One should also make mention of a small gold plate (less than one inch in height) found at Amphipolis which contains an inscription of ten lines of magical names and formulae, e.g. "Baruch, Adonai, Uriel, Gabriel, Michael," etc.[30] Another gold plate, unearthed in Gallep on the Lower Rhine, the site of a Roman camp, contains an inscription of magical names and incantations which Sieburg identified as Egyptian, Jewish, Phoenician, and Babylonian.[31] Similar texts have been found inscribed on silver and bronze,[32] as have prescriptions for writing protective and religious spells on tablets of gold, silver, bronze, and tin.[33] The gold plates with the magical spells date from the Roman period, however, while the lead plates with the curses date from the classical age of Greece. In seeking to establish historical compatibility for the Book of Mormon, one might look for gold plates from the earlier period with religious texts inscribed upon them.

The Orphic gold plates provide perhaps the best examples of such early religious texts inscribed on tablets of gold and buried in the ground. There are at least seventeen such plates known at present, found in ancient burial sites in such widely scattered areas as Italy, Greece, and Crete.[34] The plate known longest was probably discovered in the eighteenth century, although it was not published until 1836,[35] and the most recently discovered plate came to light in 1972 and was published in 1976.[36] Dating the plates is difficult, due to lack of similar texts with which they may be compared, but Zuntz and Burkert date them from as early as the fifth century B.C. in one instance to as late as the third century A.D. in another (most are dated to the fourth century B.C. or earlier).[37] Zuntz hypothesizes the existence of a larger text which was the ancestor of the gold plate texts and which, when read to an audience of initiates, was accompanied by ritual acts, although he does not accept the earlier opinions of Wieten and Harrison that they were celebrations of mystery acts relating to a mystic death and resurrection for the living.[38] Despite Zuntz's reluctance to acknowledge the hypothetical earlier text to be a "didactic poem," a recently found Orphic papyrus, dated to the fourth century B.C. and discovered in a tomb near Thessaloniki, contains a commentary on an authoritative Orphic poem, perhaps a form of the one which preceded the fragments on the gold tablets.[39] Because of this ancient commentary, Burkert assumes a date for the original poem to be at least the fifth or sixth century B.C.

Commentators agree that the material on the gold plates was not indigenous to Greece but represents foreign influences from the sixth century or earlier. Zuntz suggests that the apparent cultic influence on the earlier version of the ritual formulary could well have come from Egypt,[40] an hypothesis also proposed by others before him.[41] Harrison, however, attributes the enrichment of the poem with ritual elements to Iranian influence.[42] The influence was certainly from the ancient Near East, even if there is no agreement on where the ideas were originally found. This necessarily brief and incomplete background material must suffice as an introduction to a consideration of the text itself.

Commentators also agree that the texts on the plates are related to one another, even though various plates contain different parts or aspects of the original work. This presentation is not concerned with reconstructing the parts into the original order of the whole or determining how each aspect of the original has been altered or preserved on the different plates. For our purposes, the various elements of the poem are as important as the place they occupied in the original work. Following Guthrie, Zuntz, Burkert, and others, the text is here translated and presented as concisely as possible in order to place the general story before the reader.[43]

> "This is the tomb (rule) or remembrance if someone is about to die.[44] You go to the well-fashioned houses of Hades (realm of departed spirits)."

> "You shall find to the left of the House of Hades a spring . . . to this spring you must not come near."[45]

> "Go to the right as far as one should go, being right wary in all things."[46]

> "There is to the right a spring, near which is standing a white cypress. There the souls of the dead who descend refresh themselves."[47]

> "Further on, you shall find another, the Lake of Remembrance, and cold water flowing forth, and there are guardians above it.[48] They will ask you in their astute minds, 'For what purpose are you searching (wandering) about the dark regions of the destructive netherworld?'"[49]

> "Who are you? Whence are you?"[50]

> (The answer follows)

"Here I stand before you, pure from impurity, Queen of those below,[51] and Eukles and Eubouleus, and the other immortal gods and daemons,[52] for I also profess that I am one of your blessed race, and I have paid the penalty for unrighteous deeds." "Say, 'I am a son of earth and of starry heaven, but my race is of heaven alone. This you yourselves know.'"[53]

"'But I am parched with thirst and I am about to perish. Give to me quickly the cold water which flows forth from the Lake of Memory.'"[54]

"And they will have pity under the king of the under-world, (or perhaps, "And they will initiate you to the king of the underworld") and they themselves will give you to drink from the holy spring, and thenceforth among the other heroes you shall have lordship."[55]

(The gods speak:)

"Hail, you who have suffered the suffering. This you have never suffered before.
You are become god from man.
A kid you are fallen into milk.
Hail, hail to you journeying the right hand road by the holy meadows and groves of Persephone."[56]

"You are going a long way, which others also (go), initiates and Bacchoi, heirs of the holy way . . ."[57]

One should not understand the preceding text to be a conjectured reconstruction of the textual archetype of the plates. It is rather a composite of the various texts which are acknowledged as being associated in origin and thought.[58] The following commentary on the text, necessarily as brief and incomplete as was the introduction, represents a sampling of the scholarly opinions presently held concerning the material.

The major difficulty for many has been to specify the religious movement with which the plates are to be identified. They have long been known as the "Orphic gold plates," but Zuntz observes that on no plate is there a clear hint pointing to Orpheus or Dionysius, and "no reason remains for describing the religion to which they witness as 'orphic.'"[59] Still, these texts correspond to the claim in Pseudo-Plato *Axiochos* that the subject of the ancient bronze plates was the fate of the soul in the spirit world.[60] It is further assumed that the bronze plates of Pseudo-Plato are the same as the "Thracian tablets which tuneful Orpheus carved out," mentioned by Euripides in the *Alcestis*.[61] There is considerable harmony in subject matter between the no longer extant bronze plates of Thrace as reported in ancient sources and the gold plates which have been recovered in modern times. Guthrie summarizes the message of the gold plates as follows:

> The purpose of the plates is clear from their contents. The dead man is given those portions of his sacred literature which will instruct him how to behave when he finds himself on the road to the lower world. They tell him the way he is to go and the words he is to say. They also quote the favourable answer which he may expect from the powers of that world when he has duly reminded them of his claims on their benevolence.[62]

Zuntz suggests that the text and some unspecified accompanying rites, "in which the journey of the deceased to Persephone was symbolically enacted," were celebrated by the living at the burial of the dead. These rites "were considered indispensable if a soul was to attain to its 'proper and blissful consummation.'" He attempts to identify the ritual drama with Pythagorean rites and argues that "the preservation, through the centuries, of these texts, and the custom of inscribing them on gold leaves to accompany the dead, became understandable . . . as elements, and evidence, of these Pythagorean rites. . . ."[63] The ritual nature of the text is further suggested by observing that although the engraved Hipponios tablet was found in the grave of a female, line ten says, "I am a *son* of earth and of starry heaven" (unless the engraver simply did not wish to be very accommodating to his subject).[64] A separate study of related sources would reveal the necessity of performing such ritual acts during mortality, as well as some specific references to performing them on behalf of the deceased.

As the spirit of the deceased enters Hades, or the realm of

departed spirits, it is counseled to avoid the path of the left and to keep to the one on the right. Plato may be drawing upon the same tradition when he has Socrates say of the path to Hades:

> To be sure, the journey is not as Aeschylus has Telephos speak of it. For he states that the path leads straight to Hades, but it seems to me to be neither straight nor single. Otherwise there would not be any need of guides, for surely one would not go astray if there were only one path.[65]

Plato is more explicit in the *Gorgias,* where in the final pages Socrates gives a mythical account of the judgment which takes place in Hades, suggesting that after death men go to a great meadow where there is a crossroads. Those who are deemed just in the judgment may take the path which leads to the Isles of the Blest, while the unjust must take the path which leads to Tartaros.[66] Finally, in the *Republic,* Plato appears to allude to the same source as that which is behind the gold plates. Socrates tells Glaucon of a story in which, after the judgment of souls, the unjust had to take the path which led to the left and downward, while the just could take the path which led to the right and upward.[67] In the gold plates, then, the avoidance of the spring on the left must be equivalent to the avoidance of a place of suffering, or hell.

Despite the apparent confusion in the various plates about the number of springs of water (the *spring* near the cypress is not always identified with the *lake* of Memory, nor is the distinction always clear between the spring on the left and the one on the right), scholars generally assume that there are only two springs.[68] Zuntz suggests that the spring near the tree may actually be flowing from the Lake of Memory,[69] but the essential unity of the two springs on the path to the right is still maintained. The spring of *Lethe,* or forgetfulness, is likely because the spring and lake on the right are associated with *Mnemosyne,* or remembrance.[70]

Lethe appears as a personified goddess first in Hesiod's *Theogony,* but she is found in rather bad company:

> But abhorred Strife bare painful Toil and Forgetful-
> ness and Famine and tearful Sorrows, Fightings also,
> Battles, Murders, Manslaughters, Quarrels, Lying
> Words, Disputes, Lawlessness and Ruin, all of one
> nature, and Oath who most troubles men upon earth
> when anyone wilfully swears a false oath.[71]

This description occurs in the context of the goddesses who, as
the offspring of Night, have the task of punishing sinners with
appropriate penalties.[72] By the time of Plato, *Lethe* had become
a river which was destructive to the unjust and which was to be
avoided by the just. Plato tells the myth of Er, the Pamphylian,
who had died in war and had miraculously been restored to life.
In this tale, obviously well known to the point of being prover-
bial in the fifth century, Er describes the nature of the world of
departed spirits, and Socrates concludes from the myth that
only the souls of the just can escape the punishment of drinking
from the river of *Lethe* and forgetting everything.[73] Elsewhere
Plato speaks of the soul which has not followed in the path of
the gods as one which falls to the earth burdened with a load of
forgetfulness and wrongdoing.[74] Zuntz states that "death is forgetting," whereas to seek the drink from the spring or lake of
memory is to seek life, and "they who retain memory are those
who are ripe for a higher form of life."[75]

The tree beside the spring has been consistently identified as
a "Tree of Life," although the Greek phrase, "white cypress," is
troublesome for many, including Zuntz:

> This white cypress indeed has never ceased puzzling
> students; for the cypress is not white, (and) even if the
> Greek adjective is taken in its wider and basic (shining),
> its application to this dark tree remains unexplained.[76]

Guthrie also admits his uncertainty concerning the description
of the cypress tree:

> Concerning the white cypress I do not see that it helps
> towards an explanation to say that by white cypress the
> writer meant a white poplar (as Comparette in *Laminetti
> Orfiche,* Florence, 1910), an admittedly common, as
> well as extremely beautiful tree, and one, moreover,

which had associations with the dead. It is a striking feature of the poem, and I hope that some day our knowledge of infernal history may be widened sufficiently to include it.[77]

A. B. Cook proffers the suggestion that "on the whole it seems most likely that the tree of the tablets was a miraculous cypress. . . ." As such, he continues, the white cypress is in line with such marvelous trees as the silver apple tree of the Celts or the twelve-fruited tree of the Revelation.[78] One should also note that, according to Pseudo-Kallisthenes, when Alexander the Great consults the two oracular trees of the Sun and the Moon in Prasiake, the trees are described as being similar to cypresses, although nothing is said concerning their color.[79]

The ritual nature of the plates has been noted above, but just what comprised the ritual actions or how they accompanied the text has not been agreed. Zuntz argues for Pythagorean mysteries, Guthrie for Orphic rites, and Harrison for Cretan adaptations (in an Orphic manner) of Egyptian funerary ceremonies. Guthrie notes that it is impossible even to tell whether the dialogue occurs between the initiate and the gods of Hades or the initiate and his guide.[80] All do agree on one matter concerning the plates: they originated in or were influenced by Near Eastern culture and religion.

THE NEAR EASTERN CONNECTION

One of the earliest commentators to make the connection between Orphic beliefs and Egypt was Herodotus. In his book on Egypt, the historian states that Egyptians did not permit woolen articles in their temples, nor would they be buried in woolen garments. "In this," he continues, "they agree with the so-called Orphika or Bacchika, which are really Egyptian and Pythagorean. For in these rites also, if a man share in them it is not lawful for him to be buried in woolen garments."[81]

In the present instance of the so-called Orphic texts, virtually all modern scholars have suggested an Egyptian origin for them, because of the reference in some of the gold tablets to cold

water. This connection is usually based on some funeral monuments bearing the following inscription: May Osiris give cold
water [to you].[82] These monuments date no earlier than the
Roman Empire, however, and their relevance to the gold plates
has been disputed.[83] Language similar to the plates has also been
found on a magical papyrus from Egypt: "Hail to the water
white and the tree with the leaves high hanging."[84] Similarity of
both the gold plates and the Egyptian sources just quoted to the
early Christian term *refrigerium* denoting the "refreshment" of
the dead in Paradise has also been of great interest to students of
early Christian doctrines.[85]

The Greek word ψυχϱόν not only means "cold" but also
suggests "refreshing," and it is also related to the term ψυχή, or
soul. Jane Harrison made the following observation regarding
the ψυχϱόν ὕδωϱ of the well of Osiris and the water and the tree
in the magical papyrus: "The well would be both cool and fresh
and *life*-giving; by it the soul would revive (ἀναψύχειν), it
would become 'a living water, springing up into everlasting
life.'"[86] The tree growing by the fountain or spring of living
water is thus a Tree of Life, and "it is only the soul whose purity
is vouched for which is to be allowed to drink from it."[87]

Much earlier than the funeral monuments and the magical
papyrus, and therefore much more significant for similarities to
the gold plates, are the Egyptian funerary texts frequently
placed in graves from the Old Kingdom through the Roman
period. Zuntz summarizes the relevance of the *Book of the Dead*
literature for the tablets:

> Concerned lest their dead, at their resting-places on the
> edge of the desert, should lack the vital moisture, the
> Egyptians sought to provide it for them by including
> suitable spells and pictures in the *Book of the Dead.*
> Hence we find in it representations of the dead, on their
> way through the Netherworld, scooping water from a
> basin between trees, or catching in a bowl water poured
> out either by an arm which grows from a tree beside a
> large basin, or by a goddess inside that tree.[88]

Chapter 58 of the *Book of the Dead* is entitled "Spell for
Breathing the Air and of Having Power over the Water in the

Underworld." The accompanying illustration on the Ani Papyrus shows Ani and his wife, Thuthu, scooping water with their right hands from the pool which is bordered by palm trees loaded with dates.[89] The text presents the spell to be spoken by the god Osiris: "Open to me! Who are you, and where were you born? I am one of you. . . ." The next chapter has a similar heading, and the accompanying illustration shows Ani kneeling beside a pool of water next to which is growing a sycamore tree. The goddess Nut is in the tree offering food and pouring water into Ani's hands from a pitcher.[90] The text with the illustration begins: "Hail, thou sycamore tree of the goddess Nut. Grant that I may drink the water and breathe the air which are in you." In chapters 107 and 109 a spell is given to enable the initiate to enter the regions of heaven. Two sycamore trees are described as being at the door of the Lord of the East, and one approaches the trees and the door by being guided in a boat, the barge of the god. South of the trees and the door are the lakes of a thousand geese and the fields of the god, which Piankoff associates with a type of paradise composed of green pastures and hunting grounds.[91] Also in the *Book of the Dead* are spells in which the initiate is required to give specific secret or ritual names and responses to questions of identity and purpose before he is allowed to enter the realm of the god.[92]

Elsewhere in Egyptian funerary literature, the water of the god Osiris is spoken of as *cold* water, just as in the examples from the Roman period cited above. "This cold water of yours, O Osiris, this cold water of yours, O King, has gone forth to your son, has gone forth to Horus."[93] One can also find warnings in which the soul of the deceased is told to avoid the lake of the evil-doer.[94] The purpose of the warnings, instructions, and dialogues is implied in one of the Pyramid Texts: "Thou art departed that thou mayest become a spirit, that thou mayest become mighty as a god, an enthroned one like Osiris."[95]

Despite the obvious similarities shared by the gold plates and the Egyptian literature, in addition to the proven contacts between the Greek and Egyptian civilizations from the critical seventh century B.C. and later, sufficient differences have been noted to show that some modification accompanied the borrowing of motifs. The only refreshment mentioned in the gold tablets is a drink of water, but the soul in Egyptian texts is refreshed "not only with water but also with fruit and frankincense." The plates always refer to a cypress tree, while the Egyptian literature consistently mentions a sycamore, and Zuntz states "there could not easily be trees more different than these two."[96] The drinking of a "living water" by the soul parched with thirst is common to both sources, but, so far as is known, Egyptian literature did not have springs of *Lethe* or *Mnemosyne*. While chapter 25 of the *Book of the Dead* gives a formula to make a man possess memory in the Netherworld,[97] no mention is made of a well or drinking of water in that context. Jane Harrison considers the designation of the two springs as *Lethe* and *Mnemosyne* to be a Greek development from the neutral fountains mentioned in the Egyptian literature.[98] Because the Egyptians are not commonly known to have used inscribed gold plates before the Roman period, either for the living or the dead, Zuntz suggests that this practice was also a Greek innovation upon the Egyptian tradition.[99] Nevertheless, F. S. Harris collected ample evidence to show that Egyptians did use metal plates (including gold ones) for inscribing treaties and religious texts in the pre-Hellenistic era.[100]

The differences in the two civilizations allow for independent development within a common tradition, or better, development in one tradition which borrows from another. Zuntz summarizes his views on the relationship between the gold plates and the Egyptian sources:

> In both countries these texts are equally designed to accompany the dead into their graves in order to tell them what awaits them in the other world and how they are to meet it. In Egypt this had been the custom for hundreds and even thousands of years, while in Greece there is no trace of it, apart from the few Gold Leaves, whose texts witness to a set of very specific persuasions. Hence it can reasonably be argued that the narrowly confined and recent Greek usage derives from that older civilization to which Greeks owed so much and which they often proclaimed as their teacher of "wisdom."[101]

The burial of the texts with the dead does not preclude the sacred significance of the materials to the living, especially when one considers the ritual purposes commentators attach to them. The recitation of the text, or at least part of it, on special ritual occasions, would be necessary to prepare the living initiate for his journey into the world of departed spirits. The burial of the text with the deceased insures that he will have a familiar and faithful guide for his journey, one whose warnings and reminders will protect him and assist him in achieving his divine potential.

THE BOOK OF MORMON AND THE DREAM OF LEHI

By now it is obvious that the accounts of Lehi's dream in the Book of Mormon have much in common with the gold tablets and the related Egyptian literature. The Book of Mormon narrative claims Egyptian ties,[102] probably quite similar to the mercantilistic connections of the Greeks in Egypt.[103] The Book of Mormon begins at the close of the seventh century B.C.,[104] coinciding with the seventh/sixth-century origins of the religious materials on the Greek gold plates. The use, or borrowing, of typically Egyptian motifs and the inscription of religious writings upon gold plates are of considerable significance for the student of the Book of Mormon, and the striking resemblances in all the materials under discussion would be remarkably coincidental if they were not connected to a common source or origin. Since the Greek gold tablets appear to have an Egyptian origin which agrees in time and content with the Egyptian associations of the Book of Mormon, the most feasible and plausible explanation for the internal characteristics shared by both is that seventh/sixth-century B.C. Egypt is the common meetingground for the two traditions.

In the first narration of the dream in 1 Nephi, the one given by Lehi, the following descriptive elements are noteworthy. Lehi's dream begins in a dark and dreary wilderness, through which he can advance safely only with the assistance of a guide.[105] Following his guide through the "dark and dreary waste" for a long time, Lehi reaches a large field, or meadow, through which flows a river.[106] Near the river stands a tree, laden with a sweet white fruit which refreshes the wanderer. At this point Lehi himself becomes a guide to some of his own family, who are apparently lost in the dark wilderness and have nobody else to guide them.[107] As details of the dream come into focus, Lehi further describes a path leading to the tree[108] and many other paths which lead to doom and destruction.[109] Some of the multitude of souls wandering in the dark world are assisted in their journey by a "rod of iron,"[110] but many are drowned in the hitherto unidentified fountain, or river.[111] In addition to those drowned in the river, many enter into a "great and spacious building," described as being on the opposite side of the river from the tree.[112] The building is superterrestrial and is filled with people of wealth who scorn those eating from the fruit of the tree.[113] Not all who come to the tree for refreshment enjoy the experience, suggesting they are not properly prepared to receive the fruit, and others wander off and are lost in a great mist of darkness, indicating they have not secured an adequate guide to help them achieve the goal of the tree.[114]

In this brief account, narrated from the perspective of Lehi, the only two elements not accounted for in the gold plates or the Egyptian literature are the "rod of iron" and the "great and spacious building."[115] It was noted above that despite differences between the gold plates and Egyptian texts (*Lethe* and *Mnemosyne*, the writing upon gold plates, and the white cypress tree all differ from their counterparts in Egyptian sources), scholars note that the paths, tree, springs, and dialogue with divine beings argue for an original relationship with independent development in the Greek texts. The differences in the Book of Mormon are likewise not sufficient to disprove the Egyptian connection and are in no way incompatible with the ancient world origin claimed by the Book of Mormon.

The second narration of the dream, given by Lehi's son Nephi, displays an even greater affinity with the Greek and Egyptian materials considered above than does the earlier abbreviated account. In the expanded version, there is much that at first appears extraneous to the symbols of the dream, particularly the prophetic history of Jesus, the Christian tradition, and some aspects of world history as they relate to the family of Lehi. One observes that the dream symbols are very much like the elements of a ritual drama which function as vehicles for transmitting the history of man and for conveying redemptive knowledge to the participant. The common Near Eastern elements of the Tree of Life, springs or rivers of water, etc., which are part of the Egyptian redemption ritual for the dead, and which are adopted and adapted on the gold plates for an Orphic or Pythagorean mystery drama, are also found in the Book of Mormon Tree of Life dream. These elements of the vision or dream assist in Nephi's prophetic and visionary portrayal of the Christian message of redemption for mankind.[116]

In a manner which has been recognized only recently as typically apocalyptic, Nephi was transported to a high mountain where the vision given earlier to his father was opened to his view and understanding.[117] Before he was permitted to see the vision of the tree, however, Nephi was asked two questions by his angelic guide, and only satisfactory answers to these questions allowed him to proceed.[118] The dialogue pattern of preparing Nephi for further visionary insights continues throughout the account, including such questions from his angelic guide as, "What desirest thou?"[119] "What beholdest thou?"[120] "Knowest thou . . . ?"[121] and "Rememberest thou?"[122]

As the vision opened, Nephi first saw the tree, which he described as being white.[123] As it continued, he saw all that his father had seen, but in many instances he recounted new details which were not included in the earlier narrative. The unidentified river of water in the first version of the dream is a "fountain of filthy water" in the second account, and is further identified as "the depths of hell."[124] Especially noteworthy in the expanded account is the mention of a second spring called "the fountain of living waters," which flows beside the Tree of Life.[125] The other symbols in Lehi's vision, such as the rod of iron, the great building, and the dark mists, are repeated and explained in Nephi's account of his own vision.

The symbols discussed in the present essay are reminiscent of the symbols studied by Goodenough in his extensive work, *Jewish Symbols in the Greco-Roman Period.* Goodenough argues that symbols in the ancient world could be transferred from one religion or culture to another and not lose their usefulness in a new setting.[126] He refers specifically to the Tree and Water of Life when stating that such symbols had a constant religious value, although they "could be used with gods whose mythologies were utterly dissimilar."[127] It is the constant religious value behind the symbols which permits their use in divergent traditions. The Tree and Water of Life may signify refreshment and life-giving power in one instance and the bestowal of memory (the essence of life) in another; the river of filthy water can be hell, forgetfulness, or the water of the evildoer in different mythologies; but the *value* of the symbols remains constant.

Through all this type of literature is the need for a personal or textual guide to aid the traveler and initiate along the divine path. The mists of darkness in the dream of the Tree of Life prevent many from seeing their way or from finding such a guide and thus prevent them from traveling the *one* path which will lead to the Tree. Just as the Egyptian and Greek sources used above to test the historical compatibility of the Book of Mormon were written as guides for adherents of their respective traditions, so also the Book of Mormon states that it is a guide for those who wish to be redeemed by Christ and find the path to the Tree of Life.[128] It is this challenge of the book, more than its demonstrable compatibility with the ancient Near Eastern origin which it claims, that gives it significance in modern setting, and it is not a challenge which can be ignored or taken lightly.

NOTES

1. Hal Hougey, *The Truth About the "Lehi Tree-of-Life" Stone* (Concord: Pacific Publishing Co., 1963).

2. Both authors refer to the first edition of Lucy Smith's biography, pp. 58-59, although the account of the dream has not been changed in the revised edition (the one used by the present author was published by Deseret Book Co. in 1953) pp. 48-50.

3. Hougey, p. 24.

4. There is no evidence that Lucy Mack Smith committed her material to writing before 1845, and because the Book of Mormon was written in 1829, some question exists regarding the influence of the Book of Mormon phrasing on her work. According to Lucy's chronology, the particular dream of her husband which is used by the above critics in their comparison occurred in 1811, some eighteen years before the Book of Mormon was written in English and thirty-four years before Lucy's work was written. The complex nature of possible influences in narrating a dream experience over so lengthy a period of time is beyond any certain reconstruction. Hougey argues polemically and tendentiously that if one suggested that the Book of Mormon account influenced Lucy Smith in her phrasing or working in recounting the dream of Joseph Smith, Sr., he must then admit "that Joseph Smith's mother was dishonest, and that she willingly and purposely jeopardized the reputation of her son" (p. 25). He then states that such could not have been the case "in view of all the things she says about him," returning to his simplistic theory that the only direction of influence was from Lucy Smith to her son.

5. Because it also claims to be a translation, any modern language source material which the translator found useful or helpful in his translating efforts cannot be used *ipso facto* as evidence against the authenticity of his work.

6. Nibley's three major works in this area are: *Lehi in the Desert and The World of the Jaredites* (Salt Lake City: Bookcraft, 1952); *An Approach to the Book of Mormon* (Salt Lake City: Deseret Book Co., 1964); *Since Cumorah* (Salt Lake City: Deseret Book Co., 1967). The debt of any writer in this field, including that of the author, will be obvious to anybody familiar with Nibley's treatment of the subject, even when, as in the present instance, materials relating to Book of Mormon origins are being considered for the first time in that context.

7. Morton Smith, *Clement of Alexandria and a Secret Gospel of Mark* (Cambridge: Harvard University Press, 1973), p. ix.

8. Ibid., p. 1. Smith submitted photographs of the manuscript to a number of specialists who generously supplied opinions on the date of the hand. Although different dates were favored by the scholars, Smith states that all agreed on the possibility of an eighteenth-century date.

9. Ibid.

10. Clement to Theodore, Folio 1, recto 11. 22-23.

11. Ibid., 1. 17.

12. M. Smith, *op cit.,* p. 4.

13. Ibid., p. ix.

14. Kirk and Raven, *The Pre-Socratic Philosophers* (Cambridge: Cambridge University Press, 1971), pp. 37ff.; Jane Harrison, *Themis* (New York: Meridian Books, 1962 [reprint of 1927 ed.] p. 462; W. K. C. Guthrie, *Orpheus and Greek Religion* (New York: W. W. Norton and Co., 1966), p. 11; Kath-

leen Freeman, *Companion to the Pre-Socratic Philosophers* (Cambridge: Harvard University Press, 1966), p. 1.

15. E. R. Dodds, *The Greeks and the Irrational* (Berkeley: University of California Press, 1968), p. 147: "But I must confess that I know very little about early Orphism, and the more I read about it the more my knowledge diminishes. Twenty years ago, I could have said quite a lot about it (we all could at that time). Since then, I have lost a great deal of knowledge. . . ." New discoveries tend to upset old theories.

16. The Thracian origin is argued in Dodds, p. 147; Freeman, pp. 1-2; on the story relating to Orpheus and Orphic rituals, see Guthrie, pp. 25ff. Cornford, *From Religion to Philosophy* (New York: Harper and Row, 1957), p. 99; p 178n., mentions possible connections with Iranian or Persian influences on Orphism, suggesting a more eastward origin for the theology of the movement.

17. Diels-Kranz, *Die Fragmente der Vorsokratiker* (Berlin: 1960, reprint), p. 3, citing Ibykos, fr. 17.

18. R. Sealey, *A History of the Greek City States, 700-338 B.C.* (Berkeley: University of California Press, 1976), p. 52. Bury and Meiggs, *A History of Greek*, 4th ed. (New York: St. Martin's Press, 1975), pp. 84-85. Chester G. Starr, *The Economic and Social Growth of Early Greece, 800-500 B.C.* (New York: Oxford University Press, 1977), pp. 49-51. That religion spread with trade during this period is suggested by Guthrie, p. 11: "It is generally agreed that there was considerable activity, whether nascent or renascent, in the sphere of Orphic and kindred religion, in the sixth century B.C."

19. Guthrie, p. 10.

20. Ibid., p. 9. I. M. Linforth, *The Arts of Orpheus* (Berkeley: University of California Press, 1941), stated that before 300 B.C. the description of "Orphic" was applied to all sorts of ideas associated with every manner of ritual.

21. See note 15 and Harrison, pp. 462ff.

22. Freeman, p. 5.

23. Freeman, p. 4. In Plato, see examples of the hexameters attributed to Orpheus in *Cratylus* 402b, *Philebus* 66c; and a reference to Orphic hexameters in *Ion* 536b.

24. Euripides, *Alcestis* 965ff. The scholiast on the passage, a contemporary of Plato, states that the tablets actually existed at that time on Mt. Haimos.

25. Pseudo-Plato, *Axiochos*, 371a.

26. Günther Zuntz, *Persephone* (Oxford: Clarendon Press, 1971), p. 278.

27. *Inscript. Graec.* V.2, 387. Cf. I.G.V.2, 390 and 566.

28. Zuntz, *Persephone*, p. 278 n. 7, referring to Kern, *I.G.* 1.1., Pls. 8, 10 and 21. Pl. 8 is a bronze plaque from Mycenae and pl. 10 one from Thetonium in Thessaly; cf. Arangio-Ruiz and Olivieri, *Inscriptiones Sicilae et M. Graeciae* (1925) for numerous examples, e.g. an archaic bronze plaque from Policastro

(p. 47). These date from the sixth and fifth centuries B.C., and numerous examples from later periods could also be cited.

29. Zuntz, *Persephone,* p. 279.

30. *British Museum Catalogue,* p. 378, no. 3153, cited in Zuntz, pp. 29ff. No. 3150 in the British Museum is a similar gold plate, and others have been found.

31. F. Sieburg, *Bonner Jahrbucher* 103 (1898), pp. 123ff.

32. A. Wiedemann, *Bonner Jahrbucher* 97 (1895), pp. 215ff., and Sieburg, pp. 123ff.

33. Sieburg, pp. 136ff.

34. In addition to the list of plates and their origins listed in Zuntz, *Persephone,* p. 286, two others are known to the author. One is in the J. Paul Getty Museum in Los Angeles and the other was discovered in southern Italy (Hipponios) in 1972, and published by Zuntz in *Wiener Studien* 89 (1976). The last-mentioned plate will be discussed in some detail.

35. Ibid., p. 355.

36. Zuntz, *Wiener Studien* 89 (1976), esp. p. 132 for text.

37. Zuntz, *Persephone,* pp. 294ff., and 355ff. Walter Burkert, while visiting U. C. Berkeley as the Sather Classical Lecturer in 1977, gave some information and opinions concerning the plates which will be used in this paper.

38. Zuntz, *Persephone,* p. 343.

39. This papyrus was discussed in some detail by Prof. Burkert, who stated that it clearly predates the tomb in which it was found. Pre-Socratic concepts from Anaxagoras and Democritus are found in the text, but nothing later than the fifth century can be seen.

40. Zuntz, *Persephone,* pp. 342ff., and pp. 370ff.

41. Guthrie, pp. 177, 198, 208; Freeman, pp. 7, 14, etc.

42. Harrison, pp. 462ff.

43. The author's translation is given where another translator is not named.

44. The first part of the text is taken from the Hipponios tablet found in 1972. It is one of the earliest of the plates, dating perhaps to the fifth century. There is some question whether "tomb" or "rule" should be read, but the author follows the editors of the text.

45. Petelia Plate (B1), (lines) 1-3. In this plate alone, the tree mentioned below is found by the forbidden spring on the left. Elsewhere the tree is beside the spring on the right, where commentators agree it belongs.

46. Plate from Thurii (A4), 2, trans. Guthrie, p. 173.

47. Hipponios plate, 2-4.

48. Combined from B1, 4-5, and Hipponios, 6-7.

49. Hipponios plate, 8-9.

50. Plates from Crete B3-B8, 3.

51. This text comes from the plates from Thurii, designated A1-A3, and from B1. A composite rendering of the four is given below. The more common rendering, "I am come from the pure, pure Queen of those below," is rejected by Zuntz (*Persephone* p. 306), following Rohde, *Psyche II*, p. 218, *et al*. The adjective is unsuitable for the goddess, and ritually speaking, it is the soul which has become Καθαρὰ ἐκ καθαρων. No agreement exists on the identification of the goddess.

52. Zuntz notes that the words "suggest an assembly of gods which it is hard, even so, to visualize" (*Persephone,* pp. 311-12).

53. Hipponios plate, 10, and B1, 6-7.

54. Ibid., 11-12, and B1, 11. 8-9.

55. Ibid., 13-14, and B1, 10-12. The alternative translation was suggested by an emended spelling proposed by M. West. It is left in parentheses in favor of the reading on the plate, although spelling difficulties exist in line 13 as it stands.

56. A4, 3-7, transl. Guthrie.

57. Hipponios plate, 15-16.

58. Analysis of the metrical difficulties in the poetic lines, and also of the presence of some prosaic elements in certain of the plates, has led to attempts to determine which portions of the texts were original and which were added later. There is no real agreement at present on solutions to such problems, and even suspected additions must be earlier than the basic composition given above, i.e., prior to the fourth century.

59. Zuntz, *Persephone,* p. 326. The single exception is the term *Bacchoi* in line 16 of the Hipponios plate, not known to Zuntz when he wrote *Persephone.* Burkert considers this at best a slender thread to connect with "Orphism."

60. Pseudo-Plato, *Axiochos* 371a.

61. Euripides, *Alcestis* 967-70.

62. Guthrie, p. 172.

63. Zuntz, *Persephone,* p. 343.

64. This example argues that the same text is necessary for all participants, and it is thus unnecessary to make a distinction between male and female in the basic formulary.

65. Plato, *Phaedo* 108a.

66. Plato, *Gorgias* 523ff., esp. 524a.

67. Plato, *Republic* 614ff.

68. Jane Harrison, *Prolegonema to the Study of Greek Religion* (Cleveland: World Publishing Co., 1959, reprint), p. 574; cf. note 63.

69. Zuntz, *Persephone,* p. 378.

70. Guthrie, pp. 177ff.; Zuntz, *Persephone,* pp. 378ff.; Harrison, *Prol.,* pp. 574ff.

71. Hesiod, *Theogony* 226-30.

72. Ibid. 211-25.

73. Plato, *Republic* 621. *Lethe* is forgetting, and the Greek word for truth, *alethelia*, has been seen as "non-forgetting." The reward for the just is to have knowledge preserved or restored, just as the punishment for the unjust is to forget what they know.

74. Plato, *Phaedrus* 248c.

75. Zuntz, *Persephone*, p. 380, 381.

76. Ibid., p. 373.

77. Guthrie, p. 182.

78. A. B. Cook, *Zeus* (Cambridge: Cambridge University Press, 1940), III:420-21.

79. Pseudo-Kallisthenes, *Hist. Ales. Magn.* 17.27ff.

80. Guthrie, pp. 176ff.

81. Herodotus, *Hist.* 2.81.

82. Inscript., Graec. *(It. et Sic.)* XIV., 1488, 1705, 1782.

83. Zuntz, *Persephone*, p. 370.

84. Dietrich, *Abraxos*, p. 97, cited in Harrison, *Prol.*, p. 576.

85. Zuntz, *Persephone* p. 370; cf. Harrison, *Prol.* p. 575 n.2; Guthrie, p. 192 n.14; etc.

86. Harrison, *Prol.*, p. 576.

87. Guthrie, p. 177.

88. Zuntz, *Persephone*, p. 177.

89. T. G. Allen, *The Book of the Dead*, Chicago: University of Chicago Press, 1974. See also Wallis Budge, *The Egyptian Book of the Dead* (New York: Dover Publishing Inc., 1967, reprint) p. 314.

90. Ibid.

91. A. Piankoff, *The Wandering of the Soul* (Princeton: Princeton University Press, Bollingen Series XL. 6, 1974), pp. 4-8.

92. *Book of the Dead*, chapter 125, cited in Piankoff, pp. 8-10.

93. R. O. Faulkner, *The Ancient Egyptian Pyramid Texts* (Oxford: Clarendon Press, 1969), Utterances 32, 33, 423, etc.

94. Ibid., Utterances 214 and 500. Zuntz appears to have missed such sources, for he states that the Egyptians have nothing corresponding to the two springs of some of the plates.

95. Spell 752b, cited in Piankoff, p. 3.

96. Zuntz, *Persephone*, p. 372.

97. Budge, pp. 87ff.

98. Harrison, *Prol.*, p. 576.

99. Zuntz, *Persephone*, p. 376.

100. F. S. Harris, *The Book of Mormon, Message and Evidences* (Salt Lake City: Deseret News Press, 1953), pp. 96-99.

101. Zuntz, *Persephone,* p. 376.

102. 1 Ne. 1:2; Mosiah 1:4; Morm. 9:32.

103. Nibley, *Lehi,* pp. 36ff.

104. 1 Ne. 1:4; 5:13; 10:4; etc.

105. 1 Ne. 8:4-7.

106. 1 Ne. 8:9-13.

107. 1 Ne. 8:14-16.

108. 1 Ne. 8:20-22.

109. 1 Ne. 8:23, 28, 32.

110. 1 Ne. 8:19, 24, 30.

111. 1 Ne. 8:32.

112. 1 Ne. 8:26.

113. 1 Ne. 8:27ff., 33.

114. 1 Ne. 8:24ff., 28, and 8:23, 32.

115. Nibley, *Approach,* pp. 211ff., gives evidence which would suggest that the great building may have come from the Arab world, which in turn was imitating earlier Babylonian architecture. The height, sometimes ten or twelve stories, is even described as making the building appear to stand in the air, high above the earth. He further notes that in Arab tradition, spaciousness is the index of elegance and comfort. There is some possibility that the rod of iron came from the Jewish world of Lehi, especially in relation to the temple, but that must be dealt with properly within its own cultural context.

116. This often-repeated aspect of the redemption drama in the Book of Mormon must be reserved for another study, since the dream symbols as they related to the ancient Near East are the focus of the present paper.

117. 1 Ne. 11:1; the author has given a brief treatment of this theme in "Manichaeism, Mormonism, and Apocalypticism," *Sperry Lecture Series,* Provo: BYU Press, 1973, pp. 18-25, and the volume of recent literature on the subject attests to its new-found importance in the study of ancient religious history and literature.

118. 1 Ne. 11:2-6. The two questions were: "What desirest thou?" and "Believest thou that thy father saw the tree of which he hath spoken?"

119. 1 Ne. 11:10.

120. 1 Ne. 13:2.

121. 1 Ne. 11:16, 21.

122. 1 Ne. 14:8.

123. 1 Ne. 11:8. In the earlier account only the fruit was mentioned as white (8:11), perhaps because of the emphasis on partaking of the fruit. The tree receives greater emphasis in Nephi's experience.

124. 1 Ne. 12:16.

125. 1 Ne. 11:25.

126. E. R. Goodenough, *Jewish Symbols in the Greco-Roman Period*, 13 vols. (New York: Bollingen Foundation, 1954), esp. vol. 4.

127. Ibid., 7:116.

128. 1 Ne. 13:33-37; 14:18-30.

Two Shots
in the Dark

*Hugh W. Nibley, linguist, classicist, and historian, is Pro-
fessor of History and Religion at Brigham Young University,
where until recently he was Director of the Institute of Ancient
Studies. Adept in some fourteen languages, he graduated from
UCLA with highest honors, received his Ph.D. from the University of California at Berkeley, and has done specialized language
study at Berkeley and Chicago. He is a prolific writer, having
published hundreds of articles and books both on secular topics
and on pioneering historical, linguistic, and cultural studies of
the Book of Mormon and Mormonism. In "Two Shots in the
Dark," Nibley examines two passages in the Book of Mormon—
the account of Lehi's exodus from Jerusalem and the account of
Christ's ministry in the Americas—in light of recent scholarship.
He rigorously compares the Lachish letters, discovered in 1935,
with Lehi's story, and finds truly astonishing parallels in form,
style, subject matter, and even mention of specific names and*

*events. He also compares early Christian writings called "Forty-
Day Literature" to 3 Nephi in the Book of Mormon, and again
finds striking parallels and similarities. The article suggests that
either Joseph Smith was "extravagantly lucky" or the Book of
Mormon is indeed a translation of an ancient document that is
historically, linguistically, culturally, and factually accurate.*

---

i. DARK DAYS IN JERUSALEM:
THE LACHISH LETTERS AND THE
BOOK OF MORMON (1 NEPHI)

The Lachish Letters are the best evidence so far discovered
for the authenticity of Bible history. "In these letters," wrote
Harry Torczyner, whose edition and commentary remain the
standard work on the subject, "we have the most valuable discovery yet made in the biblical archaeology of Palestine and the
most intimate corroboration of the Bible to this day."[1] They are
also the star witness for the correctness of the Book of Mormon,
the opening scenes of which take place in exactly the same
setting and time as the Letters. Both records paint pictures
which are far removed from those supplied in any other known
sources, and yet the two pictures are as alike as postcards of the
Eiffel Tower.

The first contribution of the Lachish Letters to ancient
studies was the revelation that such documents existed. Until
their discovery in 1935, it was thought that the Hebrew alphabet of that time (shortly after 600 B.C.) was used only for the
writing of inscriptions; indeed, all known inscriptions of comparable antiquity to the Letters are so scarce and scanty that it
has been impossible even to put together a complete exemplar of
the Hebrew alphabet from their contents. But with the finding
of the Lachish Letters, it suddenly became clear that "the ancient
Jews could write quickly and boldly, in an artistic flowing
hand" (T. 15). The same arresting discovery was repeated at
Qumran, where again the revelation of writing in common use

among the Jews of another Jerusalem six hundred years later came as a distinct surprise. While the Lachish Letters were written on potsherds, the scrolls were kept in the pots, both practices reminding us that since prehistoric times symbolic marks on pottery had been used to convey messages.

Potsherds, however, do not lend themselves to convenient filing, and the contents of important Lachish Letters were duly abridged for transfer to the official archives (T. 80) in the form of *delathoth,* as would appear from Letter 4 in which the writer reports that he is writing *'al ha-DLT.* What is a *delet*? Torczyner is puzzled that such a word should be used to indicate "a sheet or page of papyrus," since the word originally meant "door-board, then board in general," being applied according to the dictionary to a "board, placque, plate, or tablet."*

Torczyner finds the root meaning of the Accadic word *edeln,* from *wdl, ydl,* "to lock or shut," the collective noun indicating things locked, hinged, or joined together—a reminder that the very ancient codex form of the book was joined pages of wood, ivory, or metal. The scanty evidence, confined to the time of Jeremiah, is enough to justify speculation of the possibility of the *delathoth* being such "plates" or metal tablets as turn up in the Book of Mormon story.

More specific resemblances in the records are evident, beginning with the same obsessive concern with writing and recording and the same association with the name of Jeremiah. Nephi informs us that Jeremiah's words had been put into writing from time to time (rather than appearing as a single completed book), and that the process was still going on at the time his family left Jerusalem (1 Nephi 5:13). From the Lachish Letters we learn that Jeremiah himself made use of other writings circulating at that time, including the Lachish Letters

---

*The one passage in the Old Testament that would justify calling a *deleth* a roll of papyrus is Jer. 36:23: "when Jehudi had read three or four leaves (delathoth = pagellas) he cut it with a knife and cast it into the fire, until all the roll (megillah, volumen) was consumed with fire." Papyrus tears easily, yet instead of ripping the roll to shreds in his wrath, the king had to go after it with a knife—surely it was solider than paper.

themselves, which may be "some of the actual documents" upon which the prophet based his account of his fellow prophet Uriah—Jeremiah 38:4, in fact, is a direct quotation from Letter 6 (T.18). (Jeremiah could hardly have visited the enemy strong-hold of Lachish to consult the original potsherd text.)

Nephi's father, Lehi, kept a written account of things as they happened, including even his dreams and visions (1:16), which things Nephi faithfully transfers to his record, but only after he has abridged them and added his own account. This process of transmitting, abridging, compiling, and commenting as we find it at Lachish goes on throughout the Book of Mormon. Preser-vation on *delathoth* was no invention of Lehi's, since the story begins with the fetching of records written on bronze plates from the archives of Laban, the military governor of Jerusalem. Is metal plates carrying delathoth too far? The Copper Scroll of the Dead Sea Scrolls assures us that it is not. That scroll was made of separate plates riveted together, admittedly an unusual and inconvenient arrangement but nonetheless one necessary to insure the survival of particularly precious records. Joseph Smith's insistence on books made of metal plates was a favorite target of his detractors, metal plates were strange enough to seem ludicrous, and impractical enough to cause difficulties. This was *not* the normal way of writing; John Allegro comments that "the scribe [of the Copper Scroll], not without reason, appears to have tired toward the end, and the last lines of writing are badly formed and rather small. One can almost hear his sigh of relief as he punched out the last two words in the middle of the final line."² Compare this with the sighs of Nephi's younger brother:

> . . . and I cannot write but a little of my words, because of the difficulty of engraving our words upon plates . . . But whatsoever things we write upon anything save it be upon plates must perish and vanish away; but we can write a few words upon plates. . . . and we labor dili-gently to engraven these words upon plates, hoping that our beloved brethren and our children will receive them." (Jacob 4:1-3)

Equally significant for the Book of Mormon study is Torczyner's emphasis on the *Egyptian* manner of keeping records in
the days of Zedekiah. The Lachish Letters were written on potsherds, he notes, only because of a severe shortage of papyrus,
the normal writing material. With the use of Egyptian paper
went the Egyptian scribal practices in general: "The new writing
material first appears under Tiglath Pileser III," that is, its
general use throughout the Near East begins a century before
Lehi's day, "and thereafter [writes A. T. Olmstead] every expedition has its two scribes, the chief with stylus and tablet, his
assistant with papyrus roll or parchment and Egyptian pen."[3]
More than sixty years before Lehi left Jerusalem the kings of
Assyria were also pharaohs of Egypt, their Egyptian scribes
glorifying them in Egyptian records. At the same time the
Assyrian court "found it necessary to possess an Aramaic
scribe" as well, to record in that language.[4] Thus the idea of
Lehi's bilingual record keeping, which caused considerable
trouble to the recorders, is not entirely out of place. The reason
given for it is economy of space. In Lehi's day a new type of
Egyptian writing, demotic, was coming to its own, as much
quicker and briefer than hieratic as hieratic was than hiero-
glyphic. This is perhaps what Lehi would have used. Only a
thousand years later do we learn of "characters which are *called
among us* the reformed Egyptian," something not recognizable
to any Egyptologist today, altered beyond recognition even as
"Hebrew hath been altered by us also" (Mormon 9:32-33, italics
added). It should be noted however, that the only known
example of supposed Nephite writing, the so-called Anthon
Transcript, is compared by specialists with *Meroitic* writing—
another type of "reformed Egyptian" developed at the same
time as the Nephite script by people also fleeing from destroyers
of Jerusalem, who in a short time transformed demotic or
hieratic into their own new and mysterious writing.

The dates *post and ante quem* of the Lachish Letters are
neatly bracketed by two layers of ashes representing two
destructions of the city, one in 597 and the other in 588 B.C.
between which they were found. Letter 4 "can date only a few

weeks before the fall of Lachish," while others "possibly cover a period of a few years" (T.18). There is definitely a conflict in the record as to who was the king at the time. The scribe of Jeremiah 27:1-3 says that Zedekiah was not yet king, but scholars now insist that he was wrong and that Zedekiah was ruling earlier than the Masoretic text says he was, so 1 Nephi 1:4 may not be an anachronism. While Lehi's story begins in the *first* year of Zedekiah "the background of our ostraca," according to Torczyner, "actually happened in the *last* year of the reign of Zedekiah" (T. 69). After his vision in the desert Lehi spent some time at Jerusalem entering into the activity of the other prophets and getting himself into the same trouble: "In that same year there came many prophets, prophesying unto the people that they must repent, or the great city Jerusalem must be destroyed" (1:4). This was the very message ("not good!") that "caused the hands to sink even the hands of (those in) the city and the country," according to the Lachish Letters (6:6-7).

The *proper names* in the Lachish Letters and the Book of Mormon belong to *one* particular period in Jewish history—the same period. Seven of the nine proper names in Letter 1 end in -yahu, which later became -iah, and during the Babylonian period lost the "h" entirely. In all the letters there are no Baal names and no El names—the lack of which was once thought to be a serious defect in the Book of Mormon. Torczyner finds "the spelling of the names compounded with -iah" to be most important. The -yahu ending is *also* found as -yah about a century later among the Jews in Elephantine, who were "perhaps the descendants of those Jews who, after the fall of the Judaean kingdom, went down to Egypt, taking with them the prophet Jeremiah" (T. 27). Here we have another control over the Lehi story. The discovery of the Elephantine documents in 1925 showed that colonies of Jews actually did flee into the desert in the manner of Lehi, during his lifetime, and for the same reasons; arriving in their new home far up the Nile, they proceeded to build a replica of Solomon's Temple, exactly as Lehi did upon landing in the New World. Both of these oddities, especially the latter, were once considered damning refutations of the Book of Mormon. The -yahu ending of personal names abounds at Elephantine, but in a more abbreviated form (-iah) than at Lachish (-yahu) a hundred years earlier. The same variety of endings is found in the Book of Mormon, e.g., the Lachish name *Mattanyahu* appears at Elephantine as *Mtn,* and in the Book of Mormon both as Mathonihah and Mathoni. The Book of Mormon has both long and short forms in the names Amalickiah, Amaleki and Amlici, cf. Elephantine MLKih (T. 24). The Assyrian inscriptions show that the final "ll" was dropped in the Hebrew spelling after Lehi left, when the Jews "lost their pronunciation of the consonant "ll" under the influence of the Babylonian language" (T. 25). Of the two names in Letter 1 *not* ending in -yahu, the one, Tb-Shlm (which Torczyner renders Tobshillem), suggests Book of Mormon Shilom and Shelem, while the other Hgb (T. Hagab), resembles Book of Mormon Hagoth.

More significant are the indications that the -yahu names are "certainly a token of a changed inner Judaean relationship of Yhwh." "This practice," Torczyner suggests, "is in some way *parallel* to . . . the first reformation by *Moses*"; what we have in the predominance of -yahu names reflects "the act of general reformation inaugurated by King Josiah (Yoshiyahu) [the father of Zedekiah]" (2 Kings 22 and 23) (T. 29). Another interesting coincidence: A Book of Mormon king 450 years after Lehi undertook a general reformation of the national constitution and revival of the religious life of the people. He and his brothers had been rigorously trained by their father, King Benjamin, "in all the language of his fathers, that thereby they might become men of understanding," familiar with the writings of the ancient prophets and also "concerning the records which were engraven on the plates of brass," without which records, he tells them, "even our fathers would have dwindled in unbelief." "And now, my sons, I would that ye should remember to search them diligently, that ye may profit thereby . . ." etc. (Mosiah 1:2, 3, 5, 7). Fittingly, this king named his eldest son, the great reforming king, Mosiah, suggesting both the early reform of Moses and its later imitation by Josiah. This would be altogether too much of a coincidence were it not that the Book of Mosiah supplies the information that fully accounts for the resemblances when it explains just how Nephite names and customs were preserved intact in the transplanting of cultures from the Old World to the New. Lehi's ties to the Yahvist tradition are reflected in the only female name given in his history, that of his wife, Sar*iah*; such feminine names turn up at Elephantine—Mibtahyah, though in female names the yahu element usually comes first (T. 27-28).

The action of the Lachish Letters centers around the activities of the prophets in the land, who are causing grave concern to the government. The Book of Mormon opens on a similar note: "and in that same year there came many prophets, prophesying unto the people that they must repent, or the great city Jerusalem must be destroyed" (1:4). The identity of all but two of these prophets has now been lost, but it is clear from both the Lachish Letters and the Book of Mormon that there were more of them. "It must certainly be admitted," writes Torczyner, "that there was more than one prophet at this time" (T. 65). The central figure is of course Jeremiah, but it is only by chance that we even know about him, for he is not mentioned in the book of Kings—it is the prophetess Huldah, "an otherwise quite unknown figure," whom Josiah consults (T. 70). Jeremiah in turn mentions the prophet Uriah "in only a few passages." and his name turns up nowhere else, though Uriah's "religious influence must have been of great extent and long standing!" (T. 70). Uriah "prophesied against this city and against this land according to all the words of Jeremiah" (Jeremiah 26:20). The words of such prophets were dangerously undermining morale both of the military and the people. Lachish Letter 6:5-6: "Behold the words of the . . . are not good, (liable) to weaken the hands . . . the hands of the country and the city" (T. 64). This passage is cited intact by Jeremiah 38:4.

As the Book of Mormon opens, we see Lehi as one of those citizens distressed and discouraged by the preaching of the "many prophets." "As he went forth," apparently on a business journey, for he was a rich merchant, he "prayed unto the Lord, yea, even with all his heart, in behalf of his people" (1 Nephi 1:5). In reply to his prayer he received a vision which sent him out to join the prophets: "my father . . . went forth among the people, and began to prophesy and to declare unto them . . ." (1:18). He indeed was teaching "in the spirit of Jeremiah," for Nephi explicitly links him to the prophet's vicissitudes: ". . . for behold, they have rejected the prophets, and Jeremiah have they cast into prison. And they have sought to take away the life of my father, insomuch that they have driven *him* out of the land" (7:14, italics added). Torczyner suggests that Uriah "may have *hidden in the hills* of Western Judah . . . for a long time" (T. 70), and we find Lehi doing the same thing. Indeed, as Torczyner points out, what we are dealing with here is a type of thing, Uriah's story being told only "as a *parallel* to Jeremiah's not less dangerous position. . . ." (T. 69). To their number we may add Lehi, whose story has every mark of authenticity.

As the Book of Mormon leads us into a world of Rekhabites and sectaries of the desert, so the Lachish Letters give us "for the first time . . . authentic and intimate contemporary reports from Jews, faithfully following their God, about their inner political and religious struggles. . . ." (T. 18). Torczyner sees in the -yahu names a sure indication of "a loyal reformist faction which included even the highest military officers—." Ya'ush and his men are the prophet's followers (T. 66) even though they are necessarily the king's defenders. We see Uriah hiding out in the wilderness "where he had friends and followers, for a long time" (T. 70). The Dead Sea Scrolls have put flesh on these sectarian bones, showing how from the earliest times communities of the faithful would withdraw from Jerusalem to bide their time in the wilderness. Lehi's activities were not confined to the city, he was in the desert when he received the manifestation that sent him hurrying back to his house in Jerusalem, from which later he "went forth among the people" as a prophet (1:18). Badly received, he was warned in a dream that his life was in danger (2:1) and ordered to go into the wilderness and leave all his worldly things behind (2:2). It was the idea behind the Rekhabites (Jeremiah 35) and the people of Qumran: Nephi, inviting a new recruit to come and "have place with us," points out to him that only so could he "be a free man like unto us," and that to "go down into the wilderness" was the only way to "be diligent in keeping the commandments of the Lord"

(4:33-34; 1QS 1). This is the firm conviction of the sectaries of the desert, later expressed in the writings of St. Anthony. So Zoram duly takes an oath and joins the pious company (4:35).

One important aspect of Lehi's account has surfaced very recently in the light of what Klaus Koch calls the rediscovery of *Apocalyptic.* It seems that almost every ancient patriarch, prophet, and apostle is credited with having left behind a *"Testament"* or *"Apocalypse"* bearing his name. A key figure is Jeremiah, whose two assistants, Ezra and Baruch, are responsible for two of the six basic Jewish Apocalypses. Some of these stories are very old, and a consistent pattern emerges from the telling of them, widely scattered though they are in space and time. Briefly summed up, the general plot is this: A righteous man, sorely distressed by the depravity of the world or of Israel, prays fervidly for light and knowledge, and in due time receives a divine manifestation, when a heavenly messenger comes to teach him and takes him on a celestial journey, climaxing in a theophany, after which he returns to earth and reports his experience to family and friends; often this is just before he dies, bestowing a patriarchal blessing—his testament—upon his sons. Often also he goes forth to preach to the people, who reject his message with scorn, whereupon he departs into the wilderness with his faithful followers to establish a more righteous if tentative order of things in the desert, a sort of "church of anticipation." All of which things Lehi also does in due and proper order; the first part of Nephi's writing, he says, is but an abridgment of his father's record, which may properly be called the Testament or Apocalypse of Lehi. It also relates to the Lachish Letters, for Jeremiah was the champion of the Rekhabites (Jeremiah 35) and his assistants (cf. 4 Ezra and 2 Baruch) both headed such communities of refugees. Lehi is definitely doing the accepted thing for men of God in his time.

That the Rekhabite ideal of the desert sectaries was in full flower in Lehi's day, as many other sources now indicate, is clear from the accusation that Nephi's elder brothers brought against him, that he was planning to set up such a society with himself as "our ruler and our teacher . . . ," leading them by his false claims of prophetic inspiration to believe "that the Lord has talked with him . . . thinking, perhaps, that he may lead us away into some strange wilderness [some unoccupied tract]; and after he has led us away, he has thought to make himself a king and a ruler over us. . . ." Plainly they know about that sort of thing (16:37-38). When, after eight years of wandering, the party was commanded to build a ship and sail on the waters, they were all at their wit's end, because they had never dreamed of such a thing as a promised land beyond the sea; theirs was strictly the tradition of the desert sectaries, "a lonesome and a solemn people," as Nephi's younger brother put it.

Against the larger background of national calamity, which is never lost from view, both the Lachish Letters and the Lehi story are concerned with relatively narrow circles of friends and relations.* Clandestine flights from the city in both stories involve friends and families; Nephi and his brethren go back to town to persuade Ishmael and his family to join them in flight (7:2-5). But soon the group begins to split up as Laman, Lemuel, and the two daughters of Ishmael whom they later married, as well as two of Ishmael's sons, vote to return to Jerusalem (7:6, 7). They find the whole idea of giving up their opulent life-style and renouncing their fashionable friends quite unacceptable:

> Behold, these many years we have suffered in the wilderness, which time we might have enjoyed our possessions and . . . been happy. And we know that the people . . . of Jerusalem were a righteous people; for they kept the statutes and judgments of the Lord . . . they are a righteous people; and our father hath judged them. . . . (17:21-22).

They are especially disgruntled at having to defer to a quality in their father for which the Lachish Letters have a particular

---

*Torczyner, p. 18, "The Lachish Letters are the first personal documents found, reflecting the mind, the struggles, sorrows and feelings of ancient Judah in the last days of the kingdom, within the typical form of ancient letter writing. . . . here for the first time we have authentic and intimate contemporary reports from Jews, faithfully following their God, about their inner political and religious struggles, as told in the book of Jeremiah." The Lehi history, as we showed in the book *Lehi in the Desert,* is nothing if not intimate.

expression characterizing the man of prophetic calling as
ha-piqqeah, which Torczyner finds to mean "the open-eyed" or
visionary man, (T. 53) "the seer," "the man whose eyes God had
opened to see," (T. 65) i.e., to see things that other people do
not see. So in the Book of Mormon the brothers use it in a
critical sense against their father, arguing that he is being un-
realistic and impractical:

> . . . they did murmur in many things against their
> father, because he was a *visionary* man, and had led
> them out of the land of Jerusalem, to leave the land of
> their inheritance, and their gold, and their silver, and
> their precious things, to perish in the wilderness. And
> this they said he had done because of the *foolish
> imaginations of his heart.* (2:11, italics added)

They make fun of their father for being *piqqeah,* a "visionary
man." Torczyner explains the word by referring to the instance
in 2 Kings 6:17, where Elisha asks the Lord to open the eyes of
his servant so he could see realities, horses and chariots, which
otherwise only Elisha could see. In the same way the uncoopera-
tive brothers of Nephi hiding out with him in a cave in the
Judean wilderness had their eyes opened so they could see "an
angel of the Lord" while he was reprimanding them (3:29; 7:10).

When feelings run high the Lachish Letters resort to an
unpleasant expression which Torczyner notes because of its
peculiarity: "another interesting phrase may be 'to curse the
seed of somebody,' used apparently in the form ya-or zera
ha-melek, 'he curses (the) seed to the King,' (V, 10) reminding us
of . . . the Arabic curse: 'May Allah destroy thy house.'" (T.
17). The exact Lachish practice however is not found in the
Bible, but the closest thing to it is found in Alma 3:9: "And it
came to pass that whosoever did mingle his seed with that of the
Lamanites did bring the same curse upon his seed."

If the Lachish Letters reflect "the mind, the struggles,
sorrows and feelings of ancient Judah in the last days of the
kingdom" (T. 18), so to an even greater extent does the book of
Nephi, where families split along political lines in a tragic conflict of loyalties. And if the situation of Uriah *parallels* that of

Jeremiah, as Torczyner points out, even more closely does it parallel that of Lehi when we learn from the Letters of "*a warning from the* prophet to one of *his* friends [Slm], who is apparently in the same danger as he himself [cf. Ishmael]. It is, therefore, a prophet fleeing from his home and his friends, a prophet wanted by the military authorities" (T. 64).

The leading character of the Letters is a high military officer Hosha'yahu at Qiryat-Ye'arim, suspected by one party, as reported to his superior Ya'ush, of treachery to the king in aiding the prophet, and by the other of betraying the prophet by revealing the contents of his warning letter to the king: this letter revealed to the king that the prophet was fleeing to Egypt. Likewise his superior officer Ya'ush, who has been ordered to investigate him, "appears to be on the best of terms with the king. But still both men respect the prophet and believe in him, in spite of the king's attitude to him, and their hearts ache that they should be responsible for his destruction" (T. 113). The same tragic confusion as in the Lehi story. This is borne out in the relationship of the actors to the Egyptians in both dramas. Though Lehi supports the anti-Egyptian party, his sons have Egyptian names and Egyptian educations and they keep their records after the Egyptian manner. Moreover, the party flees toward Egyptian territory. The same anomaly confronts us in the Lachish Letters, which tell of a certain general sent down to Egypt to fetch a prophet back to Jerusalem for execution (T. 63). But why on earth, asks Torczyner, would the good man flee to Egypt, of all places, when his crime was supporting Jeremiah in calling "for peace with *Babylonia?*" Our informant finds "this astonishing fact," that he fled towards Egypt instead of Babylonia, quite inexplicable (T. 67).

As the main actors in the Lachish drama are high military officers, so also in the Book of Mormon the key figure in the Jerusalem episode is another high military officer. This was Laban, whose official position resembles that of Ya'ush in Lachish very closely. "Thus Ya'ush must be the military governor of Lachish . . . this greatest fortress of Judah . . ." (T. 87); along with that ". . . 'lord Ya'ush' may have been Governor of the City, whose *archives* would probably have been housed in the region of the palace-fort or keep, or perhaps he was only the senior military officer" (T. 12). All of which applies with equal force to Laban, the military governor of Jerusalem, "a mighty man" who "can command fifty," in his garrison (1 Nephi 3:31) and "his tens of thousands" in the field (4:1). Among the non-biblical names in the Book of Mormon which excited amusement and derision among its critics, we remember one *Josh,* identified in Reynold's Concordance as "a Nephite general, who commanded a corps of ten thousand men" at Cumorah—an interesting comment on the conservatism of Nephite tradition (Mormon 6:14). Where is the king in all this? In both stories he appears as a rather shadowy character in the background. As for Ya'ush, "the king appeals to him in everything concerning this part of the country" (118), that is, the whole western part of the kingdom (87)—he left things pretty much up to his general, as according to the Book of Mormon he also did in Jerusalem. Laban was of noble descent, of the same ancestry as Lehi himself and of a more direct line to the patriarch Joseph. For the genealogy was kept in his family (5:16) and the archives were housed at his official residence as the archives of Lachish "would probably be housed" at the headquarters and residence of Ya'ush. When Lehi's sons went to get the letters from Laban, they talked with him intimately as he sat in his house, and proposed buying the plates. He refused to give up the brass plates and so they decided to bribe him with what was left of their own family treasures. They knew their man, but not quite well enough, for he kept the treasure but chased them out of the house and sent his servants after them to get rid of them (3:24-25). The young men escaped and hid out in a cave, but the cat was out of the bag—Lehi's flight was now known to Laban as Uriah's was to Ya'ush, and Laban's troops would soon be on the trail of the refugees as Ya'ush's were already in pursuit of Uriah. Lehi was spared, however, because Laban never got into action on the case. That very night Nephi found him dead drunk in a street near his house and dispatched him with his own sword (4:5-18). Going toward the house, he met Laban's servant and got the keys to the treasury and archives from him by a ruse. In the dark the man thought that Nephi was Laban, for he was expecting his boss to be returning very late (and drunk) from an emergency council of "the elders of the Jews . . . Laban had been *out by night* among them" (4:22, emphasis added). There is a world of inference in this—secret emergency sessions, tension, danger, and intrigue—as there is in Lachish Letter XVIII, which must be forwarded from Ya'ush to the king through the village of Qiryat Ye'arim *by night* (T. 183). Lehi's boys took Laban's servant along with them "that the Jews might not know concerning our flight . . . lest they should pursue us and destroy us" (4:36). Even so we see in the Lachish Letters "a prophet fleeing from his home and friends, a prophet wanted by the military authorities" (T. 64). Zoram was carried along by force but was persuaded that it was in his own interest to join a pious escape-group in the desert, and he duly exchanged oaths with his captors, his conscience not overly bothered by the change of sides; displaying the same hesitant and divided loyalties as everyone else in the Book of Mormon and the Lachish Letters. The military correspondence of the Lachish Letters with its grim suspicions of disloyalty and double-dealing, fervid denials, charges, investigations, and reports, reminds one of the much later Bar Kochba letters (discovered in 1966) which in turn present truly astonishing parallels to some of the military correspondence in the Book of Mormon.*

One peculiar situation in the Lachish Letters casts a good deal of light on an equally peculiar and highly significant episode in the Book of Mormon. Hosha'yahu protests to his boss in Lachish, "and the letter (which) Nedabyahu, the NKD of the King, had brought, has the slave sent to my Lord" (p. 64 n. 1). The title NKD suggests that "the prophet's warning letter . . . could have been sent while the prophet was still near his hometown, through a little boy, most suited as an unsuspected messenger," in view of the fact that little boys performed such offices in the time of David (2 Samuel 15:36; 17:17-21), and that "such small boys are used also today in Palestine, often for quite responsible missions . . ." (68). What suggests the idea to Torczyner is the mention of "Nedabyahu, the NKD of the

---

* Discussed by Hugh Nibley in *BYU Studies* 14 (Autumn 1973), pp. 120-24.

King," as the one who delivered a letter from the prophet to SHLM warning him of the danger he was in (LL III, 19-21). The word NKD suggests first of all grandson. There is a Nedabiah, grandson of King Jehoiakim, in 1 Chronicles 3:18, and Tor-czyner finds it "possible and even probable" that he is the very one named here. What, the king's own grandson bearing letters for his opponent the prophet? The exact meaning of NKD is "unfortunately . . . not definitely established" so that the king referred to may be "either Jehoiakim . . . or less likely, Jeconiah, . . . or Zedekiah. . . ." (T. 61). It is not a direct line of descent, Jeconiah being not the father but the nephew of Zede-kiah; but since most scholars maintain, along with LXX, that NKD simply means offspring or descendant, "it would be quite possible . . . to call somebody the 'grandson' [NKD] of his grandfather's brother" i.e. in this case of Zedekiah. ". . . the Hebrew *nekedh* may certainly have been used at least for *grand-nephew* as well as for grandson" (T. 61). This Nedabiah, whose title "may equally well mean the grandson of Jehoiakim as the grandnephew of Zedekiah," was quite young; "one would prefer the age of 10-13 to that of 5 years" (T. 69), carrying dangerous letters between the towns and camps for the prophet's people. Since he was running errands for the opposi-tion party, the boy was, of course, away from home most of the time; and since he was specifically carrying letters of warn-ing telling people to decamp and save their lives, he could surely count on escaping with them. When news reached them that the royal family was wiped out, only one course of action was open to the child (as survivor) and his friends. Where would they go? Torczyner suggests *"the date of 590-588,"* for this episode, i.e. the year 589, just eleven years after 600 B.C. According to the Book of Mormon, eleven years after Lehi left Jerusalem, i.e., 589, a company escaped from the land of Jerusalem bearing with them the youngest son of Zedekiah, the only member of the family not put to death when Jerusalem was taken. From the descendants of these people, arrived in the New World, the Nephites learned that Jerusalem actually did fall as prophesied: ". . . will you dispute that Jerusalem was destroyed? Will ye say that the sons of Zedekiah were not slain, all except it were *Mulek*? Yea, and do ye not behold that the *seed* of Zedekiah are with us, and *they* were driven out of the land of Jerusalem?" (Helaman 8:21, italics added). By an interesting coincidence, the LXX translates the word NKD by which Nedabyahu is designated in Hebrew simply as "seed" (T. 61), as apparently does the Book of Mormon—"the seed of Zedekiah." The land north where they settled in the New World "was called Mulek, which was after the son of Zedekiah; for the Lord did bring Mulek into the land north. . . ." (Helaman 6:10). Nowhere are we told that Mulek was the leader of the company, and indeed at his age that would be unthinkable—his father Zedekiah was only about thirty-one when he was taken prisoner and blinded. But as the sole survivor of the royal family and heir presumptive to the throne, he was certainly the most important person in the company, a source of legitimate pride to the group. The name tells everything—"Mulek" is not found anywhere in the Bible, but any student of Semitic languages will instantly recognize it as the best-known form of diminutive or caritative, a term of affection and endearment meaning "little king." What could they call the uncrowned child, last of his line, but their little king? And what could they call themselves but Mulekiyah or Mulekites?

And so the coincidences go on accumulating. It is time to turn to the computer, as we do today whenever questions and problems arise. What are the chances of the many parallels between the Lachish Letters and the opening chapter of the Book of Mormon being the product of mere coincidence?

1. First consider the fact that only one piece of evidence could possibly bring us into the Lehi picture, and that one piece of evidence happens to be the *only* first-hand writing surviving from the entire scope of Old Testament history. Lehi's story covers less than ten years in the thousand-year history of the Book of Mormon, and the Lachish Letters cover the same tiny band of a vast spectrum—and they both happen to be the *same* years!

2. Not only in time but in place do they fit neatly into the

same narrow slot; and the people with which they deal also belong to the same classes of society and are confronted by the same peculiar problems.

3. With the Book of Mormon account being as detailed and specific as it is, it is quite a piece of luck that there is nothing in the Lachish Letters that in any way contradicts its story—that in itself should be given serious consideration. Is it just luck?

4. Both documents account for their existence by indicating specifically the techniques and usages of writing and recording in their day, telling of the same means of transmitting, editing and storing records.

5. The proximity of Egypt and its influence on writing has a paramount place in both stories.

6. Both stories confront us with dynastic confusion during a transition of kingship.

7. Both abound in proper names in which the yahu ending is prominent in a number of forms.

8. In both, the religious significance of those names gives indication of a pious reformist movement among the people.

9. The peculiar name of Jaush = Josh, since it is not found in the Bible, is remarkable as the name borne by a high-ranking field officer in both the Lachish Letters and the Book of Mormon.

10. In both reports, prophets of gloom operating in and around Jerusalem are sought by the government as criminals for spreading defeatism.

11. The Rekhabite background is strongly suggested in both accounts, with inspired leaders and their followers fleeing to the hills and the caves.

12. Political partisanship and international connections cause division, recriminations, and heartbreak in the best of families.

13. The conflicting ideologies—practical vs. religious, materialist vs. spiritual—emerge in two views of the religious leader or prophet as a *piqqeah*, "a visionary man" a term either of praise or of contempt—an impractical dreamer.

14. For some unexplained reason, the anti-king parties both flee not towards Babylon but towards Egypt, "the broken reed."

15. The offices and doings of Laban and Jaush present a complex parallel, indicative of a special military type and calling not found in the Bible.

16. Almost casual references to certain doings by night create the same atmosphere of tension and danger in both stories.

17. Little Nedabyahu fits almost too well into the slot occupied by the Book of Mormon Mulek, "the Little King" who never came to rule but escaped with a party of refugees to the New World.

18. The whole business of keeping, transmitting, and storing records follows the same procedures in both books.

Other parallels may be added to taste, but this should be enough to show that Joseph Smith was either extravagantly lucky in the opening episodes of his Book of Mormon—that should be demonstrated by computer—or else he had help from someone who knew a great deal.

ii. Christ Among the Ruins

The great boldness and originality of writings attributed to Joseph Smith are displayed in their full scope and splendor in the account, contained in what is called Third Nephi in the Book of Mormon, of how the Lord Jesus Christ after his resurrection visited some of his "other sheep" in the New World and set up his church among them. It would be hard to imagine a project more dangerous to life and limb or perilous to the soul than that of authoring, and recommending to the Christian world as holy scripture, writings purporting to contain an accurate account of the deeds of the Lord among men after his resurrection, including lengthy transcripts of the very words he spoke. Nothing short of absolute integrity could stand up to the consequences of such daring in nineteenth-century America. We know exactly how his neighbors reacted to the claims of Joseph Smith, and it was not (as it has become customary to insist) with the complacent or sympathetic tolerance of backwoods "Yorkers," to whom such things were supposedly everyday experience: nothing could equal the indignation and rage excited among them by the name and message of Joseph Smith.

And yet the particular part of the Book of Mormon to which we refer, the post-resurrectional mission of Christ in the New World, has not been singled out for condemnation; it has in fact met with surprisingly little criticism. Why is that? Experience has shown, for one thing, that the tone and content of this particular history are so elevated and profoundly sincere as to silence and abash the would-be critic. When the austere Dean of the Harvard Divinity School can take Third Nephi seriously as a religious outpouring, who can laugh at it?[5] More to the point, the story of Christ's ministry among men during the forty days following his return from the tomb is one to which the churchmen have always given a wide berth, frankly disapproving of the crass literalism of Luke's almost clinical accounts. What can one say about events for which, as one scholar puts it, "no metaphysical or psychological explanation can be given?" What controls does one have for testing matters that lie totally beyond our experience?

Of recent years the discovery and rediscovery of a wealth of very early Christian writings suggests at least one type of control over the illusive history of the forty days. For with surprising frequency the oldest of these texts purport to contain "The Secret Teachings of Our Lord to His Disciples" after his return from the dead, or titles to that effect. Since this is the theme of the history in Third Nephi, ordinary curiosity prompts us to ask how that document compares with the ancient ones in form and content. That question in turn waits on the prior necessity of comparing the older writings with each other to see whether, taken all together, they tell anything like a consistent story. When this writer brought a number of the "Forty-Day" texts together some years ago (the amount of available material has grown considerably since then) it became at once apparent that they do have certain themes and episodes in common.[6] At that time nothing could have been farther from this person's mind than the Book of Mormon, and yet if we set those findings over against the long account of Nephi, the latter takes its place in the bona fide apocalyptic library so easily and naturally that with the title removed, any scholar would be hard put to it to detect its irregular origin. That is only our opinion, but fortunately copies of the Book of Mormon are not hard to come by in our society, and the reader is free to control the whole thing for himself. Permit me to run down the list of common features in the forty-day writings in the order in which we presented them in the article referred to.

First, we noted that the large literature of the Forty-Day Mission of the Lord was early lost from sight by the Christian world because it was never very popular, and that for a number of reasons. In almost all the accounts, for example, the Apostles, who are about to go forth on their missions and establish the Church throughout the world, anxiously ask the Lord what the *future* of that church is to be, and are given a surprisingly pessimistic answer: the Church will fall prey to the machinations of evil and *after two generations* will pass away. "The Apostles protest, as we do today: Is this a time for speaking of death and disaster? Can all that has transpired be but for the salvation of a few and the condemnation of many? But Jesus remains unyielding: that is not for us to decide or to question."* A strangely negative message for the Church, understandably unacceptable to the conventional Christianity of later times. One would hardly expect such a thing in the Book of Mormon, but there it is, the same paradox: the glad message of the resurrection and the glorious unifying of the Saints is saddened, dampened by the forthright declaration that the Church is only to survive for a limited time. To speak of the world in negative terms is permissible—but the Church?

> 3 Nephi 27:30. And now, behold, my joy is great, even unto fulness, because of you, and also this *generation . . .* for none of them are lost.
> 31. Behold, I would that ye should understand; for I mean them who are now alive of this *generation. . . .*
> 32. But behold, it sorroweth me because of the fourth generation [in the Old World it was the *second* generation] from this *generation,* for they are led away

---

*H. N. in *Vigiliae Christianae*, 20 (1966), pp. 6-7.

captive by him even as was the son of perdition; for they
will sell me for silver and for gold. . . . And in that day
will I visit them, even in turning their works upon their
own heads (italics added; cf. 17:14; Chs. 21-23).

On both hemispheres the people of the Church were only
too willing to forget such disturbing prophecies and insist that
God would never desert his church.

The loss of the "Forty-Day Literature" was clearly hastened
by the secrecy with which the various writings were guarded.
The usual title or instruction to the texts specifies that "these are
the secret teachings" of the risen Lord, and as such they were
treasured and guarded by the communities possessing them.
This *secrecy* made possible all sorts of sectarian misrepresenta-
tions, forgeries, and *Gnostic aberrations,* which flourished
throughout the Christian world of the second century and
served to bring the final discredit and oblivion on the writings
and the sects that exploited them. The apocryphal literature
contains no better explanation of the original observance of
secrecy than the book of Third Nephi itself:

26:6.   And now there cannot be written in this book
even a hundredth part of the things which Jesus did truly
teach unto the people;

10.   And if . . . they will not *believe* these things,
then shall the greater things be *withheld* from them,
unto their condemnation.

11.   Behold, I was about to write them, all which
were engraven upon the plates of Nephi, but the Lord
forbade it, saying: I will try the faith of my people.

27:23.   Write the things which ye have seen and heard,
save it be those which are *forbidden.*

Besides things which *should* not be recorded were those which
by their nature could not be:

17:17.   And no tongue *can* speak, neither *can* there be
written by any man . . . so great and marvelous things
as we both saw and heard Jesus speak . . .

29:32.   And tongue *cannot* speak the words which he
prayed, neither *can* be written by man the words he
prayed.

34. . . . so great and marvelous were the words
which he prayed that they *cannot* be written, neither
can they be uttered by man.

Peculiar to the "Forty-Day Literature" is the emphasis on
certain teachings neglected or vigorously opposed by the intellectual churchmen of later Christianity. Whether or not one
chooses to accept them as authentic, it is their presence in the
preachings of the risen Lord in Third Nephi which interests us
here. One aspect of his activity which does not receive particular attention in Luke's accounts is the worldwide circulation
of the Savior among his servants in the apocalyptic versions.
Luke has the Lord come and go with great freedom and frequency among his people in Judaea, but in the "Forty-Day
Literature" he appears to them in all parts of the world. So also
in the Book of Mormon:

3 Nephi 16:1. . . . I have other sheep which are not of
this land, neither of the land of Jerusalem, neither in any
parts of that land round about whither I have been to
minister.
2. . . . they . . . have not as yet heard my voice.
3. But . . . I shall go unto them, and . . . they shall
hear my voice, and shall be numbered among my sheep
(cf. 15:14-24; 17:4; 27:2ff.).

In the early Christian texts, the teaching of the risen Lord is
prophetic and apocalyptic, reviewing the history of God's
dealing with men on earth from the beginning and carrying it
down to its glorious culmination at the Parousia; the story is
usually presented in a series of *"dispensations,"* alternating
periods of light and darkness through which the world and the
saints must pass. The Third Nephi version faithfully follows the
pattern in a long exposition which goes back to the beginning of
the law, its presence among peoples scattered in divers places,
not in just one place (ch. 15); its future among them and its
spread throughout the world among the Gentiles (ch. 16), with
the vicissitudes through which both Israel and the Gentiles must
pass (ibid.). Chapter 20 carries the coming history of Israel and
especially of the Nephites themselves right through to the end,
including the climactic events of our own day, as chapter 21 sets

forth God's dealings to come with the people on this hemisphere until the establishing of the New Jerusalem.

The most natural questions to ask anyone returning to earth after being away would be, Where did you go and what did you see? These questions, put by the disciples in the Old World accounts, lead to discussions of the *Descensus and the Kerygma,* i.e., the Savior's descent to the prison-house to preach to those spirits who were disobedient in the days of Noah (1 Peter 3:19-20). This theme became the subject of the "Harrowing of Hell" drama of the Gospel of Nicodemus and the medieval mystery plays. Does the Book of Mormon version have anything about that? Yes, and the Descensus and the Kerygma described there are uniquely glorious. Let us recall that the Descensus closely parallels the earthly mission of John the Baptist "to give light to them that sit in darkness and in the shadow of death" (Luke 1:79). In the Book of Mormon, the hosts that sit in darkness are the Nephites themselves, exhausted and in utter despair and desolation after three days of destruc- tion followed by *total darkness,* and awful *lamentations* followed by even more awful silence. The Lord, three days after his crucifixion, leaves the spirits in prison and *now* descends to *them* as a figure of light "descending out of heaven . . . clothed in a white robe" exactly as he does to the spirits in hell in the Old World writings; announcing to them "I am the *light* and the *life* of the world" (11:11) who has come directly from the agony of the "bitter cup" to bring light and deliverance to them. And they accepted him as such as "the whole multitude fell to the earth" (11:12); then he identified himself to them and an- nounced his mission, and "they did cry out with one accord, saying: Hosanna! Blessed be the name of the Most High God! And they did fall down at the feet of Jesus, and did worship him" (11:16-17). For they knew that he had come to lead them out of their prison. The first thing he did was to address them as disobedient spirits (11:32), "And this is my doctrine . . . that the Father commandeth all men, everywhere, to *repent* and believe in me"—we are all *disobedient spirits* in prison! The next thing was to insist that they all be *baptized*—exactly as in the "Descensus" accounts; he must give the "Seal" of baptism to all to whom he preaches in the underworld before they can follow him out of darkness up into his kingdom. Jesus puts it to them as an act of deliverance. Then the Lord says a striking thing to the Nephites (11:39-40). "Verily, verily . . . this is my doctrine, and whoso buildeth upon this buildeth upon my rock, and the *gates of hell* shall not prevail against them. And whoso shall declare more or less than this . . . the *gates of hell* stand open to receive such when the floods come and the winds beat upon them." He has come to deliver them from the *Gates of Hell* that hold them in bondage; this is the "smashing of the Gates theme," the "Harrowing of Hell" motif all the way through. As he is about to leave there is a great sorrowing among them as if they were being left behind in darkness. This vividly recalls like situations in the royal Parousias of Egyptian rulers, a concept going back at least as far as the text of the Am Duat.

To show his people that he is really a resurrected being and not a spirit, both in the New Testament account and in the apocryphal version, Jesus calls for food—real food—and insists that they share it with him in a sacred meal. The meal usually follows the baptism, putting its seal upon the initiation and the union of those who follow the Lord. In Third Nephi the sacral meal with the risen Lord, repeated more than once, is an event of transcendent importance, to which we shall refer below.

Most scholars and theologians have seen the purpose of the Forty Days to be the laying of a firm foundation for the sending out of the disciples into all the world to lay a foundation for the Church. At the time of the Crucifixion they were utterly demoralized and scattered, in no condition to go forth as powerful ambassadors of the Lord into all the world. The Forty-Day teaching has the object of *preparing them for their missions.* This is exactly the case in the Book of Mormon. After the founding of the Church among the people come two chapters (27-28) dealing exclusively with the preparation of the chosen disciples for their special missions into the world, upon which after his departure they immediately set forth.

As might be expected, the appearances of the Lord to the astonished multitude, as well as his departures from them, are events of *celestial splendor,* nowhere more movingly described

than in chapter 11 of Third Nephi. The utter glory of his
presence among the people or with the disciples is a constant
theme in both the Book of Mormon and the other sources. And
yet it is combined with a feeling of the closest and most loving
intimacy, especially moving in the Book of Mormon accounts
of his dealings with the children.

The comings and goings of God himself, moving between
heaven and earth, must needs be surrounded by an aura of
mystery and excitement. Can such things really be? Luke in his
meticulous, almost clinically exact and factual reports, wants us
to know once and for all that they really *can* be. The wonder of
it, something akin to the excitement of Christmas, quickens the
reader's pulse, but how could we describe the state of mind of
those who actually experienced it? The apocryphal writings go
all out to make us feel with them, but it is Third Nephi who
really catches the spirit:

> . . . when Jesus had ascended into heaven, the multitude
> did disperse, and every man did take his wife and his
> children and did return to his own home.
>
> And it was noised abroad among the people immedi-
> ately, before it was yet dark, that the multitude had
> seen Jesus . . . and that he would also show himself on
> the morrow unto the multitude.
>
> Yea, and even all the night it was noised abroad con-
> cerning Jesus; and insomuch did they send forth unto
> the people that . . . an exceedingly great number, did
> labor exceedingly all that night, that they might be on
> the morrow in the place where Jesus should show him-
> self unto the multitude (19:1-3).

Nothing could convey the atmosphere of the electrifying
"Forty-Day" message better than that.

But now it is time to turn to a particular text. When E.
Revillout announced the discovery of a Coptic manuscript of
the Gospel of the Twelve Apostles in 1904, he declared it to be
the text which Origen and Jerome "considered . . . to be
perhaps earlier than Saint Luke and referred to by him in his
prologue," a work esteemed by the Church Fathers as of
"capital importance," uniquely free of any hint of heresy, carrying the tradition of Christ's visits to the earth beyond the scope

of Luke—even to an event fifteen years later.[7] German scholarship promptly and routinely minimized the claims of Revillout, and went too far in the process. If the fragments of the Coptic Gospel of the Twelve Apostles do not necessarily occur in the order in which Revillout arranged them (the order which we will follow), subsequent discoveries make it clear that they really are connected parts of a single—and typical—Forty-Day manuscript, and that they belong to the earliest stratum of early Christian writing. Revillout's arrangement does not follow quite the same order as Third Nephi, either, but a comparison of the two may be instructive.

The Lord's condescension: He came and ate with them:

Ev.XII; Aps. Frg. 2 PO 2:132

. . . friends: Have you ever seen, Brethren, such a loving lord, promising his apostles his own kingdom? where they would eat and drink with him upon a heavenly table even as he had eaten with them on earth at an earthly table.

Thereby he put them in mind of the heavenly table, considering the things of this world (kosmos) as nothing.

3 Nephi 10:18. And it came to pass that in the ending of the thirty and fourth year, behold, I will show unto you that the people of Nephi who were spared, and also those who had been called Lamanites who had been spared, did have great *favors* shown unto them, and great *blessings* poured out upon their heads, inasmuch that soon after the ascension of Christ into heaven he did truly manifest himself unto them—

19. Showing his body unto them, and ministering unto them; and an account of his ministry shall be given hereafter.

3 Nephi 26:13. Therefore, I would that ye should behold that the Lord truly did teach the people, for the space of three days; and after that he did show himself unto them *oft, and did break bread oft, and bless it, and give it unto them.*

To make them one with him and with each other:

If you really want to know, listen and I will tell you. Did not God

3 Nephi 19:23. . . . that they may believe in me, that I may be in

feel an equal love for all his Apostles? Listen to John the Evangelist, testifying how the Christ used to plead with (*sops*) his Father on their behalf, even that "they become One *even as we are one.*"

Do you want to know the truth about that? It is that he chose the Twelve. . . .

"Listen to John the Evangelist testifying."
[On this matter he refers them back to the testimony of John.]

them as thou, Father, art in me, that we may be one.

29. Father, I pray . . . for those whom thou hast given me out of the world . . . that they may be purified in me, that I may be in them as thou, Father, art in me, that we may be *one,* that I may be glorified *in them.*

3 Nephi 28:6. (In another matter also he refers the disciples back to John): ". . . I know your thoughts, and ye have desired the thing which John, my beloved . . . desired of me."

The Loaves and Fishes:

. . . upon them, saying, I feel concerned (pity) for this multitude; for behold they have been with me for *three days,* and (now) they have nothing to eat. I don't want to let them leave here hungry, lest they faint by the wayside.

Andrew said to him, My Lord, where will we find bread in this wilderness? . . .

Jesus said to Thomas: Go to a certain (pei) man who has with him five loaves of barley bread and two fishes, and bring them to me here.

Andrew said to him, Lord, how far would five loaves go with such a huge crowd?

Jesus saith to him: Bring them to me and there will be enough.

3 Nephi 17:6. And he said unto them: Behold, my bowels are filled with *compassion* towards you.

3 Nephi 8:23. ". . . for the space of *three days*" preceding all had been deprived. The place was now desolate.

3 Nephi 20:6. Now, there had been no bread, neither wine, brought by the disciples, neither by the multitude;

[While they go for the food Jesus *talks with a little child.*]

3 Nephi 18:2. And while they were gone for bread and wine, he commanded the multitude that they should sit themselves down upon the earth.

And so they went [for the food]. A small child was brought to Jesus and straightway he began to worship him.

3 Nephi 17:11. And it came to pass that he commanded that their little children should be brought.

The small child said to Jesus, Lord I have suffered much because of these [i.e., at the hands of people. The puzzled scribe connects this with the loaves: the child must have suffered because of *them*, as if the child had been sent to fetch them], Jesus saith to the child, Give me the five loaves which have been entrusted to you.

3 Nephi 17:12. So they brought their little children and set them down upon the ground round about him, and Jesus stood in the midst; and the multitude gave way till they had all been brought unto him.

Thou has not saved (rescued) this multitude in time of need, but it is the toikonomia (arrangement, ordinance, divine intent) that (they) behold a marvelous thing, the *remembrance* of which shall never pass away, nor the food with which they are filled.

3 Nephi 26:14. And it came to pass that he did teach and minister unto the children of the multitude of whom hath been spoken, and he did loose their tongues, and they did *speak unto their fathers great and marvelous* things, even greater than he had revealed unto the people; and he loosed their tongues that they could utter.

Note here the *strange precocity of* the child and the sacramental (memorial) nature of the meal.

3 Nephi 18:5. And when the multitude had eaten and were filled, he said unto the disciples . . .

7. . . . this shall ye do in *remembrance* of my body, which I have shown unto you . . . that ye do always *remember* me. And if ye do always *remember* me ye shall have my Spirit to be with you.

11. And this shall ye always do to those who repent and are baptized in my name; and ye shall do it in *remembrance* of my blood,

which I have shed for you, that ye
may witness unto the Father that
ye do always *remember* me. And
if ye do always *remember* me ye
shall have my spirit to be with
you.

The Sacrament administered:

And Jesus (1) took the loaves

3 Nephi 18:3. And when the disciples had come with bread and
wine, he (1) took of the bread

and (2) blessed them (gave thanks
over them)

and (2) brake

and (3) divided them

and (3) blessed it;

and (4) gave them to the Apostles

and (4) he gave unto the disciples
and commanded that they should
eat.

(5) *that they might bear them to
the multitude.*

4. And when they had eaten
and were filled, he commanded
that (5) they should give unto the
multitude.

The Sacrament withheld:

For Judas (had been) the last to
partake of the loaves (refers back
to the Last Supper, to illustrate a
principle).

3 Nephi 18:28. And now behold,
this is the commandment which I
give unto you, that ye shall *not*
suffer any one knowingly to partake of my flesh and blood *un-
worthily*, when ye shall minister
it;

Andrew said to Jesus, O Master
(sah), Judas did not receive a
kleronomia (of) loaves . . . to
bear to the multitude . . . (such as
. . . we were to give to them. . .

29. For whoso eateth and
drinketh my flesh and blood un-
worthily eateth and drinketh
damnation to his soul; therefore
if ye know that a man is unworthy
to eat and drink of my flesh and
blood ye shall forbid him.

. . . That is because he to whom I
did *not* give a share of the loaves
from my hands was *not worthy* of
a part (share) of my flesh.

Neither did he care to share with the poor, but thought only of the glosogomon (finance)

The Sacramental Prayer:

It is a mystery of my Father . . . which con(cerns) . . . the partaking (dividing) of my flesh.

The actual words of the prayer (Moroni 4:1-2) are given by Moroni, 4:3:

And forthwith he blessed them, saying, O my *Father*, root (source) of all good, *I ask thee to bless these* five barley *loaves* that *all these* (multitude) may be filled, that thy son may be glorified in thee; and that those whom thou hast drawn to thee out of the world might *hearken to* (after, obey) *him.*

O God, the Eternal *Father, we ask thee* in the name of thy Son, Jesus Christ, *to bless* and sanctify *this bread* to the souls of *all those* who partake of it; that they may eat in *remembrance* of the body of thy Son and . . . always remember him, and *keep his commandments* which he hath given them, that they may always have his Spirit to be with them. Amen.

And straightway his word came to pass in exousia (authority, as requested). His blessing fell upon (shope) on the bread in the apostles' hands.

Moroni 5:2. . . . wine . . . that they do always *remember* him, that they may have his *Spirit* to be with them. Amen.

And all the people ate and were filled. They *gave praise* to God.

3 Nephi 20:9. Now, when the multitude had all eaten and drunk, behold, they were filled with the Spirit; and they did cry out with one voice, and gave *glory* to Jesus, whom they both saw and heard.

Jesus prays three times:

You have seen, O my beloved ones, what love Jesus had toward his Apostles, insomuch that he kept (hid) nothing from them of any of the things touching upon his godhead (relationship to God).

3 Nephi 28:13. And behold, the heavens were opened, and they were caught up into heaven, and saw and heard unspeakable things.

14. And it was forbidden them that they should utter; neither was it given unto them power that they could utter the things which they saw. . . .

(1) the first time while blessing the five loaves of barley-bread.

(1) 3 Nephi 19:19. And it came to pass that Jesus departed out of the midst of them, and went a little way off from them and bowed himself to the earth, and he said:

20. Father I thank thee that thou hast given the Holy Ghost unto these whom I have chosen . . . out of the world.

24. . . . When Jesus had thus prayed . . . he came unto his disciples, and . . . 25 . . . blessed them as they did pray unto him . . . and behold they were as white as the countenance and also the garments of Jesus.

(2) The second time in his giving thanks to his Father. [Without quoting.]

(2) 3 Nephi 19:28. Father, I thank thee that thou hast purified those whom I have chosen . . . and also for them who shall believe on their words. . . .

29. Father, I pray not for the world, but for those whom thou hast given me out of the world. . . .

30. And [Jesus] . . . came again unto his disciples . . . and behold they were white, even as Jesus.

(3) The third time in giving thanks for the seven loaves. [The prayer is not quoted.]

(3) 3 Nephi 19:31. And . . . he went again a little way off and prayed unto the Father.

32. And tongue cannot speak . . . *neither can be written* by man the words which he prayed.

33. And the multitude did hear and do bear record; and their hearts were open and they did understand in their hearts the words which he prayed.

The Lord invites the disciples to ask for higher things:

Have you seen (considered) O my beloved ones, the love of Jesus towards his Apostles? Insomuch

3 Nephi 27:2. And Jesus again showed himself unto them, for they were praying unto the Father

that he did not conceal anything from them, even all the things concerning his godhead:

in his name; and Jesus came and stood in the midst of them, and said unto them: What will ye that I shall give unto you?

They are abashed and have to be encouraged:

Jesus saith to Thomas: Thomas my friend, you and your brethren are free to ask me whatsoever you please and I will keep nothing back from you. Insomuch that you may see, and feel (palpitate) and be convinced in your heart. If you want to see those in their tombs revived, you do well to ask for a sign of the Resurrection. For it was I myself who said to you, "I am the Resurrection and the life." And also "If the ear of wheat does not die, there will be no yield (karpos). And if you yourselves do not see with your eyes (1 John 1:1), your heart will not be confirmed in this. . . .

Thomas wept and said to Jesus: Thou hast taken all this trouble to come to the tomb *because of my incredulity.* Let thy will be done and this tomb receive me until the day of the Resurrection.

Jesus said: *Thomas, be not afflicted;* that which I do you know not . . . I told you to move the stone so that a witness of the Resurrection might appear in the tomb of death. . . .

You likewise, if you do not see with your eyes will not be strengthened in your hearts.

Have I not told you: More blessed are ye who have not seen and have

3 Nephi 28:1. And it came to pass when Jesus had said these words, he spake unto his disciples, one by one, saying unto them: What is it that ye desire of me, after that I am gone to the Father?

6. And he said unto them: Behold, I know your thoughts, and ye have desired the thing which *John,* my beloved, who was with me in my ministry, before that I was lifted up by the Jews, desired of me.

3. And he said unto them: Blessed are ye because ye desired this thing of me; therefore, after that ye are seventy and two years old ye shall come unto me in my kingdom; and with me ye shall find rest.

4. . . . he turned himself unto the three, and said unto them: What will ye that I should do unto you, when I am gone unto the Father?

5. And *they sorrowed in their hearts, for they durst not speak* unto him the thing which they desired.

6. And he said unto them: Behold, *I know* your thoughts, and ye have desired the thing which *John* . . . desired of me.

3 Nephi 19:35. And it came to pass that when Jesus had made an end of praying he came again to the disciples, and said unto them: So great faith have I never seen *among all the Jews;* wherefore I

believed than *ye who have seen* and not believed.

Ye had seen how many wonders and miracles I did in the presence of *the Jews,* and they *believed not* on me.

could not show unto them so great miracles, because of their unbelief. 36. Verily I say unto you, there are *none of them* that have seen so *great things as ye have seen;* neither have they heard so great things as ye have heard.

The disciples are understandably embarrassed at having to ask questions which argue a lack of faith in the very presence of the Resurrection. Here was the living Jesus before them, risen from the dead; and yet he knows that they are still unsettled in their minds. For how could they be guaranteed their own resurrection? After all, Jesus was a special case, the Son of God; but the men, women, and children he raised from the dead all had to die again. What about this? Are there levels and degrees of immortality? Is there a transition zone between the living and the dead? On these questions both of our sources at this point launch into earnest discussions. For the type of the human who is dead but not dead, raised from the dead but still not resurrected, the Gospel of the XII Apostles gives us Lazarus, while the Book of Mormon discusses the same matters as represented by the strange case of the Three Nephites.

Thomas said to Jesus: My Lord, behold thou has granted us every favor in thy goodness. *There is just one thing* which we would like you to bestow on us. We want to see, O Lord, those people who were dead and buried, whom you revived (raised up), as a sign of thy *resurrection* which is to take place for us.

We know, Lord, that thou didst raise up the son of the widow of Nain. But we are thinking of *another kind* of miracle, for you met with that multitude going along the road. What we want to see is the bones that have fallen apart in the tombs and are able to join together so that they can speak on the spot. . . .

Didymus boldly (took heart) said to him: My Lord, how shall we go to him since the Jews are seeking to stone thee?

He said this because he was worried by the things which Jesus had said about Lazarus and did not want to go.

Didyme (Thomas), come with me, let us go to Bethany, so that *I can show you the TYPE of the Resurrection* at the Last Day in the grave, that your heart may be strengthened that I am the Resurrection and the Life.

3 Nephi 28:7. Therefore, more blessed are ye, for ye shall never taste of death. . . .

8. Ye shall never endure the pains of death; but . . . ye shall be changed in the twinkling of an eye from mortality to immortality; and then shall ye be blessed in the kingdom of my Father.

Come with me O Didymus, and I will show you the bones that have come apart in the tomb uniting themselves together again . . . I will show you the body hollow putrefied eye-sockets . . . devoid . . . the tongue of Lazarus, rotted away, which *will speak again* with thee . . .

3 Nephi 28:13. . . . and they [all the disciples] were caught up into heaven. . . .

15. And whether they were in the body or out of the body, they could not tell; for it did seem unto them *like a transfiguration* . . . changed from this body of flesh into an immortal state. . . .

17. . . . now, whether they were mortal or immortal, from the day of their transfiguration, I know not. . . .

see that which the worm have eaten coming forth at my voice when I call. . . .
Thou seekest a sign of the Resurrection, Thomas, come and I will show it to you at the tomb of Lazarus.

37. . . . there must needs be a change wrought upon their bodies . . .

38. Now this change was not equal to that which shall take place at the last day; but there was a change wrought upon them. . . .

You have asked about the stretched out hands; come and I will show you the hands of Lazarus wrapped in their bandages, tight in their shroud, which will be raised up as they come out of the tomb.

Didymus my friend, come with me to the tomb of Lazarus, for *my mouth desires what thou hast thought.* . . .

3 Nephi 28:6. . . . *I know your thoughts* 3. . . . Blessed are ye because *ye desired* this thing of me. . . .

Jesus said to him: Didymus, *he who walks in the LIGHT trembleth not* (or, is not offended) Jesus said this to Thomas to console him when he saw that he was afflicted because of the death of Lazarus. . . .

3 Nephi 18:16. And as I have prayed among you even so shall ye pray in my church, among my people who do repent and are baptized in my name. Behold *I am the light; I have set an example for you.*

And these are the things which Jesus said to his Apostles.

Jesus cried out, saying: *My Father, My Father, root of all goodness, I pray unto thee,* for the moment has come to *give glory to thy Son,* that all may know that it is Thou who hast sent *me* for this. Glory unto thee unto the eternity of the eternities. Amen.

3 Nephi 19:29. *Father, I pray . . .* for those whom thou hast given me . . . that I may be in them as thou, Father, art in me, that we may be one, *that I may be glorified* in them.

No passage of scripture has puzzled theologians more since the days of the primitive Church than 1 Peter 3:18f, 4:6, the brief notice of the Descent of Christ to preach to the dead, "regarded by some," as MacCulloch observes, "as wholly enigmatic" because "the plain meaning of the passages conflicted with the interpreters' views of the nature of life beyond the grave."[8] Descent to *what?* was the question. Not to the Underworld, certainly, was St. Augustine's conclusion—too primitive and naive for words.[9] To what, then? There are three missions of Christ, three descents in the Gospels: 1) As a mortal condescending to mortals, 2) as a spirit, ministering to spirits in their deep prison, 3) as a glorified resurrected being who frequently descends during the forty days to minister to certain mortals who share in his glory in special manifestations, as described in the Gospel of the XII Apostles and 3 Nephi. Since the second mission is rejected by the Doctors of the Church, in the allegorizing spirit of the times they had no trouble in making the Petrine passage refer to the first: The Lord descended to those in this life only who sat in the dark prison of ignorance, who were disobedient *like* those of Noah's day, etc. Thus they confine the Petrine doctrine to the Lord's mortal mission, as does the modern Catholic explanation, that "the *effect* of Christ's preaching extended to the lost [in Limbo, not in Hell], without His having actually descended to them. . . ."[10]

But that third mission was hard to shake. "Whether the Petrine passages referred to the Descent or not, the doctrine itself, wherever derived, soon became a most vital one in early Christian thought."[11] And the farther back we go in the record the more conspicuous it becomes. The famous Harrowing of Hell mystery play is only its final expression, taken from the earlier Gospel of Nicodemus and other still earlier sources well attested at least in the second century.[12] Indeed, MacCulloch suggests that "Jewish belief in the possibility of good news being announced to the dead," goes clear back to the ancient prophets, including Isaiah (51:1; 52:7; 49:9).[13]

In this third realm we run into a strangely ambiguous state of things, confronted by an impressive cast of characters who have died, are raised from the dead as an earnest of the Resurrection, and then have to die again! There was the host of those risen from the dead in Galilee; the pair Leucius and Karinus who went to Jerusalem to deposit their written affidavits to the Resurrection and then returned to their tombs;[14] or the two in Arimaethea who, "having given up their writings . . . were transfigured, exceeding white, and were no more seen." On the way to enlist the testimonies of Karinus and Leucius, Nicodemus, Joseph and three rabbis "meet twelve thousand who have risen."[15] All of these were raised from the dead only to return to the grave.

Since none of these risen ones are mentioned in the scriptures, however, the test case would have to be Lazarus, who appears at all three levels in the Gospels. We find *a* Lazarus speaking from "Abraham's bosom" on high to one in the depths of hell—communicating between the worlds (Luke 16:20-25). On earth we find a very human Lazarus, the friend of Jesus, who goes the way of mortality only to be recalled from the tomb (John 11:1-43). He is the obvious candidate to witness

what went on in both worlds; the perfect living example of
those ambivalent beings who in their persons prove the Resurrection and yet are still subject to death, like the three Nephites
and the host of witnesses mentioned above. Lazarus's experience is put to good use in the early Christian dramatizations. In
the dialogue between Death and Hades that is the opening scene
of the Harrowing of Hell, Hades is distressed at the prospect of
one who has but recently snatched Lazarus from his power
". . . have mercy on me," cries Hades, "do not bring Him here,
for he is great!"[16] Lazarus is the test case, the proof of the reality
of the whole thing. As such he appears frequently in the
accounts of the Kerygma.[17]

Viewing the three types of descent, we must admit that one
is not more miraculous than the other; actually, Christ's visits
during the Forty-Day Mission are no more incredible than the
other two, and all are attested by an interesting interweaving of
documents which deserve much closer study in which the Book
of Mormon scores many points.

In early Christian ordinances ties are clearly established
between the three levels. Thus, the designation of baptism as
photismos or "light-bringing" was by the early Saints "sometimes symbolized as an actual light, the result of Christ's
presence, shining in the gloom of hades," which is mentioned as
early as the Odes of Solomon. Does that mean baptism was
connected with the Lord's visits to the world below as well as to
the world above? MacCulloch thinks so, for the preaching must
be followed by baptism: "All this is in keeping with the custom
of vicarious baptism . . ." (1 Corinthians 15:29).[18] So the over-
poweringly dramatic appearance of the Lord to the Nephites
sitting in darkness, identifying himself to them as "the Light and
the Life," has its counterpart in the world below. Baptism was
an initiation into the Church, and an important part of the
Lord's Descent to the Underworld is the way in which he gal-
vanizes the spirits there (*excitavit* et *erexit*), and organizes them,
as they form up in special marshaling areas[19] or form into a pro-
cession behind Adam and the Patriarchs, the grand parade that
is the climax and conclusion of the Harrowing of Hell.[20] In a
word, the Lord organizes the Church, as he does in the Book of

Mormon, of those who are about to be saved and led out of darkness.

NOTES

1. Torczyner, Harry, *Lachish I* (Tell ed Duweir): *The Lachish Letters* (Oxford University Press, 1938), p. 18.

2. Allegro, John M., *The Treasure of the Copper Scroll* (New York: Doubleday, 1960), p. 27.

3. Olmstead, A. T., *History of Assyria* (Chicago: The University of Chicago Press, 1960), p. 583.

4. Ibid., pp. 581-82.

5. See Krister Stendahl, "The Sermon on the Mount and Third Nephi," Truman G. Madsen, ed., *Reflections on Mormonism* (Provo, Utah: Religious Studies Center, Brigham Young University, 1978), pp. 139-54.

6. See Nibley, H., "Evangelium quadraginta dierum," *Vigiliae Christianae* 20 (1966), pp. 1-24.

7. Revillout, E., *Les Apocryphes Coptes*. Première Partie, *Les Évangiles des douze Apotres et de Saint Barthélemy* (Paris: Firmin-Didot, 1904), in *Patrologia Orientalis,* Tome II, Fascicule 2, 1907.

8. J. A. MacCulloch, *The Harrowing of Hell* (Edinburgh: T. Clark, 1930), p. 30.

9. Ibid., pp. 50f.

10. Ibid., pp. 50-56, discusses six different interpretations.

11. Ibid., p. 65.

12. In such early Christian classics as Ignatius, Clement, the Odes of Solomon, etc. Ibid., p. 241, the Shepherd of Hermas, and the Epistle of the Apostles, all very early, p. 246.

13. MacCulloch, *The Harrowing of Hell,* p. 252.

14. Ibid., pp. 158ff.

15. Ibid., pp. 158f, 170f.

16. Ibid., pp. 163f.

17. Ibid., pp. 177, cf. 290, 333.

18. Ibid., ch. XV, pp. 240-52; quote is from p. 248.

19. Ibid., pp. 260 ff. ch. XV.

20. The most available text of the Harrowing of Hell is in the popular reprint volume entitled *The Lost Books of the Bible and the Forgotten Books of Eden* (Cleveland: World Publishing Co., 1926).

6

Eugene England

Through the Arabian Desert to a Bountiful Land: Could Joseph Smith Have Known the Way?

Eugene England, Associate Professor of English at Brigham Young University, has published widely on topics as diverse as Brigham Young and the poetry of Frederick Goddard Tuckerman, and his original poetry appears in various magazines and journals. England received an A.B. from the University of Utah, then won a Danforth Graduate Fellowship, and earned his M.A. and Ph.D. at Stanford University. Co-founder of Dialogue, A Journal of Mormon Thought, *he has been an LDS Institute Instructor and has taught literature and writing at several colleges and universities. He has carefully studied the passage in the Book of Mormon recounting the emigration of Lehi from Jerusalem, thoroughly reviewed the information about Arabia accessible to Joseph Smith, and examined the reports of explorations since then, particularly the records of a journey in 1975 along the route described in the Book of Mormon as reported by Lynn M. and Hope Hilton in their book*

In Search of Lehi's Trail. Comparison of the details of the Book of Mormon account, published in 1830, with subsequent cultural and geographical findings reveals no contradictions and numerous remarkable correspondences. In this article England develops the argument that the Book of Mormon account of Lehi's journey across the Arabian peninsula could not have been written in the 1820s. More than twenty significant geographic details accurately described in the Book of Mormon but not known in America in Joseph Smith's time serve us evidence that it is indeed an ancient document, written from firsthand information.

There is an obvious test for the claim that the Book of Mormon is an ancient document: 1) determine if the details of geography, culture, language, literature, etc., are actually true to the ancient places and peoples it claims to be describing, and then 2) find out if those details could reasonably have been known in 1830 when it was published. In other words, it may have been possible for an early nineteenth-century American who was uncommonly imaginative and coherent in his thinking to produce a reasonable, even captivating, fiction about an emigration of sixth-century B.C. Hebrews across essentially unknown Arabia and the Pacific Ocean and about their development as a culture in America. But if the story claims to be literally *true*, it must hold up against all the subsequent 150 years of detailed scientific explorations and linguistic study of these areas and cultures. In this essay I will look only at the *route* taken by the Book of Mormon emigrants from Jerusalem across Arabia to the sea, testing the hypothesis that Joseph Smith, or one of his contemporaries, made up the account of that journey on the basis of information available in the 1820s.

A clever, or even sensible, writer of fiction would have been wise to choose a different route, if he had planned to go into detail. Much better information was available about the Mediterranean, including the Phoenician coast, where, for instance, material and skill for building an ocean-going ship would more likely have been known by Joseph Smith to have existed anciently. Much less could have been known of the Arabian Peninsula south of Jerusalem. The standard geographies of the time, those that were possibly available to Joseph Smith in the public libraries at Canandaigua, Ithaca, and Rochester in western New York, were consistently spare in describing Arabia as "generally a barren uncultivated waste,"[1] with sometimes a little information on the "bizarre" customs surrounding the Islamic holy cities of Mecca and Medina. Some of them added (based on the surviving ancient references to "Arabia Felix" and on Karsten Niebuhr's account of his explorations of Yemen and the Hijaz, published in English in 1792) this kind of misleading generality: "The southern division is fertile in a high degree, and produces rice, maize, etc., and abounds in frankincense, gums, balsams, honey, wax, spices, and all the tropical fruits."[2] And this is the extent of the knowledge reasonably available to "an unlettered farm boy" in western New York. But suppose Joseph Smith were a clever, multilingual researcher—or at least had access to one. What was the *most* he could possibly have known about Arabia?

Actually it turns out that the more he had known based on contemporary expertise the more wrong he is likely to have been, especially in details he included about large river courses, the particular directions traveled, and the specific location of an isolated luxuriant spot (that his emigrants called "Bountiful"), where there were not only flowers and fruit trees but also ore for toolmaking and large trees good for shipbuilding. For instance, had he read Niebuhr in detail he would have known of the littoral zone on the northeast shore of the Red Sea as a possible route, but he would have gotten the impression there was not any such system of wadis (valleys of the seasonal river-beds) as became important in his story.[3] And if in some way he had gotten hold of John Burckhardt's information before it was published in 1829 and 1831, or of reports of the British experience in Muscat, he would have been convinced that the earlier popular geographies and gazetteers were far too optimistic about southern Arabia being a comparatively fertile area. For instance, under the impact of the information that became generally available by the 1830s, McCulloch's *Universal Gazetteer* (New York, 1843) was willing to assert that the ancient references to Arabia Felix were "erroneous" and that the southern coast was dreary and unproductive. This was based on explorations that did not move inland and especially on the reports from Muscat at the eastern end of the southern shore of what is now Oman. Europeans could read imaginative descriptions of heat so great it roasted animals on the plain and fowls in the air; a sailor's account commented "there is only a sheet of brown paper between here and Hell."[4]

Conder's Arabia (London, 1825), the most complete general guide possibly available to Joseph Smith, describes the whole southern coastline as "a rocky wall . . . as dismal and barren as can be; not a blade of grass or a green thing."[5] It is this kind of information, the most up-to-date available for potential explorers, that led James Wellsted, a British naval officer who was able to travel in eastern Oman in the mid-1830s, to write in great surprise about his visit to oases near Minna:

> As we crossed these, with lofty almond, citron, and orange-trees yielding a delicious fragrance on either hand, exclamations of astonishment and admiration burst from us. "Is this Arabia," we said, "this the country we have looked on heretofore as a desert?" . . . I could almost fancy we had at length reached that "Araby the blest," which we had heretofore regarded as existing only in the fictions of our poets.[6]

The same expedition explored the coast southwest of Muscat and got some better information on Dhofar (the area in western Oman that corresponds best to Joseph Smith's "Bountiful," the fertile coast where the emigrants built and launched their ship). There they found the same surprising luxuriance reported by Wellsted and noted the promontory just west of Dhofar, "from which coasting vessels had turned for nearly two thousand years, their monsoon filling sails as their prows pointed to India."[7] And ten years later the same navy ship that had brought Wellsted, the *Palinarus,* returned to Dhofar, and Surgeon H. T. Carter went ashore and made the first modern examination of the frankincense trees that grow there. But as a twentieth-century account of "the unveiling of Arabia" notes, the reports of these were neglected and their names forgotten, so that in 1894, when Mr. and Mrs. James Theodore Bent went inland in Dhofar, they reported, "That arid Arabia could produce so lovely a spot, was to us one of the greatest surprises of our lives."[8]

As late as the 1920s Bertram Thomas was surprised at the "thickly wooded wadis"[9] of Dhofar, and even in 1939 a scholarly journal of exploration could write, "It is quite probable that Solomon had to transport his ships, or the material for them, from the Mediterranean, for where on the shores of the Red Sea could timber be found for shipbuilding?"[10]

Clearly the information on Arabia available to Joseph Smith was vague, inaccurate, contradictory. He would have been wise to choose a better-known route—or at least to be vague and general himself about the journey through Arabia and the ship-building. But he is not. The account is extremely detailed, leaving itself open on nearly every page to easy falsification through subsequent discoveries. We are told that Lehi, one of the many prophets that came forth (like Jeremiah) to call the Southern Kingdom of Judah to repentance before their captivity under Nebuchadnezzar, is warned by God in about 600 B.C. to flee for his life. He had dwelt "at Jerusalem"[11] and was apparently wealthy but now "took nothing with him, save it were his family, and provisions, and tents, and departed into the wilderness" (2:4). The route and times were quite specific, even somewhat mysteriously so: "He came down by the borders *near* the shore of the Red Sea; and he traveled in the wilderness in the borders which are *nearer* the Red Sea" and "when he had traveled *three days* in the wilderness, he pitched his tent in a valley by the side of a river of water . . . And when [he] saw that the waters of the river emptied in the *fountain* of the Red Sea, he spake unto Laman, saying, O that thou mightest be like unto this river, *continually* running into the fountain of all righteousness!" (2:5, 6, 9; italics added).

Using a manner of poetic exhortation that we have since learned was common among the Arabic peoples[12] and a metaphor that, though unusual to Westerners, is exact for that land where seasonally dry watercourses are the most enduring features,[13] Lehi also addressed his other wayward son, Lemuel: "O that thou mightest be like unto this valley, firm and steadfast, and immovable in keeping the commandments of the Lord!" (2:9). Lehi's family remained in this "valley of Lemuel" for some time, while the sons were sent back to Jerusalem to obtain the scriptural and historical records of their tribe and family and then to bring another family to provide for intermarriage in the developing colony. Then they took "provisions" and "seeds of every kind," grown during their stay in this valley, and "traveled for the space of four days, nearly a south-southeast direction" to a place they called Shazer (16:11, 13).

At Shazer they began to kill animals for food with bows and arrows and started traveling again, "following the same direction, keeping in the most fertile parts of the wilderness, which were in the borders near the Red Sea" (16:14). After they had traveled "many days" through an area of "sufferings and afflictions" and stopped again to hunt food, Lehi's son, Nephi, the narrator, "did break my bow, which was made of fine steel" and the bows of the others "lost their springs" (16:18, 21). But Nephi found wood to make a new bow and used that and a sling to "slay wild beasts" on the "top of a mountain" in that area (16:23, 30, 31). They then again traveled "nearly the same course as in the beginning . . . for the space of many days . . . and . . . did pitch our tents again, that we might tarry" (16:33). In this place, "which was called Nahom," the father of the second family died and was buried (16:34).

After living at Nahom "for a space of time"[14] (16:33), probably another growing season, the group started out again, but traveled "nearly eastward from that time forth" (17:1). This was a more difficult area of wilderness where they "did wade through much affliction" and "did live upon raw meat" because the Lord directed that they should "not . . . make much fire" (17:12). But then, after a total of eight years traveling and camping, sometimes settling for a season, they "did come to a land which we called Bountiful, because of its much fruit and also wild honey; and . . . beheld the sea, which we called Irreantum . . . many waters" and "did pitch our tents by the seashore" (17:4, 5). Here Nephi went up "into a mountain" and was given directions by the Lord to "construct a ship" (but "not after the manner of men") and shown where to find "ore to molten" for tools (17:7, 8, 9). At one point the rebellious brothers threatened to throw Nephi "into the depths of the sea" (17:48), but finally he was able to get them to cooperate, and they "did work timbers of curious workmanship" (18:1) until they had a ship capable of ocean voyage. They loaded it with "much fruits and meat . . . and honey . . . and provisions . . . and seeds and . . . put forth into the sea and were driven forth before the wind toward the promised land" (18:6, 8), which was America.

If we assume Joseph Smith is the author of this story, he has provided us with a daring abundance of unique details about matters unknown in his time, which ought to make it a simple matter to show him factually wrong in the light of later discoveries. Most dramatic—and most easy to falsify—would be the references to campsites at specific locations capable of producing crops; the conditions near a mountainous area supporting wild game that would break a steel bow and cause others to lose their spring and yet where wood for new bows could be found; and most of all, of course, the abrupt turn in direction and travel eastward—over an unusually desolate area but directly to a remarkably fertile area (fruit, flowers, honey) on the seashore that also meets a unique combination of unusual conditions: a beach, but also cliffs from which someone could be thrown into a deep sea; ore for toolmaking; timbers of sufficient length and quality for shipbuilding; and a prevailing wind to take them toward America. But the exploration of the Arabian peninsula by Westerners, which has occurred mainly in the twentieth century, especially since the penetration of Bertram Thomas into the Empty Quarter (1920s) and Wilfred Thesiger into Dhofar, has produced *no single contradiction* of Joseph Smith's daringly detailed "conjectures" and most remarkably has shown a high correlation of the actual discoveries to his specific details.

Modern research has recovered knowledge of an ancient caravan route, "The Frankincense Trail," from Dhofar, the ancient source of that precious material, to near Jerusalem; the trail conforms in detail to Joseph Smith's account of distances, turns, and specific geography. And modern travelers along that route have described details that fit the implications of his descriptions of topography, relative desolateness, weather conditions, etc. Of course, this route, and its remarkable beginning point, the uniquely fertile Salalah area in Dhofar, were known and written about anciently, for instance in the work of Strabo and Pliny,[15] but not with sufficient detail to account for more than a few of the correspondences, even if those documents had been available to Joseph Smith or if they were considered trustworthy or were detailed enough to be related to specific geography by anyone who did have access to them. The real state of popular and educated belief about the nature of Arabia is best indicated in the sketchy gazetteer accounts I have reviewed, and especially in the great surprise of educated explorers such as Wellsted, when they first came upon totally unexpected realities like the fertile Salalah.

To review, then. The details that we know now, through direct, modern observation and research into ancient sources unknown to Joseph Smith, correspond to what the Book of Mormon describes: An ancient caravan route passed to the east of Jerusalem from Damascus to what is called Salalah in modern Oman, the source of frankincense. Israelite merchants, living in the area of Jerusalem and serving as intermediaries between users of the route and the city, knew the trails and the sheikhs who controlled them, and had the means and knowledge to travel in the desert. Lehi (who lived "at Jerusalem," and had tents, etc.), when warned to flee for his life, most likely went directly to the Frankincense Trail where it moves along the Wadi Al Araba, part of the same geologic rift valley that forms the Sea of Galilee, the Jordan River and the Dead Sea and thus essentially determines the only route south, to Aqaba on the Red Sea. Aqaba is an ancient metal-smelting and shipbuilding area where Lehi's son Nephi certainly could have learned those skills "after the manner of men"—or at least what he had not learned in the metal-working centers of Jerusalem and Damascus. The ancient route then moves long the beach for eighteen miles but turns east in the face of impassable cliffs, up the Wadi Umm Jurfayn and then down the Wadi El Afal ("the borders *near* the Red Sea") to the coastal plain again ("the borders *nearer* the Red Sea").

Studies of a number of travel accounts show that the average desert caravan speed for a group the size of Lehi's is nearly twenty to twenty-five miles a day.[16] About "three days in the wilderness" from Aqaba (seventy-six miles) along the Frank-incense Trail is the large oasis of Al Beda, in an impressive valley with a riverbed that flows dramatically after rain and a flowing stream that waters substantial crops, all conditions that fit exactly the "valley of Lemuel" where Lehi's party stayed for some time. In addition the water flows into the Gulf of Aqaba, an arm of the Red Sea which in ancient Hebrew was likely called (in order to distinguish it from an ocean or large sea) a *yam,* a "source" or "fountain," Joseph Smith's exact word.[17] Now paralleling the coast again, the Trail, like that in the Book of Mormon, lies in a "nearly south-southeast direction." After traveling for "the space of four days" Lehi's group camped at a place they called "Shazer," which by normal traveling distance (about a hundred miles) would correspond to the prominent ancient oasis now called Wadi Al Azlan. Here they began to hunt wild game with bows and arrows and continued to do so after traveling for "many days" in the "same direction," which would have taken them into the general area of modern Jiddah.

This area, midway down the eastern shore of the Red Sea, is known for a combination of heat, humidity, sand, and salt that rusts car fenders in a few months and turns limber any dry wood brought from other areas. Here Nephi broke his steel bow and the wooden bows "lost their spring," but Nephi found wood for new bows and then found wild game nearby at the top of a mountain. Around Jiddah grows the pomegranate tree, excellent for bowmaking, and to the east, as there are farther north, are mountains with wild asses, gazelles, grouse, partridge, etc., which are still hunted with "slings," as Lehi's group hunted.[18] After again traveling "many days" in "nearly the same course," Lehi's group stopped "for the space of a time" in a place "which was called Nahom," evidently a well-established oasis on the route, and then turned and traveled "nearly eastward from that time." The ancient Trail did indeed take exactly such a turn (because of the interruption of high mountains coming directly to the seacoast) at modern Al Kunfidah, then going up the wadi system to the ancient caravan city of Najran and branching there. The main route then went south to ancient San'a, which by 600 B.C. had developed into an alternate source of frankincense, and the other route continued east, through the southern edge of the desolate sand desert known to modern explorers as "the Empty Quarter," until it came out to the fertile Qara Mountains in Dhofar, the original ancient scource of frankincense and the only such spot (about twenty miles long) on the entire fourteen-hundred-mile southern coast. Joseph Smith's account got the turn exactly right and also the area of increased desolation and "much affliction," including the interesting detail that the emigrants lived on raw meat, not being allowed "much fire," in this the one area of the trail where we now know they would have been in greatest danger of Bedouin raiders.[19]

Most startling, the Book of Mormon provides exactly all the details (now proven, but which no one knew in the 1820s) of *Salalah:* This small, unique spot is favored six months of the year by southwest monsoon winds that cloak the mountains in mist and produce the anciently precious frankincense which brought the caravan trail there—and also produce flowers, honeybees, fruit, and huge "sycamore-figs." These trees Thomas and Thesiger first described for western man;[20] they can produce long timbers of strong hardwood, remarkably free from knots and resistant to sea water and used even today to make ocean-going dhows. There is also iron ore in the mountains, a beach where Lehi's emigrants could "pitch . . . tents by the seashore" but one which terminates abruptly on the west in cliffs that drop a hundred feet "into the depths of the sea." And the seasonal monsoon winds that produce the fertility of this unique area also provide a unique source of power that we now know opened up trade across the open sea to India in the first century A.D.[21] and by which Nephi's ship would have been "driven forth . . . towards the promised land" of America. In Joseph Smith's time, as we have seen, neither the shipbuilding skills and materials nor the favorable winds on this desert shore of Arabia were known about in the west.

What can we make of this remarkable lack of mistakes and the even more remarkable number of correspondences in a nineteenth-century attempt to produce an ancient document? Simply that the hypothesis that the Book of Mormon was written in the 1820s is untenable. It would be equivalent to an average modern person sitting down right now and writing an account of an expedition down a river in ancient Siberia. There are certain popular beliefs about Siberia—that it is forested, with north-running rivers that end in an icebound arctic sea—parallel to those available to Joseph Smith about Arabia. But suppose your account moved your expedition through various turns and a variety of topography and climates, including waterfalls, swamps, and deserts at specific locations, and ending in a *warm water current* that took your travelers through the supposedly ice-bound Arctic Ocean *to the Pacific.* You would be dismissed as a forger. But if it turned out, on later exploration, that you were right in every detail it would have to be assumed that you had actually had access to a true firsthand account.

For Joseph Smith to have so well succeeded in producing over twenty unique details[22] in the description of an ancient travel route through one of the least-known areas of the world, all of which have been subsequently verified, requires extraordinary, unreasonable faith in his natural genius or his ability to guess right in direct opposition to the prevailing knowledge of his time. Of course, any particular detail might be coincidental, and I do not claim that such things as distances traveled can be exactly proven, but the piling up of parallel detail after detail, with *no* contradictions, is conclusive. As Occam first made clear, and many subsequent logicians have reminded us, of two rationally possible explanations for a phenomenon, the one less demanding of our credulity, the one less dependent on a series of coincidences or complex possibilities, is by that made the most persuasive. If we have to choose between explaining the origin of the Book of Mormon as a nineteenth-century forgery of an ancient account that luckily got a whole series of specific details right, even against the claims of contemporary knowledge, and accepting it as a genuine ancient document, the second possibility is by far the more reasonable.

NOTES

1. Frederick Butler, *Elements of Geography and History Combined*, 4th ed. (Wethersfield, Conn.: Deming and Francis, 1828), p. 245.

2. Ibid. I have examined the great variety of the geographies or "gazetteers" that could possibly have been available to Joseph Smith. They range from R. Brooke's *General Gazetteer*, published in London in 1794 and very popular, republished in a number of editions (finally, with revisions by John Marshall, in the U.S. in 1844), to Nathaniel Dwight's *Short but Comprehensive System of the Geography of the World . . . Designed for Children* (Northampton, Conn.: Simeon Butler, 1811), which was also republished many times. All of these are sketchy, very general and vague, and though generally consistent with each other, even obviously all dependent on Brooke's early work, they are contradictory about a central matter, the nature and location of any fertile areas in Arabia. All of those before 1835, when more careful explorations began to have their effect, subscribe to the ancient Romantic idea of an "Arabia Felix" in the south, but some identify the whole southern third as that poetic area (Butler, op. cit); some speak of "some few fertile spots [in the interior], which appear like islands in a desolate ocean"—Jedediah Morse, *A New System of Geography, Ancient and Modern, for the Use of Schools*, 24th Edition (Boston: Richardson and Lord 1824), p. 228; some identify such a fertile oasis as in "the *south-western* [italics added] extremity toward the shores of the Red Sea"—*A System of Geography: or, a Descriptive, Historical and Philosophical View of the Several Quarters of the World*, 4 vols. (Glasgow: Niven, Napier, and Khull, 1805) Vol. II, p. 273; and some claim that "in the *south-southeastern* part, called Arabia Felix, there is, in some spots, a fine soil, and luxuriant vegetation" (Dwight, op. cit., p. 109; italics added). None implies there is any timber such as would be needed for ship-building, Dwight stating specifically, "There is very little timber in Arabia of any kind." None suggests any fertile areas along the coast, some specifically denying it, such as *Conder's Arabia* (The Modern Traveller Series, London, 1825), p. 9.

3. Thorkile Hansen, *Arabia Felix* (London, 1964), p. 214.

4. See Robin Bidwell, *Travelers in Arabia* (London: Hamylyn Publishing Group, Ltd., 1976), p. 193-94.

5. Op. cit., p. 9.

6. R. H. Kiernan, *The Unveiling of Arabia: The Story of Arabian Travel and Discovery* (London: George G. Harrap and Co., 1937), p. 196. See also D. G. Hogarth, *The Penetration of Arabia, A Record of the Development of Western Knowledge Concerning the Arabian Peninsula* (London: Lawrence and Bullen, 1904), p. 138.

7. Kiernan, ibid., p. 201.

8. Bidwell, op. cit., p. 214.

9. Bertram Thomas, *Arabia Felix* (New York: Charles Scribner's Sons, 1932), p. 100.

10. J. Perowne, *Palestine Exploration Fund Quarterly,* 1939, p. 200.

11. The Book of Mormon (Palmyra, New York: Grandin Publishing Co., 1830), chapter 1, verse 4. I will give the verse notations from the "First Book of Nephi" at the beginning of the Book of Mormon as they are in the modern editions (since 1880) of The Church of Jesus Christ of Latter-day Saints, but the quotations will be from the first edition.

12. Hugh Nibley, *Lehi in the Desert and The World of the Jaredites* (Salt Lake City: Bookcraft, 1952), pp. 99ff. Professor Nibley was the first to call attention to the remarkable correspondences between the Book of Mormon claims (in 1830) about a then unknown area and the modern confirmations that have come through increased knowledge about Arabia.

13. Ibid., pp. 91ff.

14. For an analysis of possible Hebrew equivalents for that interesting phrase, see George Reynolds and Janne M. Sjodahl, *Commentary on the Book of Mormon* (Salt Lake City: Deseret News Press, 1955), vol. 1, p. 167.

15. *The Geography of Strabo,* seven volumes, translated from the Greek by Horace Leonard Jones (London: W. Heinemann Ltd., 1930), vol. 7, pp. 299-365; Pliny, *Natural History,* translated from the Latin by H. Rackham (London: William Heinemann Ltd., 1952), pp. 37-63. There is also an ancient anonymous travel account, *The Periplus of the Erythraean Sea, Travel and Trade in the Indian Ocean by a Merchant of the First Century,* translated from the Greek by Wilfred H. Schoff (New Delhi: Oriental Books Reprint Corp., 1974), with notes by Schoff. Even in the highly unlikely event that any of these esoteric classical works could have been available to Joseph Smith, they do not contain details in relation to modern geographical terms sufficient to have been helpful with the particular claims about the route we are discussing here.

16. Gus W. Van Beek, "The Rise and Fall of Arabia Felix," *Scientific American,* December 1969, p. 41, cited, with other examples of daily travel distances for desert caravans, in Lynn M. and Hope Hilton, *In Search of Lehi's Trail* (Salt Lake City: Deseret Book Co., 1976), p. 49. The Hiltons' book is a major source for my work here, since it provided many references for me to

explore, but especially since it contains the firsthand report of people who actually traveled over much of the Frankincense Trail in 1975.

17. Nibley, op. cit., pp. 88-89.

18. Hilton, op. cit., pp. 81-83.

19. Hilton, op. cit., pp. 95-97 and 101-3.

20. Hilton, p. 106; Thomas, op. cit., p. 100; and Wilfred Thesiger, *Arabian Sands* (Middlesex, England: Penguin Books Ltd., 1964), p. 47.

21. Hilton, p. 114; "Geography: Romans," *Encyclopedia Brittannica,* 1971, 10:146.

22. A quick review of these details: 1) The route south to Aqaba is an anciently primary way out of Jerusalem. 2) The ancient route, the Frankincense Trail, leaves the beach coast at Aqaba, so it is "near" the Red Sea; then it returns to it, so it is "nearer." 3) The location of a major oasis about three days' journey along the trail from Aqaba. 4) The location there of an impressive valley that could be used for poetic metaphor and 5) of a continually flowing river that 6) flows into an arm of the Red Sea called anciently a "fountain" and 7) is capable of supporting extended settlement and growth of crops. 8) Four days from this oasis, in a south-southeast direction, is another major oasis where 9) wild animals that can be hunted with bow and arrow begin to be available. 10) Further in the same direction, still along the Frankincense Trail that is in this whole area the only tenable route, with anciently dug or natural water holes at regular intervals, 11) the area (north and south of modern Jiddah) becomes more inhospitable, a source of "much affliction," with fewer water holes, 12) many sand storms and metal-destroying salt air and humidity where a steel bow would break and wooden ones lose their spring but 13) where there is excellent pomegranate wood for new bows and 14) a mountain where wild game is plentiful. 15) Many days further in the same direction is another major oasis capable of supporting a caravan through a growing season, and 16) this is where the Frankincense Trail turns sharply to the east and then 17) skirts the notorious "Empty Quarter," the worst desert in Arabia, another period of "much affliction" to the group and 18) a place where danger from Bedouin raiders could require traveling without firebuilding. 19) There is, exactly where the direct route east intercepts the southern Arabian coast, a unique fertile area of fruit and wild honey, with 20) a gentle beach and yet nearby high cliffs dropping into deep water, 21) mountains nearby with iron ore for toolmaking, 22) sycamore-fig trees growing on the mountains that are excellent for shipbuilding and 23) strong monsoon winds used anciently for sailing to India and out into the Pacific Ocean.

7

Wayne A. Larsen and
Alvin C. Rencher

Who Wrote the Book of Mormon? An Analysis of Wordprints

Wayne A. Larsen was Director of Advanced Research Systems, Eyring Research Institute, Inc., and is now a faculty member in statistics at Brigham Young University. He completed his undergraduate work at Brigham Young, after which he received his Ph.D. at Virginia Polytechnic Institute in 1967. His long list of publications includes articles on Minuteman II accuracy testing and advanced statistical analysis.

Alvin C. Rencher, a Professor of Statistics at Brigham Young University, also completed his Ph.D. at Virginia Polytechnic Institute. In addition to teaching, he has worked as a statistical consultant to the LDS Church, the state of Utah, and Kennecott Copper Corporation. He has published numerous articles on statistical techniques and applications in journals and magazines.

In this article, Larsen and Rencher report their findings from a statistical analysis of style in the Book of Mormon. Using "wordprint analysis," a method of determining idiosyncratic

*subconscious patterns in the writings of any author, they
conclude that (1) the Book of Mormon was written by many
authors, and that (2) no Book of Mormon passages resemble the
writing of any of the commonly suggested nineteenth-century
authors. The clear yet hitherto unnoticed characteristics of the
Book of Mormon discovered by Larsen and Rencher strongly
support Joseph Smith's account of the book's origin.*

The problem of Book of Mormon authorship has challenged
historians and theologians since the book was published in
1830. Opponents of the book have claimed that Joseph Smith
wrote it himself, or that an accomplice such as Solomon Spaulding or Sidney Rigdon penned it and somehow transferred it to
Joseph Smith.[1] The defenders of the book maintain that it is just
what it claims to be—a sacred record written on metal plates by
many ancient authors and translated by Joseph Smith with
divine assistance and direction (Joseph Smith—History 2:62-
65).

Both sides present arguments to strengthen their case. Pro-
ponents note that proper names and cultural traits found in the
book have been validated by recent Middle Eastern research,[2]
while opponents point out the similarities between the book's
theology and the religions of early nineteenth-century upstate
New York.[3] Book of Mormon apologists find evidence of
Hebrew and other ancient writing styles in the book,[4] but
detractors point to the grammatical mistakes in the earlier
editions as evidence that there could have been no miraculous
translation.[5] Both sides also cite archaeological evidence to
defend their points of view.

One element missing in all of this literature is an approach
that would allow for quantification of the evidence followed by
a rigorous and objective statistical analysis as a test of the
competing claims. The book purports to have been written by a
number of ancient authors. We can now test this claim scien-

tifically by combining certain assumptions of modern linguistics with new advances in the statistical analysis of texts.

For our analysis we started with a basic assumption that individual authors leave something analogous to a fingerprint in all their works. Each author's style has some subconscious individualistic patterns that are not easily altered. These patterns form his unique "wordprint." The growing number of wordprint studies includes inquiries into the authorship of letters, biblical books, and ancient Greek works.[6]

STYLOMETRY

Our approach is sometimes referred to as the science of stylometry,[7] which can be defined loosely as statistical analysis of style. It is also called computational stylistics. We do not use the word *style* in the literary sense of subjective impressions characterizing an author's mode of expression. We must deal with countable items which are amenable to statistical analysis. We look then for what is frequent but largely unnoticed, the quick little choices that confront an author in nearly every sentence. Such choices become habits, so the small details flow virtually without conscious effort.

One writer on this subject, Douglas Chretien, used the term "linguistic fingerprint" to describe an author's subconscious pattern of usage of the language features which uniquely characterize his writings. He stated: "The conscious features of style can be imitated, . . . but the unconscious and sub-conscious features surely cannot, and a test of authorship, if it is to be reliable, must be built on them."[8]

In the literature of stylistic analysis we find many references[9] claiming that for a given author these habits are not affected by (1) passage of time, (2) change of subject matter, or (3) literary form. They are thus stable within an author's writings, but they have been found to vary from one author to another. We give two examples which illustrate this approach to authorship identification.

The first concerns the controversy over the authorship of twelve of the eighty-five Federalist Papers. Although the

Federalist Papers were first published anonymously, it was later found that five were written by John Jay and that the rest were divided between Alexander Hamilton and James Madison. Although authorship of seventy-three of the papers was determined, there was still a question as to whether Hamilton or Madison wrote the remaining twelve.

Two statisticians, Mosteller and Wallace, compared the twelve disputed papers to other of Hamilton's and Madison's writings. Using frequency of usage of the small filler words, they found overwhelming evidence favoring Madison as the author of all twelve disputed papers.[10]

As a second example, when Jane Austen died in 1817 she left an unfinished novel along with a summary. A few years ago, an anonymous admirer completed this novel and published it. She was a highly skilled author and tried her best to imitate the style of Jane Austen. She succeeded very well in the conscious elements of style but failed totally in the subconscious habits of detail. When these habit patterns were examined, the difference was clearly evident.[11]

We made the same assumption, then, that has been generally accepted and proven widely applicable: each author has a wordprint. We coined the term "wordprint" to describe a writer's linguistic fingerprint or habit patterns of usage of noncontextual words.

The noncontextual words which have been most successful in discriminating among authors are the filler words of the language such as prepositions and conjunctions, and sometimes adjectives and adverbs. Authors differ in their rates of usage of these filler words.

Some previous investigators of authorship identification have oversimplified the problem. Some have chosen a definition of wordprint and then have taken several controversial passages from an author and tested for statistically significant differences in the wordprint between passages. If any statistically significant differences occurred, they assumed different individuals had authored the passages. We believe a larger view must be taken. In addition to comparing several passages written by the same author, we must also compare them with the works of a control group of contemporary authors. Conceivably, an individual author might produce wordprints which differ in a statistically significant manner and yet are consistent within themselves when compared with other authors' wordprints. We have taken this into consideration in our study by including authors who were contemporaries of Joseph Smith.

We propose to test the assumption that the Book of Mormon was written by one author (Joseph Smith or whomever) against the alternative hypothesis of multiple authorship. If the book were written by several people, we should statistically reject the hypothesis of single authorship. Showing multiple authorship would be strong evidence for Joseph Smith's account of the origin of the book, since it is the primary explanation which asserts multiple authors. Finding single authorship would not necessarily invalidate the believers' claims, however, because it is logically possible that even though Joseph Smith had divine direction in translating he might have paraphrased the text into his own words. This argument would also hold for Mormon's abridgment, but even then there would be other authors in Nephi and Moroni. That Joseph Smith could have received the translation word for word in a uniform literary mode with all style differences between authors obliterated is yet another possibility.

BOOK OF MORMON CLAIMS OF NUMEROUS AUTHORS

According to the Book of Mormon itself, numerous prophets whose lives cover a period of over a thousand years wrote the book. Three-and-one-half centuries after the birth of Christ, Mormon realized that his writing would soon come to an end, but he was shown in vision that a later people would profit from it. Acting on divine instructions, he made a very brief abridgment of the records in his charge, engraving it on gold plates. He passed these plates on to his son Moroni, who added to the record and then deposited it in the appointed place for safekeeping. With this record compiled by Mormon and

Moroni, Joseph Smith also found a much smaller record, "the small plates," which contained the early history of these people beginning with their departure from Jerusalem soon after 600 B.C. Most of this smaller record was written by Nephi and his younger brother Jacob, who were in the original group which left the Old World. Joseph Smith used this original material in place of Mormon's abridgment covering that period. Thus, according to the text, there were four major engravers of the gold plates—Mormon, Moroni, Jacob, and Nephi—and a few minor engravers as well (see Appendix A).

In addition, the abridgers of the record often appear to be quoting from other authors; for example, Mormon recorded the commandments given by Alma to his son Helaman (Alma 36, 37). Since quotation marks do not appear anywhere in the Book of Mormon, the question remains as to whether these passages are verbatim or paraphrased.[12]

For the purpose of the statistical tests, we started with two assumptions: (1) that each of the major engravers and those they quote were distinct individuals, and (2) that the writers of each verse, or partial verse, could be identified according to information given in the text. We found very little ambiguity as to who wrote what. However, identifying the source of each verse or portion of a verse required careful scrutiny, since authorship or source shifts approximately fifteen hundred times in the text of the Book of Mormon.

Through the process of assigning each quoted segment a source, we identified over one hundred authors or originators. Twenty-two of these contributed over 1,000 words; they, along with two others who had close to 1,000 words, are listed in Appendix B in descending order according to word count.[13] As expected, Mormon is first on the list, with nearly 40 percent of the book attributed to him. Nephi has the second highest word count. The third author on this list, Alma, is not one of the engravers of the book but was quoted frequently by Mormon. A very interesting facet of this list is that if all the words attributed to Deity are combined, then Deity becomes the third most-quoted source in the book,[14] with approximately 10 percent of the words.

NON-BOOK OF MORMON AUTHORS

For control and comparison purposes we analyzed the writing of several nineteenth-century authors, including that of both Sidney Rigdon and Solomon Spaulding, who have been proposed as authors of the Book of Mormon. We also included other known works by Joseph Smith and contemporary works by W. W. Phelps, Oliver Cowdery, and Parley P. Pratt.[15] Also we analyzed the Lectures on Faith plus two sections from the Doctrine and Covenants. Finally we added an article called "The Paracletes," which was published anonymously in the *Times and Seasons*.[16]

METHODOLOGY

We used three basic statistical techniques: Multivariate Analysis of Variance, Cluster Analysis, and Discriminant or Classification Analysis. These techniques will be described below. We also used three basic wordprint definitions: (1) frequency of letters, (2) frequency of commonly occurring noncontextual words, (3) frequency of rarely occurring noncontextual words. Although this paper emphasizes the frequency of commonly occurring noncontextual words, all three wordprint definitions produced similar results. Appendix C contains the 38 common and 42 uncommon words we used; they were selected from a list of words ordered by frequency.

MULTIVARIATE ANALYSIS OF VARIANCE (MANOVA)

We will first describe multivariate analysis of variance (MANOVA) and then present a few examples from the many analyses that we conducted. MANOVA is a technique that tests for homogeneity of groups,[17] the similarity of the wordprint patterns from one author to another. To illustrate the procedure, suppose that there exists a set of ten plays ascribed to Shakespeare. However, some scholars hypothesize that Shakespeare wrote only seven of the plays and that the other three were written by an unknown individual. To use MANOVA, we divide the ten plays into two groups, one containing the seven undisputed texts, the other the three disputed plays. A word-print definition is precisely chosen. MANOVA allows us to compare the wordprints for the two groups of plays and deter-mines whether the observed difference in wordprint is large in relation to the internal consistency within each group of plays. A large observed difference would support the conclusion that different authors wrote the two groups of plays, while a small difference (relative to the groups' internal consistency) would suggest that one author wrote all ten plays.

Here is an oversimplified numerical example to clarify the concept further. Consider a case where we have only two authors, with three different passages from each author. We are examining the frequency of the word *and* and find the following frequency results:

	Passage 1	Passage 2	Passage 3
Author A:	.032	.031	.032
Author B:	.063	.065	.064

Frequency in this case means relative frequency; i.e., *and* appeared 32 times per 1,000 words. It is clear that, if the three selections from each author are typical, the authors will differ in the average frequency with which they used the word *and*. However, if the results were as follows, we could not discrimi-nate between these authors on the basis of this word.

	Passage 1	Passage 2	Passage 3
Author A:	.032	.055	.068
Author B:	.042	.058	.061

On this information alone we could not rule out the possibility that A and B were the same individual.

The MANOVA technique can be applied to any number of authors and any number of words. Based on the frequencies it analyzes, MANOVA states the probability of a set of data arising if a single author wrote all of the materials examined. Certain statistical assumptions are required before this probability statement is valid. We have satisfied these sufficiently for the purposes of this study.

The writings of our 24 authors were divided into 251 blocks of text containing approximately 1,000 words apiece. Mormon was presumed to be the author of 98 of these blocks, while the last three authors—Mosiah, Enos, and the Father—had only 1 block each. The frequency of each of the words in Appendix C was computed for each of these 251 blocks.[18]

In the first analyses the blocks of words attributed to Jesus, Isaiah, and the Lord quoted by Isaiah were deleted since they agree so closely with the Bible. We thus avoid the possibility of these authors causing significant differences.

MANOVA—10 Words,
Book of Mormon Only

We first compared the 21 remaining authors by using the 10 most frequently occurring words in our list. Statistically, the differences among the authors are highly significant. Differences as large as these simply could not occur if a single author wrote the book. The statistical odds that a single author wrote the book are less than 1 in 100 billion. However, this number should not be taken too literally. It depends on several assumptions, one of which is that we have a random sample of each author's writings. The 100 billion to 1 ratio does imply, however, that the authors' wordprints vary significantly with respect to each author's own internal consistency.

The 10 words which we compared were *and, the, of, that, to, unto, in, it, for,* and *be.* Only one word, *in,* was not significantly different across the 21 authors. Seven of them were significant at less than the .0001 level; i.e., the probability that a single author would produce such disparate results is less than 1 in 10,000. In a typical research study, a difference would be labeled significant if its probability level was .05 (less than 1 in 20) or smaller. Most of the differences we found were so large that the associated probability level was very much smaller than .05.

MANOVA—38 Words,
Book of Mormon Only

The MANOVA was repeated using the 38 frequently occurring words listed in Appendix C, with similar results. Thus the 21 authors do not appear to be the same individual. We have not shown statistically the existence of 21 distinct styles but have strongly demonstrated wide divergence among most of the 21. The pattern of differences among the authors will be examined further in connection with the MANOVA which includes non-Book of Mormon authors as well.

MANOVA—Other Book of Mormon Tests

The preceding analyses were repeated using the Book of Mormon authors in a variety of contexts. These include analyses on word frequencies, analyses on all 24 authors (Jesus, Isaiah, and the Lord as quoted by Isaiah added to the data base), analyses on the 42 uncommon words listed in Appendix C, and analyses on frequency of letters. The results were the same in each case. We consistently found extremely low probabilities that the differences among these 24 groups of text could have been produced by a single author. There were no contradictory results.

MANOVA—38 Words,
Including Non-Book of Mormon Authors

We also compared the writing in the Book of Mormon with that of Joseph Smith and his contemporaries, who wrote in the time period when the Book of Mormon was published. The 90 blocks of words we used were from Joseph Smith, W. W. Phelps, Oliver Cowdery, Parley P. Pratt, Sidney Rigdon, Solomon Spaulding, the article "Paracletes," excerpts from the Doctrine and Covenants, and the Lectures on Faith. It has been suggested that certain of these men were the authors of the Book of Mormon.

As a control test we first performed a MANOVA using all 38 words on 341 word blocks from the 33 authors (24 Book of

Mormon plus 9 non-Book of Mormon authors). Probability that differences as large as those observed could occur by chance is less than 1 in 10 billion.

The overall MANOVA results for all 33 authors is of less interest than making pertinent comparisons among the 33 authors. These comparisons include direct comparisons of the Book of Mormon and non-Book of Mormon authors, along with comparisons among the book's authors grouped appropriately. The major conclusions from these statistical comparisons are:

1. There is some evidence of a wordprint time trend within the Book of Mormon; i.e., writers are more similar to their contemporaries than to writers in other time periods. This needs further investigation.

2. The passages quoting the Father do not differ from the combined passages quoting the Lord and Jesus. But there may be a little difference between quotations from Jesus and those from the Lord.

3. There is no statistical difference between the Isaiah passages and the Lord as quoted by Isaiah.

4. Joseph Smith's writing is very different from that of the author of Lectures on Faith (see Appendix E).

5. The most salient result, however, was that *none of the Book of Mormon selections resembled the writing of any of the suggested nineteenth-century authors.*[19] The Book of Mormon itself offers the strongest evidence for a clear scientific refutation of the theories that it was written in the nineteenth century.

The MANOVA tests have shown conclusively that (1) the 21 major groups of Book of Mormon text we examined were indeed written by several distinct authors, who were individually consistent as suggested in the book itself, and (2) none of the modern candidates whom we tested for Book of Mormon authorship wrote any of that text. This leaves Joseph Smith's account as the only explanation consistent with these clear yet hitherto unnoticed characteristics of the Book of Mormon. The only alternative would be that, in spite of its growing reputation in scientific circles, the theoretical basis of wordprint is not generally valid. But our own results on known nineteenth-century authors provide strong support for the wordprint concept.

To avoid the possibility that our MANOVA results might be unconsciously biased by any particular statistical technique, we included two additional analyses: cluster analysis and discriminant or classification analysis.

CLUSTER ANALYSIS

Cluster analysis takes a series of measurements on a set of observations and identifies which observations are closest to each other. In this study, the series of measurements would be the frequencies of the 38 words which form the wordprint profile, and the set of observations would be the 1,000-word blocks. "Closeness" is defined by a distance measure of the difference between two wordprints.[20] Cluster analysis can be used as an additional test of multiple authorship, but, more importantly, it can also be used as an informal method of assessing relationships between blocks of words.

The major cluster analyses we performed yielded conclusions similar to the MANOVA results discussed earlier. Mormon's word blocks clustered with other blocks by Mormon, Nephi's with Nephi's, King Benjamin's with King Benjamin's, etc. These results were the same no matter which definition of wordprint we selected—letters, common words, or uncommon words. The percent of clusterings corresponding with the multiple authors as named in the Book of Mormon was much higher than could have been produced by chance. Since these results are very similar to those presented in the MANOVA sections, we include only two examples which show a different application of clustering.

Cluster Analysis—
24 Book of Mormon Authors

This cluster analysis was for the 24 Book of Mormon authors using one observation consisting of each author's total words combined. Frequencies of the 38 common words were used as data. The purpose in combining each author's words was to determine how the authors relate to each other. To calculate a distance measure which would most clearly distinguish the authors, we chose the 9 words which discriminated best in the MANOVA.

Some results indicating that contemporaries write alike were—

1. Nephi's word blocks paired with those of his father, Lehi; together these then clustered with the group of word blocks of Nephi's brother Jacob and of Isaiah, the prophet most quoted by Nephi and Jacob.
2. The Lord's word blocks grouped with Jesus'.
3. Alma's word blocks grouped with those of Amulek, his missionary companion; once combined they paired with those of Abinadi, the man who converted Alma's father.
4. Samuel the Lamanite's word blocks paired with those of Nephi, son of Helaman. Samuel the Lamanite and Nephi were contemporary prophets.
5. The word blocks of the Lord as quoted by Isaiah paired with the Father's.

Some contrasting results were—

1. Mormon's word blocks paired with Helaman's, a bridge of 300 years.
2. Moroni's word blocks paired with Zenos's even though these two authors were most widely separated in time. Overall, Moroni's word blocks clustered less "correctly" than other authors'. Perhaps this is because much of his writing is an abridgment of the Jaredite record or quotation from unspecified earlier sources.

Cluster Analysis—Book of Mormon
and Non-Book of Mormon Authors Combined

All 33 authors were used in this analysis, with one replication per author which consisted of all blocks combined for that author. As before, 9 selected words were used for the distance calculations.

The following results were noted:

1. Joseph Smith's word blocks combined with those of Lectures on Faith; this pair then combined with Oliver Cowdery's (see Appendix E).
2. Jacob's word blocks combined with those of "The Paracletes."[21]
3. Nephi's word blocks combined with Lehi's.
4. Phelps's word blocks and Pratt's combined.
5. The word blocks of the Lord and Jesus combined.
6. Alma's word blocks, Amulek's, and Abinadi's combined.
7. Ammon's word blocks and General Moroni's combined.
8. Samuel's word blocks and those of Nephi (the son of Helaman) combined.
9. The word blocks of the Lord as quoted by Isaiah and those of the Father combined.
10. Mormon's word blocks and Helaman's combined.
11. Moroni's word blocks and Zeniff's combined.

In general, word blocks of Book of Mormon authors clustered with those of Book of Mormon authors, and word blocks of non-Book of Mormon authors clustered with those of non-Book of Mormon authors. The tendency of contemporaries to combine was also evident.

DISCRIMINANT OR CLASSIFICATION ANALYSIS

The third and most powerful statistical technique used in this study was discriminant analysis. This procedure reduced the dimensionality of differences among authors. The MANOVA has established the existence of significant differences in wordprints from one author to another. However, these wordprints are essentially 38-dimensional profiles; i.e., they are composed of the frequencies of 38 words. With 38 words to consider, it is difficult to grasp the pattern of separation between two or more authors. The discriminant procedure determines a set of functions (fewer in number than 38) which reveal the configuration of separation among the authors.[22]

A discriminant analysis is often followed by a classification analysis in which the profile of word frequencies (wordprint) of a block of words is compared to the average profile of each author, and the block of words is assigned to the most probable author. The comparisons are made by means of classification functions which measure how closely one profile matches another. We consider the techniques of discriminant and classification analysis to be the most powerful because they are self-verifying; i.e., the results tell how well the wordprint concept works on the data being studied.

Discriminant Analysis—2000-Word Blocks
for 21 Authors

The discriminant analysis we used was performed in steps. The word which best separates authors was entered first, the second best word next. This process continued sequentially until a designated critical level was reached, after which no more words were included in the analysis. In this case 18 words provided a high percentage of the discriminating power of the 38 words, and the amount of computation was thereby reduced without sacrificing much accuracy.[23] We evaluated and plotted the discriminant functions for each block of words, thus providing a visual display of the differences among authors. Some of these plots will be shown (see Figures 1 and 2).

The words selected in this discriminant analysis were then used in a classification analysis as described above. In this phase each block of words was classified with the author whose wordprint it was closest to. The percent of the correct "hits" is a measure of how well the authors can be separated, of how unique the profile of word frequencies is for each author.

In the computer run with 2,000-word blocks and 18 words selected, 93.3 percent of the blocks were correctly classified. This is a very high success rate for a situation such as this where the number of groups (authors) is so large. Typically the percent of correct classifications drops off when the number of groups exceeds four or five, and in many applications the percentage of hits is low even when the number of groups is small. The 93.3 percentage in this case was unexpectedly high.

A better method of classifying the blocks of text is to drop one or more blocks of words from the analysis, compute the classification functions, and use these new functions to classify the blocks dropped, thus eliminating the partial circularity of the previous test. This was done on the above data base and in many other cases. The results, though not as impressive as the 93 percent just mentioned, were consistently in the 70 and 80 percent range, still very high percentages for so many groups. We performed many more analyses of this type with similar results. We mention a few.

Discriminant Analysis—
Non-Book of Mormon Authors Included

Four Book of Mormon authors who had fewer than 2,000 words were deleted. This left 162 blocks of words by 29 authors. The first two discriminant functions (see Appendix F) were evaluated for all 162 observations and are shown in Figure 1. The Book of Mormon authors are rather widely separated from the non-Book of Mormon group. It should be remembered that this two-dimensional plot is essentially a projection of higher dimensional points onto a plane. The actual points in a higher dimensional space are even more separated than they appear here.

Taken together, these tests strongly reinforce previous conclusions that—

1. distinct authorship styles can be readily distinguished within the Book of Mormon, and
2. the nineteenth-century authors do not resemble Book of Mormon authors in style.

The pattern of separation which can be noticed in Figure 1 suggests another interesting observation. The 9 non-Book of Mormon authors are known to be different. Yet their pattern of

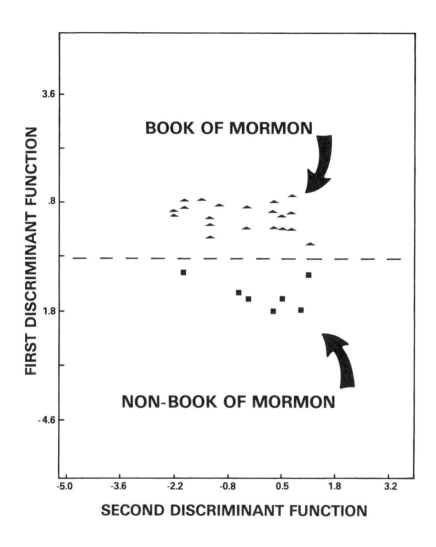

Figure 1. Discriminant Analysis of
Book of Mormon and Non-Book of Mormon Authors

variation one from another is similar to the pattern of variation among the Book of Mormon authors. This emphasizes the differences among Book of Mormon authors and helps clarify that the differences we have found are neither—

1. artifacts of the book which might possibly be typical of other books, nor
2. natural random fluctuations of word frequencies from one section of the book to another.

The presence of Isaiah among the Book of Mormon authors yielded a similar result. Believers and nonbelievers agree Isaiah is a different author than the author(s) of the rest of the Book of Mormon, yet none of our statistical tests showed Isaiah to particularly stand out. That is, Mormon, Nephi, and others appeared to be as distinctively individual as Isaiah. If Joseph Smith or any other nineteenth-century author had written the book, this would not be expected.

Discriminant Analysis of Four Major
Book of Mormon Authors and Joseph Smith

The intent in this analysis was to focus on the four major authors who together account for 62.2 percent of the Book of Mormon. These authors are Mormon, Nephi, Alma (the son of Alma), and Moroni (see Appendix B). These four were compared with each other and with Joseph Smith. Some 91 blocks of 2,000 words were available. Words of the King James Version were excluded, and 18 words were selected in the stepwise phase. We used four discriminant functions.

A plot of the first two discriminant functions is given in Figure 2. The following conclusions are apparent from the plot:

1. Alma's writing is different from Mormon's. Since *all* of Alma's words are taken from Mormon's writings, we can conclude that Mormon copied directly from Alma's writings and *Joseph Smith translated literally from Mormon's writings.*
2. Joseph Smith's writing is very definitely distinct from that of the authors in the Book of Mormon.

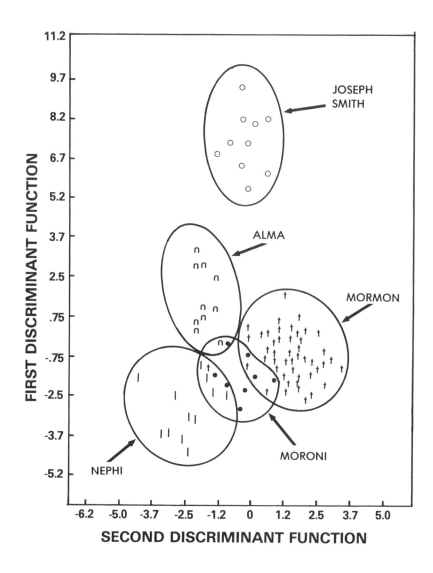

*Figure 2. Discriminant Analysis of
Four Major Book of Mormon Authors and Joseph Smith*

3. Moroni's position between Alma, Nephi, and Mormon again indicates that Moroni is consistently hard to classify.

In the classification phase, 96.7 percent of the word blocks were correctly classified. This number speaks for itself.

THREE QUESTIONS

There are three questions that may have occurred to our readers.

1. *Could Joseph Smith have altered his wordprint habits by trying to imitate the King James style?*

From all the research results with which we are familiar, the answer is no.

We mentioned the case of the lady who recently tried to imitate Jane Austen but whose own wordprint showed through the imitation when subjected to stylometric analysis. In a number of other cases, it has been shown that where an imitation is compared to the wordprint of the original, "the result resembles its creator more than it does the model."[24]

2. *Could the large differences among authors in the Book of Mormon be misleading; i.e., could we find similar differences among several works by the same author?*

In all the studies we are aware of either no significant differences were found or at most very few minor differences. As near as we can determine, the answer to this question is also no.[25]

We elaborate with a few interesting examples. One of the authors assisted in an analysis of wordprint in the Book of Isaiah.[26] Although virtually all the higher critics believe Isaiah is the product of two or more distinct authors, the Adams and Rencher work pointed to a unity of the Book of Isaiah. In fact, it showed a greater internal consistency for Isaiah than any other Old Testament book of that approximate time period.

The unity of some of Shakespeare's plays has also been questioned, but when these plays were subjected to wordprint analysis, no significant variations in wordprint were found within the given plays. An attempt to prove that part or all of Shakespeare's works were really written by Bacon resulted in what was described by A. Q. Morton as "one of history's finest examples of serendipity."[27] A man by the name of William Friedman was hired by a prominent Baconian to unravel the ciphers or code which would reveal the identity of Bacon in the text of Shakespeare. Friedman's study actually refuted the cipher idea in Shakespeare. But he became intrigued with ciphers and went on to publish some very important papers on decipherment. His work led directly to cracking the Japanese naval code in World War II.[28]

Another study examined two books by Sir Walter Scott, one written early in his career, the other just before he died. Even though Scott had suffered four strokes during the intervening time period, there were no significant differences in wordprints either within the two works or between them.[29]

3. *Can wordprints survive translation?*

A recently completed study indicates that the answer to this question is yes. (The study was conducted by Karl S. Black, Alvin C. Rencher, and Marvin H. Folsom, with no published report yet available.) Twelve German novellas, written by twelve distinct individuals, were all translated by the same American author. When the wordprints of the twelve German authors were compared by MANOVA, differences were readily apparent, with statistical significance of a very high order.

A sizable body of writing in English by the translator was also available. When his wordprint in these writings was compared with the wordprints of the twelve German authors (translated) the differences were highly significant.

As an additional check on question 2 above, the translator's own writings were divided into subgroups. These subgroups of blocks of words were compared statistically by use of MANOVA. No significant differences were found.

CONCLUSIONS

Subject to the usual statistical assumptions and allowance for error, we make the following conclusions:

1. The wordprint hypothesis appears to be justified. Based on our analysis of known non-Book of Mormon authors, each

writer appears to have a unique set of unconscious style characteristics. This profile of usage habits can serve in many cases to identify a piece of writing as belonging to a particular author, just as a fingerprint or voiceprint can be traced to its owner or originator.

2. The results of MANOVA, discriminant analysis, and cluster analysis all strongly support multiple authorship of the Book of Mormon. According to some of the MANOVA results, the odds against the Book of Mormon having a single author are more than a billion to one. Of course the assumptions for MANOVA should be checked. For example, it is unlikely that the data can be considered to have come from a multivariate normal distribution. However, we used the arc sine transformation, which partially compensated for the lack of multivariate normality.

However, the conclusion of multiple authorship does not rest on the significance tests alone. One of the most telling arguments is provided by the plots of discriminant scores in which the variation among known authors such as Joseph Smith, Sidney Rigdon, Parley P. Pratt, and others is seen to be very similar to the variation among Book of Mormon authors. Thus if one questions the highly significant results of the MANOVA by suggesting that the differences may be statistically significant but possibly reflect only minute real differences, we can clearly refer to the graphs of discriminant functions to show that the differences among Book of Mormon authors are of the same magnitude as the differences among known authors.

Conversely, the MANOVA results reinforce the discriminant function plots. These plots exhibit a very convincing pattern of separation among authors. With the backup of significance tests, this separation becomes very real and there remains little doubt of its validity.

In further support of the MANOVA results, it should be noted that most of the 38 words were individually significant; i.e., the authors differed from each other on each word considered separately.

This finding of multiple authorship has several implications.

1. It does not seem possible that Joseph Smith or any other

writer could have fabricated a work with many discernible authorship styles (wordprints). The 24 authors do not appear in 24 separate blocks of connected words but are shuffled and intermixed in a very arbitrary manner. How could any single author keep track of 38 (actually more than 38) word frequencies so as to vary them not only randomly from one section to another but also according to a fixed underlying pattern, particularly more than a century before scholars realized that word frequencies might vary with authors?

2. The implications for translation are that the process was both direct and literal and that each individual author's style was preserved. Apparently Joseph Smith was required to render the book in a rather precise format with minimum deviations from the original "wordprint." The demonstrated presence of distinguishable authorship wordprints in the Book of Mormon argues for a formal translation in which information was transferred but the imprint of the original language remained.

3. The Book of Mormon authors taken individually or collectively do not resemble any of the nineteenth-century authors which we considered, taken individually or collectively. These authors include Joseph Smith and his contemporaries who have been considered as possible contenders for authorship of the Book of Mormon. The overwhelming evidence given by MANOVA and discriminant analysis, and to a lesser extent by cluster analysis, should discredit the alternative theories that Joseph Smith, Solomon Spaulding, or others wrote it.

The separation between Book of Mormon and non-Book of Mormon authors was established by both MANOVA and discriminant analysis. Especially convincing were the plots of the first two discriminant functions. In these plots the two groups could be cleanly separated by a straight line, an extremely rare occurrence in discriminant analysis studies. This visual separation was confirmed by the MANOVA significance test, and the possibility that the observed pattern was a chance arrangement was thus ruled out.

4. An analysis of letter counts (not detailed in this paper) yielded similar results to the word count data. Letters are obviously a rough way of detecting a wordprint, since many

contextual words contribute to the letter count. The method, however, seems to be fairly effective.

5. In a cluster analysis including both Book of Mormon and non-Book of Mormon authors, the Book of Mormon authors clustered with themselves, and the nineteenth-century authors clustered with themselves.

6. Each of the discriminant analyses was followed by a classification analysis, wherein each block of words was classified according to which author's wordprint it most resembled. When all the blocks of words were used in computing the classification functions and then submitted one by one for classification, the percentage of correct classifications varied from 69 to 100. When one block at a time was withheld from computation and then submitted, the percentage of correct classifications varied from 50 to 81 percent. These percentages are rather high considering the number of authors being classified and, therefore, reinforce the multiplicity of authors conclusion shown by the MANOVA and discriminant analysis.

7. An analysis was done using 42 words which were not among the 38 words used in the previous analyses. These 42 words occurred less frequently than the 38. The MANOVA results also showed the Book of Mormon authors differ from each other in their rates of usage of these words. In fact, the indicated level of significance showed the differences to be even more highly significant than those determined with the 38 words.

The evidence to date is that many authors wrote the Book of Mormon.

APPENDIX A
Number of Words by Engravers

Engravers	Words	Percent of Book
Mormon	174,610	65.1%
Nephi	54,688	20.4%
Moroni	26,270	9.8%
Jacob	9,103	3.4%
Enos	1,157	.4%
Amaleki	919	.3%
Jarom	731	.3%
Omni	160	.1%
Amaron	154	.1%
Abinadom	96	.0%
Chemish	69	.0%

APPENDIX B
Major Book of Mormon Writers

Author	Words	Percent of Book
Mormon	97,777	36.5%
Nephi	29,320	10.9%
Alma II	19,777	7.4%
Moroni	19,408	7.2%
Lord	12,200	4.6%
Jesus	9,654	3.6%
Jacob	8,493	3.2%
Isaiah	6,478	2.4%
Helaman	5,121	1.9%
Lehi	4,634	1.7%
Lord (quoted by Isaiah)	4,355	1.6%
Zenos	4,230	1.6%
Benjamin	4,204	1.6%
Amulek	3,158	1.2%
Samuel the Lamanite	3,068	1.1%
General Moroni	2,970	1.1%
Abinadi	2,767	1.0%
Ammon	2,417	.9%
Nephi (Son of Helaman)	2,214	.8%
Angel 1	2,083	.8%
Zeniff	1,811	.7%
Mosiah	1,167	.4%
Enos	967	.4%
Father	961	.4%

APPENDIX C
Frequently Occurring Noncontextual Words

Word	Number of Occurrences	Word	Number of Occurrences
the	20015	with	1520
and	16669	yea	1245
of	11838	should	1180
that	6883	by	1201
to	6488	as	1048
unto	3642	upon	1080
in	3705	but	991
it	3100	also	1048
for	2524	from	1007
be	2513	there	820
which	2238	because	799
a	2233	these	749
not	2090	therefore	663
came	1644	when	632
pass	1525	if	648
behold	1634	even	689
all	1788	into	686
this	1454	would	612
now	1230	forth	609

Infrequently Occurring Noncontextual Words

Word	Number of Occurrences	Word	Number of Occurrences
out	591	about	262
after	507	must	244
among	582	then	224
against	557	every	227
thus	478	what	179
according	528	nevertheless	178
again	479	until	202
may	515	exceeding	175
no	474	thereof	149
wherefore	419	through	115
before	436	towards	101
might	464	verily	76
or	438	notwithstanding	67
on	420	whatsoever	72
at	397	lest	75
away	381	whether	49
an	389	nay	44
so	358	ever	36
over	323	whereby	26
O	264	thereby	37
could	281	between	32

We thank Charles Bush for these word counts which correct those published in the earlier version of this paper.

APPENDIX D

Miscellaneous Tests Internal to the Book of Mormon

We comment briefly on two questions we tried to resolve using MANOVA. The first question involves the unity of Isaiah. Many present-day Bible scholars accept the theory that there were at least two authors of the Book of Isaiah. The principle divisions are chapters 1-39 and 40-66. We compared these two using word frequencies for the portions available in the Book of Mormon. Although we ran this test four times, we could get no significant results. This means we were unable to detect any statistical difference which would support the theory that Isaiah has more than one author.

The Sermon on the Mount as recorded in Matthew was compared with Jesus' teachings to the Nephites as recorded in 3 Nephi *excluding* chapters 12-14 which contained material similar to the Sermon on the Mount. There were 2 replications (1000-word blocks) for the Sermon on the Mount in Matthew and 7 for Jesus in 3 Nephi. Due to the small number of blocks it was necessary to run 5 analyses of 4 words each. Only 1 of the 5 tests achieved a probability level as low as .05. Thus there is little evidence of a style disparity between Jesus in the New Testament Sermon on the Mount and Jesus in 3 Nephi (excluding Sermon on the Mount material).

Again, a word of caution is needed. The tests on Isaiah and Jesus involved much smaller sample sizes than the tests on the book as a whole; therefore statistical differences would be harder to find, even if there were a real difference.

APPENDIX E

Lectures on Faith

Who Wrote the Lectures on Faith?

Most Latter-day Saints attribute the Lectures on Faith to Joseph Smith. However, historians have long been doubtful of this identification, since the lectures were originally published unsigned. Recently Alan J. Phipps completed an authorship study on the Lectures on Faith.[30] Our conclusions largely support his results, with some differences as described below.

First a cluster analysis was performed on the 9 non-Book of Mormon authors. The Lectures on Faith paired with the writings of Sidney Rigdon—which is the same general conclusion that Phipps made.

Discriminant Analysis, Non-Book of Mormon Only

In this analysis each of the 7 lectures of the Lectures on Faith was counted as 1 block (there were 7 blocks for 7 lectures).

The computation set consisted of 7 non-Book of Mormon authors with 36 blocks of 2000 words. Eight words were used as dependent variables and 4 discriminant functions were retained.

A plot of the first two discriminant functions shows 6 out of the 7 lectures grouping with Sidney Rigdon's known writings. There is no overlap of this group with other writers. The fifth lecture is rather distant from this group and is somewhat closer to W. W. Phelps's group. The fifth lecture has only 772 words, which may not be sufficient for a stable estimate of word frequencies.

In the classification phase, 88.9 percent of the blocks from the computation set were correctly classified. The lectures of the Lectures on Faith were classified as follows.

Lecture	1st Choice Author	Probability	2nd Choice Author	Probability
1	S. Rigdon	1.0		
2	J. Smith	.524	S. Rigdon	.339
3	S. Rigdon	1.0		
4	S. Rigdon	.988	J. Smith	.005
5	W. W. Phelps	.461	P. P. Pratt	.367
6	S. Rigdon	1.0		
7	S. Rigdon	.995	J. Smith	.005

These results differ somewhat from Phipps's conclusions. He assigned Lectures one and seven to Sidney Rigdon and five to Joseph Smith. He claimed that Lectures two, three, four, and six possessed elements of both men's style and concluded that these four represented a collaborative effort.

APPENDIX F
Standardized Discriminant-Function Coefficients

Word	Function 1	Function 2
and	−0.35	0.15
the	0.04	0.42
of	−0.21	−0.14
that	−0.11	−0.24
to	−0.09	0.25
unto	−0.21	−0.10
in	0.07	−0.14
it	−0.01	0.16
for	−0.51	0.15
be	0.08	−0.28
which	−0.08	−0.01
a	0.05	0.11
this	0.01	−0.29
now	−0.05	0.07

with	−0.02	0.19
upon	0.04	−0.10
but	0.05	−0.02
from	0.05	0.04
therefore	−0.11	−0.24
even	−0.07	0.03

These are the coefficients for a weighted average. Thus Function 1 = $-.35Z_1 + .04Z_2 - .21Z_3 - \ldots - .07Z_{20}$ where the Z's are the standardized frequencies of the words. The sizes of the coefficients are related to their importance in separating the authors. In Function 1, the words *and, of, unto, for,* contribute heavily. In Function 2, the most important contributors are *the, that, to, be, this,* and *therefore.*

APPENDIX G
Further Questions

The study reported here is the first major computer analysis of its kind that we are aware of. It raises a number of questions for further study which we list here.

First, we need to devise better definitions of wordprints using, for example, phrases as well as words. "And it came to pass that" was undoubtedly one word in Reformed Egyptian. Conversely, some words with two or more distinct meanings should be separated in wordprint definitions.

Second, we need to determine whether the discriminant functions possess any intrinsic meaning. An investigation of this in conjunction with more precise definitions of wordprint might be particularly fruitful.

Third, we need more investigation of wordprint time trends. In particular, the Jaredite record should be compared with the rest of the book.

Fourth, we need to take a closer look at why Moroni was relatively poorly classified.

Fifth, we need to determine what differences are introduced by using the 1830 edition of the Book of Mormon rather than the present edition.

Finally, we need to determine whether some of the misclassifications are correct after all. For example, from the context of Alma 29 it is clear that Alma is writing, yet Mormon does not identify this as a quotation. This is the only instance we found of this nature. Did we miss some others? A careful misclassification study might yield some light on this subject.

NOTES

1. See Lester E. Bush, Jr., "The Spaulding Theory Then and Now," *Dialogue: A Journal of Mormon Thought* 10(1977):40-69, for an excellent summary.

2. See Hugh Nibley, *An Approach to the Book of Mormon,* 2nd ed. (Salt Lake City: Deseret Book Co., 1964).

3. See Thomas F. O'Dea, *The Mormons* (Chicago: Univ. of Chicago Press, 1957), and Eber D. Howe, *Mormonism Unvailed [sic] or a Faithful Account of That Singular Imposition and Delusion from Its Rise to the Present Time* (Plainsville, Ohio: n.p., 1834).

4. See John A. Tvedtnes, "Hebraisms in the Book of Mormon: A Preliminary Survey," *Brigham Young University Studies* 11(Autumn 1970):50-60, and John W. Welch, "Chiasmus in the Book of Mormon," *BYU Studies* 10(Autumn 1969):69-84.

5. See Brodie Crouch, *The Myth of Mormon Inspiration* (Shreveport, La.: Lambert Book House, 1968).

6. Some of these studies are Glade L. Burgon, "An Analysis of Style Variations in the Book of Mormon," M.A. thesis, Brigham Young University, 1950; Alan J. Phipps, "The Lectures on Faith: An Authorship Study," M.A. thesis, BYU, 1977; L. LaMar Adams and Alvin C. Rencher, "A Computer Analysis of the Isaiah Authorship Problem," *BYU Studies* 15(Autumn 1974):95-102; L. LaMar Adams and A. C. Rencher, "The Popular Critical View of the Isaiah Problem in Light of Statistical Style Analysis," *Computer Studies in the Humanities and Verbal Behavior* 4(1973:149-57; Roger Fowler, "Linguistics, Stylistics: Criticism?" in *Contemporary Essays on Style,* ed. Glen A. Love and Michael Payne (Glenview, Ill.: Scott, Foresman and Company, 1969); C. Douglas Chretien, reviews, *Who Was Junius?* and *A Statistical Method for Determining Authorship: The Junius Letters, 1769-1772* in *Languages* 40 (1964):85-90; Harvey K. McArthur, "KAI Frequency in Greek Letters," *New Testament Studies* 15(1969):339-49; M. Levison, A. Q. Morton, and A. D. Winspear, "The Seventh Letter of Plato," *Mind,* New Series, vol. 77(1968), pp. 109-25; David Wishart and Stephen V. Leach, "A Multivariate Analysis of Platonic Prose Rhythm," *Computer Studies in the Humanities and Verbal Behavior* vol. 3, no. 2(1970):90; S. Michaelson and A. Q. Morton, "Last Words," *New Testament Studies* 8(1972):192-208; W. C. Wake, "Sentence Length Distribution of Greek Authors," *Journal of the Royal Statistical Society* Series A. vol. 70(1957), p. 331; James T. McDonough, Jr., "Computers and the Classics," *Computers and the Humanities* 2(1967):37-40; Noam Chomsky, *Language and Mind* (New York: Harcourt Brace Jovanovich, 1972); Yehuda T. Radday, "The Unity of Isaiah: Computerized Tests in Statistical Linguistics," unpublished reports, Israel Institute of Technology, 1970, pp. 1-172; Claude S. Brinegar, "Mark Twain and the Quintis Curtis Snodgrass Letters: A Statistical Test of Authorship," *Journal of the American Statistical Association* 53(1963):85.

7. A. Q. Morton, *Literary Detection* (New York: Charles Scribner's Sons, 1979).

8. Chretien, reviews, p. 87.

9. See Morton, *Literary Detection,* p. 96.

10. Frederick Mosteller and David L. Wallace, *Inference and Disputed Authorship: The Federalist* (Reading, Mass.: Addison-Wesley, 1964).

11. Morton, pp. 189-91.

12. When Oliver Cowdery transcribed the text of the Book of Mormon as dictated by Joseph Smith, he used very little punctuation. The printer inserted most of the punctuation in the original edition of the Book of Mormon. See B. H. Roberts, *Comprehensive History of The Church of Jesus Christ of Latter-day Saints, Century I,* 6 vols. (Provo, Utah: Brigham Young University Press, 1957), 1:114.

13. These word counts were done using the computerized tapes of the Book of Mormon developed by Elden Ricks and Translation Services of Brigham Young University.

14. Some arbitrary definitions were made. Since, in Mormon theology, the term *Lord* can refer either to God the Father or to his son Jesus, we classified Deity as three distinct authors: the Father, the Lord, and Jesus. We also made the definition that the Lord as quoted by Isaiah is different from Isaiah and also from the Lord in the rest of the book. Our statistical studies showed that these divisions were largely unnecessary.

15. For excerpts from the writings of Joseph Smith, Sidney Rigdon, Parley P. Pratt, Oliver Cowdery, and William W. Phelps, we used a computer disk prepared by Alan J. Phipps (see Phipps, "Lectures on Faith," cited in note 6). We are indebted to Jim Callister for providing this disk. Joseph Smith's writings were taken from articles in the *Messenger and Advocate,* his journal, and letters to various individuals. Joseph Smith's writings included in this study are his own words. This is important, since many works attributed to Joseph Smith were actually written by his scribes or others. See Phipps, "Lectures on Faith," for further information. Sidney Rigdon's writings were taken from the *Evening and Morning Star* and the *Messenger and Advocate.* Parley P. Pratt's works were *A Voice of Warning* and *A Short Account of a Shameful Outrage.* Oliver Cowdery's writings were taken from six letters published in the *Messenger and Advocate.* W. W. Phelps's excerpts were from the *Evening and Morning Star* and the *Messenger and Advocate.* The Doctrine and Covenants sections used in this study were 101 and 104. Solomon Spaulding's writings consisted of five random selections from *Manuscript Found.*

16. We included "The Paracletes," *Times and Seasons,* 6:891-92, 917-18, to determine whether any of our 1830 contemporaries appears to be the author of this unsigned article. Our results were consistently inconsistent—a strong indication that none of the authors used in our study wrote this selection.

17. D. F. Morrison, *Multivariate Statistical Methods* (New York: McGraw-Hill, 1976), chap. 5.

18. Rather than use this frequency, we generally used the arc sine transformation of the frequency for statistical requirements. The program RUMMAGE was used on all MANOVA analyses. See G. R. Bryce, "MAD: An Analysis of Variance Program for Unbalanced Designs," *Journal of the Royal Statistical Society*, Series C (Applied Statistics), vol. 24 (London, 1974), p. 35.

19. The result remained true even when we removed formal words reflecting nineteenth-century religious style from the analyses (*hath, unto,* etc.). The results depend as much on words such as *and, of, for* as on any of the other words.

20. We used a hierarchical clustering algorithm and the Mahalanobis distance function (see P. C. Mahalanobis, "On the Generalized Distance in Statistics," *Proceedings of National Institute of Sciences* 12[India, 1936]:49).

21. See note 16.

22. The discriminant functions can also be used to examine the coefficients of each function so as to possibly identify it as a meaningful new variable. We did not attempt this, but the coefficients are available for someone who may wish to investigate further the nature of the differences among authors.

23. Eighteen discriminant functions were used even though only six were statistically significant. (The two *18's* are coincidental. These numbers will usually be different.)

24. Morton, *Literary Detection,* p. 191.

25. Ibid., pp. 132-37.

26. Adams and Rencher, "The Popular Critical View of the Isaiah Problem," pp. 149-57; Adams and Rencher, "A Computer Analysis of the Isaiah Authorship Problem," pp. 95-102.

27. Morton, *Literary Detection,* p. 185; cf. pp. 186-88.

28. Ibid., pp. 184-85.

29. Ibid., pp. 134-36, 142-43.

30. Alan J. Phipps, "The Lectures on Faith: An Authorship Study," M.A. thesis, Brigham Young University, 1977.

8

Richard L. Bushman

The Book of Mormon and the American Revolution

Richard L. Bushman, Professor and Chairman of the Department of History at the University of Delaware, is a historian of colonial America. He earned his A.B., A.M., and Ph.D. degrees at Harvard University, and was recipient of numerous fellowships, including the Guggenheim Fellowship and the Harvard National Scholarship. He has taught at six universities, including Harvard, Brown, and Brigham Young. His publications range from a prize-winning book on colonial America, to historical articles in scholarly journals, to essays on aspects of Mormonism. Bushman has studied political and social order in the Book of Mormon, and in this article he responds to the common accusation that the Book of Mormon is a restatement of provincial political opinions of early nineteenth-century America. Though critics assert that Book of Mormon societies smack of nineteenth-century American Republicanism, Bushman demonstrates that most of the

*principles associated with the American Revolution and even
the Constitution are slighted in the Book of Mormon. The Book
of Mormon is "strangely distant" from the time and place of its
publication. Bushman traces the roots of the Nephite political
order to Old World precedents—namely the Hebrew tradition
and ancient forms of monarchy.*

The Book of Mormon, much like the Old Testament, was
written to show Israel "what great things the Lord hath done for
their fathers," and to testify of the coming Messiah.[1] Although
cast as a history, it is history with a high religious purpose, not
the kind we ordinarily write today. The narrative touches only
incidentally on the society, economics, and politics of the
Nephites and Jaredites, leaving us to rely on oblique references
and occasional asides to reconstruct total cultures. Government
is dealt with more expressly than other aspects, however, perhaps because the prophets were often rulers themselves and
because the most significant reforms in the history of Nephite
government were inspired by a prophet-king. From their
comments and Mormon's editorial interjections, it is possible to
get a rough idea of the theory and practice of politics in Nephite
civilization.

While we value these scraps of information, the political
passages, it must be recognized, expose the book to attack. The
more specific the record, the more easily its verity can be tested.
Details about government make it possible to ask if the political
forms are genuinely ancient, or if they bear the marks of nineteenth-century creation. The late Thomas O'Dea, a sympathetic
but critical scholar, thought that "American sentiments per-
meate the work."

> In it are found the democratic, the republican, the anti-
> monarchial, and the egalitarian doctrines that pervade
> the climate of opinion in which it was conceived and
> that enter into the expressions and concerns of its

Nephite kings, prophets, and priests as naturally as they later come from the mouths of Mormon leaders preaching to the people in Utah.[2]

That kind of indictment would be precluded were the Book of Mormon exclusively and narrowly religious. As it is, O'Dea purports to find evidence of nineteenth-century American political culture in the Book of Mormon—for example, the prophecy of the American Revolution early in Nephi's narrative, and later, the switch from monarchy to government by elected judges. On first reading, both have a modern and American flavor. O'Dea, to be sure, wrote in the mode of higher criticism which assumes that an accurate prophecy of a specific event can occur only after the event. Even if one discounts for that assumption, however, the question remains whether the spirit and content of some of the political passages in the Book of Mormon do not partake more of American republicanism than of Israelite or ancient Near Eastern monarchy.[3]

O'Dea's observations comport with the widely accepted view of the Book of Mormon which holds that it "can best be explained, not by Joseph's ignorance nor by his delusions, but by his responsiveness to the provincial opinions of his time."[4] One of the first critics of the Book of Mormon, Alexander Campbell, noted in 1831 that the record incorporated, among other conventional American ideas, commonplace sentiments about "free masonry, republican government, and the rights of man."[5] A comparison of the political cultures of the Nephites and of Joseph Smith's America thus bears on the larger question of the origin of the English text of the Book of Mormon.

THE POLITICAL MILIEU OF JOSEPH SMITH'S NEW YORK

There is little reason to doubt that however the book originated, Joseph Smith must have absorbed the ordinary political sentiments of his time. The air was thick with politics. The Revolution, by then a half-century old, still loomed as the great turning point in American and world history. Americans annually celebrated the nation's birthday with oratory, editorials, and rounds of toasts. In 1824 and 1825, Lafayette, who had been absent from the United States for thirty-eight years, toured all twenty-four states with his son George Washington Lafayette. The following year, 1826, was the jubilee anniversary of the Declaration of Independence, and Fourth of July orators exerted themselves as never before. A few days after the celebration, news spread that on the very day when the nation was commemorating its fiftieth birthday, two of the most illustrious heroes of the Revolution, John Adams and Thomas Jefferson, had died within six hours of one another. A new round of patriotic rhetoric poured forth to remind the nation of its history and the glories of republicanism. All this was reported in the *Wayne Sentinel*, Palmyra's weekly, along with coverage of yearly electoral campaigns and debates on current political issues. Joseph Smith could not easily have avoided a rudimentary education in the principles of American government and the meaning of the American Revolution before he began work on the Book of Mormon in 1827.[6]

Patriotic orations served various purposes for the politicians who delivered them, but certain conventional usages recur: a set of attitudes and rhetorical patterns apparently shared by Americans of all persuasions. The patterns varied little from region to region, probably because newspaper editors commonly reprinted orations and essays from other areas, but we can be assured of sampling the political atmosphere in Joseph Smith's immediate environment if we rely primarily on three sources: the *Wayne Sentinel*, upstate New York oratory, and the schoolbooks for sale in Palmyra's bookstore.[7] Young Joseph may not have spent much time with any of them, but if any provincial sources influenced Joseph Smith, these must be the ones. They shaped, or expressed, the ideas of his neighbors, local politicians, and those who gathered in taverns and stores to talk politics. Presumably O'Dea would see such sentiments to be at the root of Book of Mormon political ideas.

My purpose is to test that conclusion by comparing some of the most obvious contemporaneous ideas about government and the American Revolution with political ideas and practices in the Book of Mormon. There are three that were prominent in the political literature of the 1820s: First, the depiction of the American Revolution as heroic resistance against tyranny; second, the belief that people overthrow their kings under the stimulus of enlightened ideas of human rights; and third, the conviction that constitutional arrangements such as frequent elections, separation of powers, and popularly elected assemblies were necessary to control power.

Heroic Resistance or Divine Deliverance

The most common of all conventions in orations, essays, and editorial columns was the dramatic structure of the Revolution, still familiar today. The Revolution was a struggle of heroes against oppressors, a brave people versus a tyrant king or corrupt ministry. That theme was rehearsed whenever the orators honored the Revolutionary veterans in the audience. A large portion of his hearers, one speaker said, were too young to know "the divine enthusiasm which inspired the American bosom; which prompted her voice to proclaim defiance to the thunders of Britain." It was from the soldiers themselves, the "venerable asserters of the rights of mankind, that we are to be informed, what were the feelings which swayed within your breasts, and impelled you to action; when, like the stripling of Israel, with scarcely a weapon to attack, and without a shield for your defence, you met, and undismayed, engaged with the gigantic greatness of the British power." The greatness of Jefferson was that "on the coming of that tremendous storm which for eight years desolated our country, Mr. Jefferson hesitated not, halted not . . . he adventured, with the single motive of advancing the cause of his country and of human freedom, into that perilous contest, throwing into the scale his life and fortune as of no value." Similarly Lafayette "shared in the dangers, privations, and sufferings of that bitter struggle, nor quitted them for a moment, till it was consummated on the glorious field of Yorktown." For many Americans, the courage of the heroes in resisting oppression was the most memorable aspect of the

Revolution. The editors of the "Readers" and "Speakers," the textbooks of that generation, consistently favored passages that dwelt on that theme.[8]

The narrative conventions are worth noting because of the Book of Mormon's brief description of the American Revolution. While Joseph Smith might alter costumes and the locale of the narrator, the spirit of the event was less malleable. A responsive young provincial, it would seem, would absorb this first and retain it longest. Yet coming to Nephi's prediction of the Revolution after reading Fourth of July orations, an American reader even today finds the account curiously flat. Just before the Revolution prophecy, Nephi tells of "a man among the Gentiles," presumably Columbus in Europe, who "went forth upon the many waters" to America. And it came to pass that the Spirit of God then "wrought upon other Gentiles; and they went forth out of captivity, upon the many waters." The Gentiles did "humble themselves before the Lord; and the power of the Lord was with them" (1 Nephi 13:12, 13, 16). Then the Revolution is depicted in this fashion:

> [The] mother Gentiles were gathered together upon the waters, and upon the land also, to battle against them. And I beheld that the power of God was with them, and also that the wrath of God was upon all those that were gathered together against them to battle. And I, Nephi, beheld that the Gentiles that had gone out of captivity were delivered by the power of God out of the hands of all other nations. (1 Nephi 13:17-19)

By American standards, this is a strangely distorted account. There is no indictment of the king or parliament, no talk of American rights or liberty, nothing of the corruptions of the ministry, and most significant, no description of despots or heroes. In fact, there is no reference to American resistance. The "mother Gentiles" are the only warriors. God, not General Washington or the American army, delivers the colonies.

The meaning of the narrative opens itself to the reader only after he lays aside his American preconceptions about the Revolution and recognizes that the dramatic structure in

Nephi's account is fundamentally different from the familiar one in Independence Day orations. The point of the narrative is that Americans escaped from captivity. They did not resist, they fled. The British were defeated because the wrath of God was upon them. The virtue of the Americans was that they "did humble themselves before the Lord" (1 Nephi 13:16). The moral is that "the Gentiles that had gone out of captivity were delivered by the power of God out of the hands of all other nations." The theme is deliverance, not resistance.

The theme of deliverance by God is more notable in Nephi's prophecy because it recurs in various forms throughout the Book of Mormon. Three times a people of God suffer from oppressive rulers under conditions that might approximate those in the colonies before the Revolution: Alma under King Noah, the people of Limhi under the Lamanites, and once again Alma under the Lamanites. In none do revolutionary heroes in the American sense emerge.[9] In each instance the people escaped from bondage by flight.[10] They gathered their people, flocks, and tents and fled into the wilderness when their captors were off guard. When they learned that the corrupt and spiritually hardened King Noah had dispatched an army to apprehend them in their secret meetingplace, Alma's people "took their tents and their families and departed into the wilderness" (Mosiah 18:34). Limhi's people, an exploited dominion of a Lamanite empire, departed "by night into the wilderness with their flocks and their herds" (Mosiah 22:11). Alma's people, after escaping King Noah, fell into the hands of the Lamanites who "put tasks upon them" and "taskmasters over them." When they cried to the Lord for succor, they were told to "be of good comfort, for I know of the covenant which ye have made unto me; and I will covenant with my people and deliver them out of bondage." The deliverance came in due course, but not by way of confrontation. "The Lord caused a deep sleep to come upon the Lamanites. . . . And Alma and his people departed into the wilderness. . . ." The point seemed to be that the people obtained their liberty by obedience rather than by courage or sacrifice. After successfully eluding their captors, the people thanked God because he had "delivered them out of bondage; for they were in bondage, and none could deliver them except it were the Lord their God" (Mosiah 24:9, 13, 19-21).

Godly people in the Book of Mormon defended themselves against invaders—in that sense they resisted—but they never overthrew an established government, no matter how oppressive. When we step back to look at the larger framework we can see that their actions were consistent. The deliverance narrative grew out of the Nephites' conception of history as naturally as resistance in the American Revolution sprang from Anglo-American Whig views. Book of Mormon prophets saw the major events of their own past as comprising a series of deliverances beginning with the archetypal flight of the Israelites from Egypt. Alma the Younger pictured the Exodus from Egypt and Lehi's journey from Jerusalem as the first of a number of bondages and escapes.

> I will praise him forever, for he has brought our fathers out of Egypt, and he has swallowed up the Egyptians in the Red Sea; and he led them by his power into the promised land; yea, and he has delivered them out of bondage and captivity from time to time. Yea, and he has also brought our fathers out of the land of Jerusalem; and he has also, by his everlasting power, delivered them out of bondage and captivity, from time to time even down to the present day. (Alma 36:28-29)

Among those bondages reaching "down to the present day" were those of his father and Limhi who, like their illustrious predecessors, were

> delivered out of the hands of the people of king Noah, by the mercy and power of God. And behold, after that, they were brought into bondage by the hands of the Lamanites in the wilderness . . . and again the Lord did deliver them out of bondage. . . . (Alma 5:4, 5)

Understandably the prophet-historians delighted in Alma's and Limhi's deliverances because they illustrated so perfectly the familiar ways of God with his people. Events took on religious meaning and form as they followed the established pattern of divine intervention.

Nephi's prophecy of the Revolution, therefore, makes sense in terms of its own culture as an act of divine deliverance. Any other rendition of the prophecy would have offended later Nephite sensibilities just as its present form puzzles us. In the context of the Book of Mormon, heroic resistance could not give revolution moral significance. Only deliverance by the power of God could do that.[11] Once the pattern of Nephite interpretation of history comes into focus, Nephi's account of future events becomes comprehensible.

There are two points to be made here. The first is that Book of Mormon accounts of the Revolution and of the behavior of godly people in revolutionary situations differ fundamentally from American accounts of the Revolution. The second is that there is a consistency in the Book of Mormon treatment of these events. Each deliverance fits a certain view of providential history. The accounts disregard a significant convention of American patriotic oratory of the late 1820s in order to respect one of the book's own conventions.

ENLIGHTENMENT AND POPULAR OPPOSITION TO MONARCHY

Heroic resistance did not exhaust the meaning of the Revolution for the orators of the 1820s. Beyond their display of sheer courage, the patriots of 1776 were honored for adopting the true principles of government. "This is the anniversary of the great day," the *Wayne Sentinel* editorialized on 4 July 1828, "which commenced a new era in the History of the world. It proclaimed the triumph of free principles, and the liberation of a people from the dominion of monarchical government." The adoption of free principles, namely the end of "monarchical government," and the institution of "a government, based upon the will of the People, free and popular in every feature," effected a "sublime and glorious change in the civil and moral condition" of the United States and the world. The Revolution was "the glorious era from which every republic of our continent may trace the first march of that revolutionizing spirit, which, with a mighty impetus has disseminated the blessings of free governments over so large a portion of our globe." Revolutionary principles were shaking all the nations of the earth. "Whole states are changed, and nations start into existence in a day," the jubilee orator in Palmyra declared. "Systems venerable for their antiquity have been demolished. Governments built up in ages of darkness and vassalage, have tottered and fallen."[12]

And why had this political earthquake occurred? "Knowledge and a correct estimate of moral right have opened the eyes of men to see the importance of free institutions, and the only true, rational end of existence." The principles of the Revolution were awakening people everywhere and moving them to throw down their masters. The *Sentinel,* a month after the jubilee celebration, quoted Jefferson's aspiration that the Declaration of Independence would "be to the world what I believe it will be; the signal of arousing men to burst the chains under which monkish ignorance and superstition had persuaded them to bind themselves, and to assume the blessings of free government." The American Revolution was the beginning of a world revolution in which "man, so long the victim of oppression, awakes from the sleep of ages and bursts his chains."[13]

Does any of that struggle seep into the Book of Mormon? Do enlightened people in its pages overthrow monarchs enthroned in ignorance? The most famous passage on monarchy in the Book of Mormon does in a general way echo the American aversion to monarchy. Jacob, brother of the first Nephi and son of Lehi, prophesied that "this land shall be a land of liberty unto the Gentiles. . . . For he that raiseth up a king against me shall perish, for I, the Lord, the king of heaven, will be their king. . . ." (2 Nephi 10:11, 14). Yet when we examine more closely the Nephites' own attitude toward kings, principled opposition to monarchy is scarcely in evidence. Enlightened people in the Book of Mormon do not rise up to strike down their kings as the Fourth of July scenario would have it. In fact, the opposite is true. The people persistently created kings for themselves, even demanded them. Shortly after their settlement in the New World, the followers of Nephi asked him to be their king. Nephi demurred, being "desirous that they should have no king," but they continued to look on Nephi as "a king or a protector" and by the end of his life he had acquiesced (see 2 Nephi 5:18, 6:2). As he approached death, "he anointed a man to be a king and a ruler over his people," thus initiating the "reign of the kings" (Jacob 1:9).[14] Nephi's establishment of monarchy set the precedent followed throughout Nephite political history with respect to kingmaking. When a segment of the nation migrated to another part of the continent under the leadership of the first Mosiah, they made him king over the land (see Omni 12, 19). This process was repeated not long afterwards following another migration: Zeniff, the leader of the migrants, "was made a king by the voice of the people" (Mosiah 7:9; cf. 19:26). It was quite natural that when Alma broke away with yet another band, his people should be "desirous that Alma should be their king, for he was beloved by his people" (Mosiah 23:6). Unlike Nephi, Alma firmly declined, and a few years later, kingship among the people of Nephi at large was ended.

The abandonment of monarchy, however, did not occur by revolution nor at the instigation of the people. The occasion for the change was the refusal of the sons of Mosiah II to accept the kingship. Mosiah feared the contention that might ensue from an appointment outside the royal line and proposed the installation of judges chosen by the voice of the people (see Mosiah 29). Mosiah's lengthy argument against monarchy, written down and distributed through the countryside, persuaded the people and "they relinquished their desires for a king. . . . They assembled themselves together in bodies throughout the land, to cast in their voices concerning who should be their judges. . . . And thus commenced the reign of the judges . . . among all the people who were called the Nephites" (Mosiah 29:38, 39, 44).[15]

There is nothing in these episodes of an enlightened people rising against their king. The people did not rise nor were they enlightened about the errors of monarchy. Quite the contrary. In every instance, the people were the ones to desire a king, and in three of five cases they got one. The aversion to kingship was at the top. Nephi, Alma, and Mosiah were reluctant, not the people. When monarchy finally came to an end, it was because the king abdicated, not because the enlightened people overthrew him. In the American view, despot kings held their people in bondage through superstition and ignorance until the true principles of government inspired resistance. The Book of Mormon nearly reversed the roles. The people delighted in their subjection to the king, and the rulers were enlightened.

Book of Mormon opposition to monarchy was not a matter of fixed principle either. Americans believed the patriots of 1776 had broached "a new theory" and discovered the "first principle" of government, which was "diametrically opposed" to the inequalities of monarchy. "There is no neutral ground, no midway course," a Boston orator said in 1827.[16] That was far from the case in the Book of Mormon. Alma's and Mosiah's opposition to kingship was no theoretical breakthrough, nor was it advocated as a fundamental political truth. It was simply that wicked kings had the power to spread their iniquity.

> He enacteth laws, and sendeth them forth among his people, yea, laws after the manner of his own wickedness; and whosoever doth not obey his laws he causeth to be destroyed . . . and thus an unrighteous king doth pervert the ways of all righteousness. (Mosiah 29:23)

A good king was another matter. "If it were possible that ye could always have just men to be your kings," Alma said, "it would be well for you to have a king" (Mosiah 23:8). Mosiah made the same point.

> If it were possible that you could have just men to be your kings, who would establish the laws of God, and judge this people according to his commandments . . . then it would be expedient that ye should always have kings to rule over you. (Mosiah 29:13)

There was nothing intrinsically wrong with monarchy. It was not "diametrically opposed" to good government. It was simply inexpedient because it was subject to abuse.

THE REIGN OF THE JUDGES AND AMERICAN CONSTITUTIONAL GOVERNMENT

The Nephite government was no more resistant to monarchy in practice than it was in theory, and in fact it came to occupy the very middle ground which, according to the Boston orator, could not exist. The institution of judgeships, rather than beginning a republican era in Book of Mormon history, slid back at once toward monarchy. The chief judge much more resembled a king than an American president. Once elected, he never again submitted himself to the people. After being proclaimed chief judge by the voice of the people, Alma enjoyed life tenure. When he chose to resign because of internal difficulties he selected his own successor (see Alma 4:16).[17] That seems to have been the beginning of a dynasty. In the next succession, the judgeship passed to the chief judge's son and thence by "right" to the successive sons of the judges (see Alma 50:39; Helaman 1:13). Although democratic elements were there—the judges were confirmed by the voice of the people—the "reign of the judges," as the Book of Mormon calls the period, was a far cry from the republican government Joseph Smith knew.[18] Life tenure and hereditary succession would have struck Americans as only slightly modified monarchy. The citizens of Palmyra in the middle 1820s were urged to "remember at all times the terms of office should be short—and account to the public certain and soon." A point urged in favor of Jackson in 1828 was that

> his election will break the chain of succession which has been so long practically established and by which the presidents have virtually appointed their successors, and which if not interrupted, will render our elections a mockery, and our government but little better than a hereditary monarchy.[19]

By Jacksonian standards, Book of Mormon government was no democracy. Joseph Smith's contemporaries, had they examined the matter closely, would certainly have called the elections a mockery and the government little better than a hereditary monarchy.[20]

Looking at the Book of Mormon as a whole, it seems clear that most of the principles traditionally associated with the American Constitution are slighted or disregarded altogether. All of the constitutional checks and balances are missing. When judges were instituted, Mosiah provided that a greater judge could remove lesser judges and a number of lesser judges try venal higher judges, but the book records no instance of impeachment. It was apparently not a routine working principle. All other limitations on government are missing. There was no written constitution defining rulers' powers. The people could not remove the chief judge at the polls, for he stood for election only once. There were not three branches of government to check one another, for a single office encompassed all government powers. The chief judge was judge, executive, and legislator rolled into one, just as the earlier kings had been (see Mosiah 29:13). In wartime he raised men, armed them, and collected provisions (see Alma 46:34; 60:1-9). He was called interchangeably chief judge and governor (see Alma 2:16; 50:39; 60:1; and 3 Nephi 3:1). He was also lawmaker. There is no ordinary legislature in the Book of Mormon.[21] In the early part of the Book of Mormon, the law was presented as traditional, handed down from the fathers as "given them by the hand of the Lord," and "acknowledged by this people" to make it binding (see Mosiah 29:25; Alma 1:14). But later the chief judge assumed the power of proclaiming or at least elaborating laws. Alma gave Nephihah the "power to enact laws according to the laws which had been given" (Alma 4:16). Any major constitutional changes, such as a return to formal kingship, required approval of the people, but day-to-day legislation, so far as the record speaks, was the prerogative of the chief judge (see Alma 2:2-7; 51:1-7). Perhaps most extraordinary by American standards, nothing was made of taxation by a popular assembly.[22] The maxim "no taxation without representation" had no standing in Nephite consciousness.[23] These salient points in enlightened political theory, as nineteenth-century Americans understood it, were contradicted, distorted, or neglected.[24]

ANCIENT PRECEDENTS

In the context of nineteenth-century political thought, the Book of Mormon people are difficult to place. They were not benighted Spaniards or Russians, passively yielding to the oppression of a monarch out of ignorance and superstition, nor were they enlightened Americans living by the principles of republican government. The Book of Mormon was an anomaly on the political scene of 1830. Instead of heroically resisting despots, the people of God fled their oppressors and credited God alone with deliverance. Instead of enlightened people over-throwing their kings in defense of their natural rights, the common people repeatedly raised up kings, and the prophets and the kings themselves had to persuade the people of the in-expediency of monarchy. Despite Mosiah's reforms, Nephite government persisted in monarchical practices, with life tenure for the chief judges, hereditary succession, and the combination of all functions in one official.

In view of all this, the Book of Mormon could be pictured as a bizarre creation, a book strangely distant from the time and place of its publication. But that picture would not be complete. A pattern running through the apparent anomalies provides a clue to their resolution. Book of Mormon political attitudes have Old World precedents, particularly in the history of the Israelite nation. Against that background its anomalies become regularities. The Hebrews, for example, cast their history as a series of deliverances. Moses was not a revolutionary hero from an American mold. His people fled just like Alma's and Zeniff's, and the moral of the story was that God had delivered them from captivity. Moses was not lauded for courageous resistance. The Book of Mormon deliverance narrative, incongruous amidst Fourth of July orations, is perfectly conventional biblical discourse.

The same is true for the popular demand for kings. Biblical people too raised up kings among themselves, sometimes successfully, sometimes not. The most famous instance was the anointing of Saul. There the Book of Mormon prototypes are laid down precisely. The people demanded a king of Samuel, who tried to persuade them otherwise, warning them of the iniquities a king would practice on them, just as Alma and Mosiah warned their people (see 1 Samuel 8:1-22; 10:18-25; Deuteronomy 17:14).[25] This basic plot was not singular to Saul either. Earlier, the Israelites had requested Gideon to be their king, and he had refused because "the Lord will rule over you"

(Judges 8:22-23). On another occasion, the Israelite army, after hearing of the assassination of their king, "made their commander Omri king of Israel by common consent," much as the voice of the people confirmed kings among the Nephites (see 1 Kings 16:16).[26] Whereas the Book of Mormon practice of making kings at the behest of the people clashed with American assumptions, it fit the biblical tradition.

The same holds for reliance on traditional law instead of a representative legislature and indifference to the separation of powers.[27] Not every biblical political tradition reappeared in the Book of Mormon, but there are biblical precedents for most of the Nephite practices which are not at home in provincial upstate New York. The templates for Book of Mormon politics seem quite consistently to have been cut from the Bible.[28]

With so many similarities before us, it is tempting to conclude that Joseph Smith contrived his narrative from the biblical elements in nineteeth-century American culture and leave it at that. But the problems of interpretation are not so easily dismissed. Biblical patterns work differently in the Book of Mormon than in the culture at large. While American orators blessed God for delivering them from British slavery, they never permitted their gratitude to shade the heroism of the patriots. The acknowledgment of divine aid was more a benediction on America's brave resistance. Similarly, Americans believed God inspired the Constitution, but no one suggested that it was patterned after the government of ancient Israel. No one proposed to eliminate an elected legislature or to make the presidency hereditary because a king ruled the Jews. In fact, no Americans, including the Puritans of Massachusetts Bay, followed biblical political models as closely as Book of Mormon people. Biblical language was used to sanctify American history and American political institutions, but Hebrew precedents did not deeply inform historical writing nor shape political institutions. The innermost structure of Book of Mormon politics and history are biblical, while American forms are conspicuously absent.

How does all this affect the interpretation of the book—the problem raised at the outset? At the very least, the dictum that the Book of Mormon mirrored "every error and almost every truth discussed in New York for the last ten years" should be reassessed.[29] Scholars confine themselves unnecessarily in deriving all their insight from the maxim that Joseph Smith's writings can best be explained "by his responsiveness to the provincial opinions of this time." That principle of criticism obscures the Book of Mormon, as it would any major work read exclusively in that light. It is particularly misleading when so many of the powerful intellectual influences operating on Joseph Smith failed to touch the Book of Mormon, among them the most common American attitudes toward a revolution, monarchy, and the limitations on power. The Book of Mormon is not a conventional American book. Too much Americana is missing. Understanding the work requires a more complex and sensitive analysis than has been afforded it. Historians will take a long step forward when they free themselves from the compulsion to connect all they find with Joseph Smith's America and try instead to understand the ancient patterns deep in the grain of the book.

NOTES

1. The quotation is from the title page of the Book of Mormon. The Lord's opening words to Moses on Sinai as recorded in Exodus were: "I am the Lord your God who brought you out of Egypt, out of the land of slavery" (Exodus 20:2; this and subsequent references are to the New English Bible), and the memory of that event was used ever after to recall Israel to its covenant obligations.

2. Thomas F. O'Dea, *The Mormons* (Chicago: University of Chicago Press, 1957), p. 32.

3. O'Dea's evidence is cited at ibid., p. 268, notes 19-21. Many of his references are to choices made by the "voice of the people." For a comment on the function of popular consent in monarchies as well as republics, see note 18 below. The same note also contains observations on Moroni's war for liberty which indicate it did not follow an American pattern. Alma 43:48, 49; 46:35, 36; 48:11; 51:7. The antimonarchical sentiments which O'Dea cites are shown in this essay to be strangely un-American. 2 Nephi 5:18; Mosiah 2:14-18; 6:7; 23:6-14; 29:13-18, 23, 30-31; Alma 43:45; 46:10; 51:5, 8; 3 Nephi 6:30; Ether 6:22-26. For a comment on the idea of equality see note 23 below.

4. Fawn M. Brodie, *No Man Knows My History: The Life of Joseph Smith*, 2d ed. (New York: Knopf, 1971), p. 69.

5. Alexander Campbell, *Delusions: An Analysis of the Book of Mormon* (Boston: B. H. Green, 1832), p. 13. Reprinted from the *Millennial Harbinger*, 7 February 1831.

6. An account of Lafayette's visit is found in Nathan Sargent, *Public Men and Events*, 2 vols. (Philadelphia: J. B. Lippincott, 1875), 1:89-94. The *Wayne Sentinel* reported on Lafayette's progress almost weekly. (For representative accounts, see the 7 July, 1, 8, 15, 22 September, 6, 20 October, and 3, 24 November 1824 issues.) When news of the deaths of Adams and Jefferson reached Palmyra, the *Sentinel* edged all its columns in black (see 14 July 1826 issue). Political interest in New York reached a high in the election of 1828 when 70.4 percent of adult white males voted. See Richard P. McCormick, "New Perspectives on Jacksonian Politics," *American Historical Review* 65 (January 1960) 292.

7. The relevant schoolbooks most frequently advertised in the *Sentinel* were *American Speaker, American Reader, American Preceptor, Columbian Orator,* and *English Reader*. (For illustrative ads, see *Wayne Sentinel*, 30 June, 10 November 1824; 27 October, 24 November 1826; 18 May 1827; and 28 September 1828.)

8. Caleb Bingham, *The American Preceptor; Being a New Selection of Lessons for Reading and Speaking. Designed for the Use of Schools,* stereotype ed. (New York: B. & J. Collins for C. Bingham, 1815), p. 144; *Wayne Sentinel*, 11 August 1826, 1 September 1824. Among the favorite selections were passages from the Boston Massacre orations of Joseph Warren, Thomas Dawes, Benjamin Church, and John Hancock. See William Bentley Fowle, *The American Speaker, or Exercises in Rhetorick; Being a Selection of Speeches, Dialogues and Poetry from the Best American and English Sources, Suitable for Recitation* (Boston: Cummings, Hilliard, 1826) pp. 74-90. The orator at Albany in 1817 observed that forty-one years had passed "since the dauntless representatives of an oppressed but high-minded people, having exhausted the gentle spirit of entreaty, and become persuaded of the utter uselessness of all further attempts at conciliation, dared to raise the arm of independence. . . . The country bleeding at every pore, but not disheartened, reciprocated the lofty sentiment, and confiding in the equity of their cause, looked to heaven and then aimed a deathblow at the head of tyranny. 'Twas one of the sublimest spectacles earth ever witnessed." "Patriots of '76," he said in the customary address to the veterans, "to you the scene must be most animating. You toiled, you suffered, you were willing to bleed and die in the glorious cause." Hooper Cumming, *An Oration, Delivered July 4, 1817* (Albany: Printed by I. W. Clark, 1817), pp. 5, 14.

9. In one instance an individual not numbered among the people of God attempts to assassinate King Noah, but the wily monarch escapes by subterfuge. (See Mosiah 19:2-8.)

10. Hugh Nibley discusses flight as part of the tradition of escape from crumbling societies in *An Approach to the Book of Mormon*, 2d. ed. (Salt Lake City: Deseret Book Co., 1964), pp. 107-14.

11. There is no evidence that Book of Mormon people believed revolution to be sinful. The people of Limhi considered delivering "themselves out of bondage by the sword," but gave up the idea because of the superiority of Lamanite numbers. (See Mosiah 22:2.) The point is that resistance was not necessary to make a compelling story. Flight and deliverance had a greater moral impact.

12. *Wayne Sentinel,* 4 and 18 July 1828.

13. Ibid., 21 July and 11 August 1826. The orator who pronounced the eulogy on Adams and Jefferson at nearby Buffalo in 1826 elaborated the same themes. "Looking retrospectively through the lapse of half a century, we behold these stern patriots ardently engaged in the great work of political reformation. Until then, the human mind, shackled and awed by the insignia of power, had remained unconscious of its own noble faculties. Until then, man had failed to enjoy that exalted character designed in his creation. Until then, he had yielded to the dictates of usurpation and the arrogant pretensions of self-created kings. Here and there the rays of mental light had burst upon the earth; but like the flashes of the midnight storm, they had passed away, and all again was darkness. . . . To them and a few worthy compatriots, were reserved the signal honors of broaching a new theory; of solving that, until then mysterious problem of self government; of opposing successfully the blasphemous doctrine of the divine right of kings; of redeeming the rights of man from the chaotic accumulations of ignorance, superstition and prejudice; of unfolding to the world the true source of temporal enjoyment, and the legitimate object of human society; of emancipating the human mind from the thraldom of ages, and restoring man to his proper dignity in the great scale of being." Sheldon Smith, "Eulogy Pronounced at Buffalo, New York, July 22d, in 1826," in *A Selection of Eulogies Pronounced in the Several States, in Honor of those Illustrious Patriots and Statesmen, John Adams and Thomas Jefferson* (Hartford, Conn.: D. F. Robinson & Company, 1826), pp. 92, 95.

Orators enjoyed taking inventory of democracy among the nations of the earth and analyzing the reasons for the continuance of tyranny. Why despotism in nations where conditions were otherwise favorable? asked the speaker at Troy in 1825. "If they were not debased in spirit—if they were not groping in the darkness of ignorance, or faltering in the twilight of the mind, no tyrant would strip them of their rights—no despotic throne would cast its portentous and chill shadow over the land of their birth. . . ." O. L. Halley, *The Connexion between the Mechanic Arts and Welfare of States. An Address, Delivered before the Mechanics of Troy, at their Request on the 4th of July, 1825* (Troy, N.Y.: n.p., 1825), p. 7. For the most part, Americans were optimistic about the principles of democracy. William Duer at Albany in 1826 predicted that before another jubilee, the principles of the Declaration "will take root and flourish in every soil and climate under heaven! The march of Light, of Knowledge, and of Truth, is irresistible, and Freedom follows in their train." L. H. Butterfield, "The Jubilee of Independence, July 4, 1826," *Virginia Magazine of History and Biography* 61 (April 1953):138. "The old monarchies of Europe must be entombed in some great political convulsion, if they listen not in season to the low but deep murmur of discontent, among their subjects, which is growing louder with the progress of intellectual light. . . ." William Chamberlain, Jr., *An Address Delivered at Windsor, Vt. before an Assembly of Citizens from the Counties of Windsor, Vt. and Cheshire, N. H. on the Fiftieth Anniversary of American Independence* (Windsor: n.p., 1826), p. 24.

14. Mormon reported much later that "the kingdom had been conferred upon none but those who were descendants of Nephi," implying hereditary monarchy. (See Mosiah 25:13.) Jacob, Nephi's brother, said that to honor the first Nephi, subsequent rulers "were called by the people, second Nephi, third Nephi, and so forth, according to the reigns of the kings" (Jacob 1:11).

15. Hugh Nibley suggests that rule by judges was familiar to Nephites because of precedents in Israel: "In Zedekiah's time the ancient and venerable council of elders had been thrust aside by the proud and haughty *judges,* the spoiled children of frustrated and ambitious princes. . . . Since the king no longer sat in judgment, the ambitious climbers had taken over the powerful and dignified—and for them very profitable—*'judgment seats,'* and by systematic abuse of power as judges made themselves obnoxious and oppressive to the nation as a whole while suppressing all criticism of themselves— especially from the recalcitrant and subversive prophets." Nibley, *An Approach,* p. 82. The provision for impeachment of corrupt judges in Mosiah's time could have reflected the trouble these judges had given the Israelites. Cf. Hugh Nibley, *Lehi in the Desert and The World of the Jaredites* (Salt Lake City: Bookcraft, 1952), pp. 20-26.

16. William Powell Mason, *An Oration Delivered Wednesday, July 4, 1827, in Commemoration of American Independence* . . . (Boston: From the press of N. Hale, city printer, 1827), p. 17.

17. There was a democratic element in the transmittal of authority: Alma "selected a wise man who was among the elders of the church, and gave him power according to the voice of the people" (Alma 4:16). But Alma's selection was the major part of it: "Now Alma did not grant unto him the office of being high priest over the church, but he retained the office of high priest unto himself; but he delivered the judgment-seat unto Nephihah" (Alma 4:18).

18. The confirmation of the chief judges by the voice of the people is the only element of the Nephite constitution which comes close to republicanism, and in the context of life tenure and hereditary succession, this "election" is closer to the traditional acclamation of the king than to a popular plebiscite. We forget that kings have usually been thought to rule by the consent of their people and that at the ascent of a new king to the throne this consent is normally exhibited anew. Sometimes the election is merely ritualistic; in other cases, such as the selection of William III by the Convention Parliament in 1688, the consent of the people's representatives was as essential as the popular election of an American president. There was a popular element in Nephite monarchy, too. While still monarch, Mosiah had sent "among all the people,

desiring to know their will concerning who should be their king" (Mosiah 29:1). Zeniff was earlier "made a king by the voice of the people" (Mosiah 7:9; cf. Mosiah 19:26). The army of Israel "made their commander Omri king of Israel by common consent" (1 Kings 16:16).

Marc Bloch in his study of medieval European society asks, "How was this monarchial office, with its weight of mixed traditions handed on—by hereditary succession or by election? Today we are apt to regard the two methods as strictly incompatible; but we have the evidence of innumerable texts that they did not appear so to the same degree in the Middle Ages. . . . Within the predestinate family . . . the principle personages of the realm, the natural representatives of the whole body of subjects, named the new king." Marc Bloch, *Feudal Society*, tr. L. A. Manyon, 2 vols. (Chicago: University of Chicago Press, 1961), 2:383-84.

One episode that may to a casual reader have a republican flavor is General Moroni's elevation of the "title of liberty," on which he wrote: "In memory of our God, our religion, and freedom, and our peace, our wives, and our children" (Alma 46:12). Around this emblem he rallied the people against a movement to raise up a king. While the word *liberty* and the opposition to monarchists strike a familiar note, the details of the story, beginning with the peculiar designation "the title of liberty," are strangely archaic.

Moroni made the scroll in the first place by rending his coat and proceeded to enlist the people in the cause by "waving the rent part of his garment in the air," and crying, "Behold, whosoever will maintain this title upon the land, let them come forth in the strength of the Lord, and enter into a covenant that they will maintain their rights, and their religion, that the Lord God may bless them" (Alma 46:19, 20). Responding to the call, the people "came running together with their armor girded about their loins, rending their garments in token, or as a covenant, that they would not forsake the Lord their God" (Alma 46:21). "They cast their garments at the feet of Moroni" and covenanted that God "may cast us at the feet of our enemies, even as we have cast our garments at thy feet to be trodden under foot, if we shall fall into transgression" (Alma 46:22). Whereupon Moroni launched into an elaborate comparison with Joseph "whose coat was rent by his brethren into many pieces" and expressed hope for the Nephites' preservation in similitude of Joseph's (Alma 46:23).

It is difficult to see where Joseph Smith could have encountered precedents for that ritual in his American environment. Hugh Nibley has suggested that the title of liberty resembles the battle scroll of the Children of Light in the Qumran community. (See Nibley, *An Approach to the Book of Mormon*, [Salt Lake City: Council of the Twelve Apostles, 1957], pp. 178-89; Nibley, *Since Cumorah: The Book of Mormon in the Modern World* [Salt Lake City: Deseret Book Co., 1967], pp. 273-75.)

19. *Wayne Sentinel*, 3 November 1826; 5 September 1828; cf. 12 September 1828. A common argument against an incumbent was the danger of aristocratic pretensions occurring in men held in office too long. In 1826 the party

opposing the re-election of Governor Clinton resolved "that the continuance of the office of governor in one family, for a period longer than twenty-eight years, out of forty-nine, in a state containing a population of nearly two millions, is at war with the republican principle upon which our government is founded, and would tend to the establishment of an odious aristocracy." *Wayne Sentinel* 13 October 1826. Jacksonians in 1828 argued that one of the evils of the election of 1824 was that it established a system for passing on the presidency. Were it perpetuated, "the sovereignty of the people would be an idle name. The president and his successor would save us from the trouble of an election—the heir-apparent would create the king—the king would nominate the heir-apparent to the crown." *Wayne Sentinel* 10 October 1828.

20. Under the influence of their own cultural conditioning, Mormons and non-Mormons alike have read American principles into the Book of Mormon, even though closer analysis will not sustain that view. Alexander Campbell saw republicanism in the book as did B. H. Roberts. (See Campbell, *Delusions*, p. 13; and B. H. Roberts, *New Witnesses for God: The Book of Mormon*, 3 vols. [Salt Lake City: Deseret News, 1909], 2:212; cf. p. 209.)

21. The editorial headnote to Mosiah in the most widely circulated edition of the Book of Mormon states that Mosiah "recommends a representative form of government." But there is no system of representative government suggested in the text. Rather Mosiah recommended popular approval of judges. The editorial error only emphasizes how easy it is to misread the text from a modern democratic bias. The 1981 revised edition has a more accurate editorial headnote for that chapter.

22. Despite abuses of the taxing power, no recommendation was ever made for an elected assembly. (See Mosiah 11:3, 6, 13; and Ether 10:6.)

23. The nonrepublican forms of Book of Mormon government compel us to recognize that the "just and holy principles" which protect human rights can be embodied in various constitutional arrangements.

24. The word *inequality* in Mosiah 29:32 catches the eye of modern Americans, but in context the word assumes a meaning foreign to American thought. In the preceding verses, Mosiah explains the thinking behind his image, namely, that wicked kings enact iniquitous laws and compel their people to submit, thus causing them to sin. (See Mosiah 29:27, 28.) A good king like Mosiah would enact no laws of his own, but rather would judge the people by the law handed down from the fathers, which ultimately came from God. (See Mosiah 29:15, 25.) Under bad monarchs, the king was responsible for the people's sins; under good ones, the people were responsible for themselves. One of the reasons for eliminating kings was to ensure "that if these people commit sins and iniquities they shall be answered upon their own heads. For behold I say unto you, the sins of many people have been caused by the iniquities of their kings; therefore their iniquities are answered upon the heads of the kings" (Mosiah 29:30, 31). Then Mosiah makes the reference to inequality. "And now I desire that this inequality should be no more in this land . . ."

(Mosiah 29:32). It seems clear that inequality refers to the disproportionality of one sinful man, the king, having power to lead his people into iniquity.

This must be kept in mind when reading Mosiah 29:38. It is reported that the people became "exceedingly anxious that every man should have an equal chance." An equal chance to do what? As Americans, we immediately assume an equal chance to get ahead in the world or to have a voice in government. The verse actually reads "every man should have an equal chance throughout all the land; yea, and every man expressed a willingness to answer for his own sins" (Mosiah 29:38). Having so committed themselves, the people went out to choose judges "to judge them according to the law which had been given them." With a twist of mind we can scarcely understand today, the privilege of being judged according to the traditional law was a major part of the "equality" and "liberty" in which the Nephites "exceedingly rejoiced" (Mosiah 29:39; cf. 25, 41). A similar principle underlies the American Constitution. The Lord suffered it to be established, he says in the Doctrine and Covenants, so that "every man may be accountable for his own sins in the day of judgment" (D&C 101:78).

The discourse of Mosiah, viewed against the practice of hereditary descent of the chief judgeship, raises the possibility that the major distinction between judge and king was the lawmaking power. Mosiah did not contest the right of the king to make laws, only to make iniquitous ones. A judge, however, could not even claim legislative powers and thus perforce governed by the divine law passed down from the fathers. (See Mosiah 29:15, 25.) Seemingly, by definition a lawmaker was suspect because he usurped the power of God, the maker of the traditional law. When the prophets said that the Lord should be king, they meant, at least in part, that he should make the laws.

25. There was another biblical tradition that credited God with instituting kings among the Israelites. Roland de Vaux, *Ancient Israel: Its Life and Institutions,* tr. John McHugh, 2 vols. (New York: McGraw-Hill, 1961), 1:94.

26. See also Judges 9:1-6; 2 Samuel 2:4; 1 Kings 16:21, 22; 2 Kings 8:20; 11:12.

27. de Vaux, *Ancient Israel,* 1:149-52.

28. This construction of the Book of Mormon is confirmed by the recent discovery that certain sections of the book follow the intricate patterns of chiasmus characteristic of Hebrew writing. (See John W. Welch, "Chiasmus in the Book of Mormon," chapter 2 in this volume). In many other details, which Hugh Nibley more than any other scholar has mastered, the Book of Mormon follows Hebrew and Near Eastern forms. (See Hugh Nibley, *An Approach,* 2d ed.; Nibley *Since Cumorah;* and Nibley, *Lehi in the Desert.*) Nibley points out similarities to the Egyptian as well as the Jewish culture. At the time of Lehi's exodus, the Jewish nation was under the political shadow of Egypt, and was soaking in Egyptian patterns of thought and behavior.

29. Campbell, *Delusions,* p. 13.

9

Richard Lloyd Anderson

The Credibility of the Book of Mormon Translators

Richard Lloyd Anderson, Professor of Religion at Brigham Young University, is Director of Scripture, Religious Studies Center. He received his B.A. and M.A. from Brigham Young University in history and Greek, his J.D. from Harvard Law School, and his Ph.D. in ancient history from the University of California at Berkeley. He has served on the board of editors of several journals, including the Journal of Mormon History, *and has published over seventy articles in LDS publications and professional journals. Anderson has carefully studied the early period of Mormon history, receiving the Mormon History Associate award for best article for his series on the Book of Mormon witnesses, updated and published in 1981 in a book titled* Investigating the Book of Mormon Witnesses. *He has also published many scholarly articles which concentrated on the translation of the Book of Mormon and on the organization of the Church. He was a Danforth Teacher Fellow in History, a*

Woodrow Wilson Foundation Fellow, and was Honors Pro-
fessor of the Year at Brigham Young in 1978. He has partici-
pated in field trips to Bible sites in the Mediterranean area and
Israel. In this article, Anderson examines historical evidence
that substantiates the credibility of Joseph Smith and Oliver
Cowdery. By citing documents that verify the autobiographical
claims made by both Joseph and Oliver, Anderson establishes
the argument that their private activities and writings were per-
fectly consistent with their public claims and statements. As he
states, "Religious history is blind without unflinching use of
history, but empty if history cannot include religious experi-
ence." Both history and religious experience are used in this
article to verify the credibility of the two main translators of the
Book of Mormon in their accounts of that work.

N o two people knew more about the astounding beginnings
of Mormonism. Schoolteacher Oliver Cowdery boarded with
Joseph Smith's parents the winter after the manuscript of the
first translation was lost. Joseph was then married and living
over a hundred miles away in Harmony, Pennsylvania. His
earliest record tells of frustration at spare-time progress: "My
wife had written some for me to translate . . . and I cried unto
the Lord that he would provide for me to accomplish the work
whereunto he had commanded me."[1] Oliver had never seen
Joseph Smith and was seeking answers about Joseph's ancient
records and an angelic commission to translate them. Late in life
Joseph's mother remembered Oliver's intense investigation, her
full detail of which has only recently become available.[2] One
day "he had been in a deep study all day, and it had been put in
his heart that he would have the privilege of writing for Joseph
when the term of school which he was then teaching was
closed." The "next day" he braved drenching rain and slimy
roads, determined to be with the Smiths instead of overnighting
nearer the school. With more intense resolve to help Joseph,

Oliver said that conviction of the truth of the Book of Mormon was "working in my very bones, insomuch that I cannot for a moment get rid of it."[3]

Oliver's spiritual search was not yet over, according to Lucy Smith. Although he had prayed and was sure "that there is a work for me to do in this thing," the Smiths counseled him:

> We thought it was his privilege to know whether this was the case and advised him to seek for a testimony for himself. He did so, and received the witness spoken of in the Book of Doctrine and Covenants.[4]

The mentioned "witness" is in the revelation that came through Joseph Smith soon after the two young men met, the Lord saying to Oliver, "if you desire a further witness, cast your mind upon the night that you cried unto me." The Lord asked, "Did I not speak peace to your mind?" and then emphasized: "I have told you things which no man knoweth."[5] Readers have long known that Oliver received an answer, for after the revelation he told it to Joseph, who said, "one night after he had retired to bed he called upon the Lord to know if these things were so, and the Lord manifested to him that they were true, but he had kept the circumstances entirely secret."[6] Thus a great vision is only suggested, a striking pattern in early Mormon history. The noisy braggart exaggerates his experiences and trumpets them for ego or profit. On the other hand, Joseph Smith acts like an authentic person in waiting for the appropriate time to share many details of his revelations. Both Joseph and Oliver shared deep convictions consistently but cautiously, leaving many profound dimensions to come out as their friends—and later historians—became better acquainted with their early lives. In this case, Joseph's private record almost incidentally gives the full answer to Oliver's prayer, which was never paraded for notoriety by either Joseph or Oliver:

> [The] Lord appeared to a young man by the name of Oliver Cowdery and showed unto him the plates in a vision, and also the truth of the work and what the Lord was about to do through me, his unworthy servant. Therefore he was desirous to come and write for me to translate.[7]

Oliver's many sacrifices for the restored gospel had begun. Joseph's brother Samuel had planned to spend spring with the young Prophet, evidently taking responsibility for planting his small farm. So the helpful brother and the prospective scribe faced late March as soon as school ended for farmers' children:

> The weather had for some time previous been very wet and disagreeable, occasionally freezing nights. This made the roads almost impassable, particularly in the middle of the day. But Mr. Cowdery was determined not to be detained by wind or weather and persevered until they arrived at Joseph's house, although Oliver froze one of his toes and suffered much on the road from fatigue, as well as Samuel.[8]

The meeting was a moment of destiny for both men. Oliver first wrote of it:

> Near the time of the setting of the sun, Sabbath evening, April 5, 1829, my natural eyes for the first time beheld this brother. . . . On Monday the 6th, I assisted him arranging some business of a temporal nature, and on Tuesday the 7th, commenced to write the Book of Mormon.[9]

Joseph's later history echoes Oliver's recollection, indicating that "I had never seen him" until the meeting, and that "during the month of April, I continued to translate, and he to write, with little cessation, during which time we received several revelations."[10] One revelation authorized Oliver to translate, though his lack of success brought instruction to continue as they had begun.[11] Joseph recalled May, when "we still continued the work of translation."[12] In June they moved to the Whitmer farm and completed the book. The result was that no one but Joseph and Oliver knew intimate details of the whole translation. Before moving from Pennsylvania, they were given restored priesthood authority together in daylight appearances of ancient apostles and prophets. And at noontime both of them stood before the angel as he displayed the plates to the Three Witnesses. No two knew more about the astounding beginnings of Mormonism. The reality of these events must be measured largely by the credibility of Oliver Cowdery and Joseph Smith.

These men can now be studied in depth at an early point, largely because of the historical upgrading of the extensive Mormon archives in the last two decades.

Belief in another's story is normally based on practical and instinctive tests that teachers and parents use with children, careful buyers with sellers, or discerning citizens with officials suspected of duplicity. Does the story fit known events accompanying it? Is the story verified by other eyewitnesses? Is the story told plausibly and without obvious exaggerations? Are private comments consistent with public explanations? Do details given spontaneously add up to a consistent picture? Does the person telling the story have a record of honesty? Finally, what sincerity does the teller project?

This last question is hard to pin down historically because it is hard to measure in real life. How many times are the real facts shown by the intuition of a psychologist, or a mother, or by the subtle currents of a lie detector? History cannot fully replay the manner in which something was said or watch the expressions of Joseph or Oliver telling of their visions. But it can search their private language for clues on what motivated them in life. It can furnish documents that capture their religious feelings. Above all, the religious believer asks whether true spirituality is found in the person he trusts, whether it is Christ, Paul, Wesley, or Joseph Smith and Oliver Cowdery.

The above tests can be complex when the issues are interwoven. For instance, consistency of story weaves into the manner in which the story was told. But three strong issues follow here that can be illuminated by fresh discussion. They are highlighted by subheadings.

HISTORICAL VERIFICATION

The translation story invites historical investigation. For instance, Cowdery's recollection of meeting Joseph on April 5, 1829, is given above, with his comment that they took care of "some business of a temporal nature" the next day. A land contract exists between Joseph Smith and his father-in-law, dated April 6, 1829, and signed by Oliver Cowdery and Samuel

Smith, who Lucy says arrived in Harmony the previous day
with him.[13] As another example, translating was difficult
because Joseph was poor, and the translators could not work
for a living while devoting their full time to producing a large
manuscript. Joseph's earliest record gives his financial condition
when Oliver arrived: "We had become reduced in property, and
my wife's father was about to turn me out of doors, and I cried
unto the Lord that he would provide for me to accomplish the
work whereunto he had commanded me."[14] Later he summarized their conditions during translation:

> Mr. Joseph Knight, Sr., of Colesville, Broome County,
> New York, having heard of the manner in which we
> were occupying our time, . . . very kindly and consider-
> ately brought us a quantity of provisions, in order that
> we might not be interrupted in the work of translation
> by the want of such necessaries of life. . . . [H]e several
> times brought us supplies, a distance of at least thirty
> miles, which enabled us to continue the work, which
> otherwise we must have relinquished for a season.[15]

Knight's own recollections survive, a talkative account that displays little awareness of what the Prophet had independently
said. With unique details Knight confirms translation during
poverty. Before Cowdery's coming, Joseph Smith was "poor,"
and "his wife's father and family were all against him and would
not help him." Knight mentions several visits he made back and
forth between upper Pennsylvania and his lower New York
home. He gave food, some money, and writing paper. On one
trip Knight found that Joseph and Oliver had run out of food,
suspending writing to "find a place to work for provisions." As
the Prophet said, Knight's help enabled them to continue
translating.

Verification involves one of Cowdery's two descriptions of
that period, which emphasizes his role as scribe:

> I wrote with my own pen the entire Book of Mormon
> (save a few pages) as it fell from the lips of the Prophet
> as he translated it by the gift and power of God, by
> means of the Urim and Thummim, or as it is called by
> that book, "Holy Interpreters." . . . That book is true.

> Sidney Ridgon did not write it. Mr. Spaulding did not write it. I wrote it myself as it fell from the lips of the Prophet.[16]

Remains of the original Book of Mormon manuscript match Cowdery's description. Decay took its toll after it was placed in the humid cornerstone at Nauvoo. But 30 percent of Joseph Smith's dictation to Cowdery is now preserved in LDS archives. Dean Jessee has analyzed the surviving leaves:

> Of the 144 pages of the Book of Mormon manuscript in the Church Historian's Office, 124 pages are in the handwriting of Oliver Cowdery; eleven were probably written by John Whitmer; and twelve others are the work of an unidentified scribe.[17]

This means that 86 percent of the manuscript remaining was written by Oliver Cowdery. Since the handwriting of others is limited to 1 Nephi, Cowdery very probably did all the rest, in which case he wrote 95 percent of the manuscript. Thus he is correct in saying that he wrote "the entire Book of Mormon (save a few pages)," the known exception adding up to 23 pages done by others.[18]

Oliver Cowdery's other description is familiar because it speaks on the central issue, the inspiration of the process:

> These were days never to be forgotten—to sit under the sound of a voice dictated by the *inspiration* of heaven, awakened the utmost gratitude of this bosom! Day after day I continued uninterrupted to write from his mouth, as he translated with the *Urim* and *Thummim* . . . the history or record called The Book of Mormon.[19]

Thus Cowdery reinforced Joseph Smith's terse phrases from the beginning. The Prophet's first edition preface said that the plates were translated "by the gift and power of God," that this work was completed according to "the commandments of God . . . through his grace and mercy."[20] Joseph no doubt wrote this in 1829 for publication early the following year. So Joseph Smith's words of deep faith are contemporaneous with final translation. And Oliver's earliest letter also comes from the last month of the translation, one filled with quotations from a new revelation on the value of each soul before God. Oliver encouraged Hyrum Smith to begin to share the glorious restored gospel:

> Stir up the minds of our friends against the time when we come unto you, that then they may be willing to take upon them the name of Christ, for that is the name by which they shall be called at the last day. [21]

The practical point of the letter is to thank the Rockwells for shoes, indicating a possible visit. But the writer's goal is clearly spiritual, for most of the letter stresses discipleship and follows the opening theme: "These few lines I write unto you, feeling anxious for your steadfastness in the great cause of which you have been called to advocate." The letter is unsophisticated and intense, a spontaneous burst of faith. It shows the inner elation that Oliver later claimed to have experienced while working on the Book of Mormon. Written in the third month of translation, it confirms the sustained enthusiasm of the secretary.

These sample verifications show that the Book of Mormon translators met and did practical business at the place and time that they reported, that their poverty and Knight's help were just as they claimed, and that Oliver Cowdery in fact wrote as much of the manuscript as was reported. So their memories were accurate for physical circumstances. But something more appears in the investigation—the enthusiasm of spirit, the state of mind that they claimed to have. Here history comes close to reconstructing what is spiritual, for the translators' thoughts are on record at that critical time. During 1829 Oliver Cowdery seems totally sincere and moved by altruism. From his first days in the Smith household there is the deepest desire to serve God, followed by his sacrifices in translation and his personal zeal. Such inner experience is the end product for most religions and the point of beginning for Mormon foundations. For Oliver Cowdery and Joseph Smith moved far beyond the inner light of the Pietist, Quaker, or Seeker, adding their firm witness that supernatural beings authenticated their translation, displayed the ancient metal book, and gave authority to refound Christ's church.

UNAFFECTED HISTORY

There is a credibility of modesty in supernatural claims. Paul's personality was hardly modest, but he had a healthy reserve about narrating "the abundance of the revelations."[22] Several visions in Acts are not even mentioned in his letters. His first known reference to the Damascus vision is a stark, "Have I not seen Jesus Christ our Lord?"[23] Impressive details would come later as Luke wrote Paul's early history, also including Paul's two speeches about his early visions.[24] Scholars are generally suspicious of expansion and interpolation. So although Joseph Smith has taken much criticism for not detailing his visitations at the beginning, this apparent historical weakness is really a great religious strength. One of the most obvious facts in organizations is the inverse ratio of power and assertiveness. The person with real authority needs no excess words, a truth well known to psychologists, who perceive overacting as a telling admission of weakness. Joseph and Oliver later said that their authority to baptize was first given by the miraculous appearance of John the Baptist, who then commanded them to baptize each other. In 1829 they firmly acted on such power by adding the phrase "having authority given me of Jesus Christ" to the traditional baptismal formula.[25] In 1830 they also used higher authority in performing spiritual ordinances done by New Testament Apostles, the earliest reference stating that Oliver Cowdery and David Whitmer were under Joseph and were as "Paul, mine apostle, for you are called even with that same calling with which he was called."[26] In 1830 the position of the Church was clear, as it was that year to the journalist who reported Cowdery as saying that "the ordinances of the gospel have not been regularly administered since the days of the apostles, till the said Smith and himself commenced the work."[27] But at that point no document explains the basis for this position.

Some critics charge fraud, since Joseph and Oliver did not write up their experiences then, but this is normal life. The two men later particularized as they had opportunity. The careful diarist is rare in any society. What biographers normally get are

general statements about important experiences, followed by
what further circumstances their subjects might recall if they are
writing or being interviewed. In 1832 Joseph Smith made a raw
record of his main religious experiences, and he started with a
survey in this sequence: "testimony from on high"; "ministering
of angels"; "reception of the holy priesthood by the ministering
of angels to administer the letter of the gospel . . . and the ordinances"; "reception of the high priesthood after the holy order
of the son of the living God . . . the keys of the kingdom of
God."[28] Thus Joseph privately recorded the sequence of his first
vision of God, Moroni's appearances in connection with Book
of Mormon translation, and the restoration of the lesser and
higher priesthoods—forthright but concise statements of revelation and authority. A formal summary was printed in 1835, a
revelation stating the source of priesthood authority:

> John I have sent unto you, my servants, Joseph Smith,
> Jr., and Oliver Cowdery, to ordain you unto this first
> priesthood which you have received . . . and also . . .
> Peter, and James, and John, whom I have sent unto you,
> by whom I have ordained you and confirmed you to be
> apostles . . . and bear the keys of your ministry . . .
> unto whom I have committed the keys of my kingdom.[29]

These are crisp claims, carrying little description or justification. Yet Oliver and Joseph both saw the need to make fuller
reports. In biography, elaboration is not usually invention, because those who make history are usually too busy to write it.
There are more war memoirs than war diaries. The Church
grew, obtained a stable location, and established a regular
periodical circulating to the whole Church. Then Oliver
Cowdery was driven from Jackson County and came to Kirtland to carry on the interrupted Church newspaper. Soon he
announced a decision to expand a recollection into "a full
history of the rise of the Church of the Latter-day Saints, and
the most interesting parts of its progress," a project that faded
after telling quite fully how Joseph Smith learned of the plates
and finally obtained them.[30] Cowdery started the series with the
coming of John the Baptist, a narrative filled with the spon-

taneous detail of the eyewitness. Oliver spoke of the "voice of the Redeemer," the angelic glory superimposed on the brilliant May sunlight, John's reassuring voice, which "though mild, pierced to the center," then of kneeling "when we received under his hand the holy priesthood." He poured out gratitude to God for the restored authority and for "the majestic beauty and glory which surrounded us on this occasion."[31] Cowdery's words are eloquent and convey the impact of an overwhelming experience. They are more impressive because Oliver waited for a natural opportunity and did not feel forced into a public release at the beginning.

Likewise, Joseph Smith struggled for years for the chance to write his history in depth, finally beginning in earnest in 1838, several years after Cowdery had summarized priesthood restoration.[32] Joseph added his own particulars, not at all relying on the Cowdery narrative. He described the prayer for knowledge of authority to baptize, the angel descending "in a cloud of light," the ordination, the baptism, and the subsequent ecstasy of "great and glorious blessings from our Heavenly Father" as the translators rejoiced and prophesied by the Holy Ghost.[33] If Joseph had been skilled at publicity, he would have circulated all this with the Book of Mormon at the outset. Instead, it came artlessly as his later life furnished time and scribes for his auto-biography.

The story of higher priesthood restoration was even more cautiously told. Its reality rests on the first statements quoted above; as discussed, they follow the inverse principle that real authority needs no self-conscious explanation of it. And there is a corollary operating—an inverse law of sacredness which dictates that the highest gifts will be reported guardedly and reverently. On at least seven occasions Joseph Smith alluded to higher priesthood restoration, but he never saw the need to give a full account.[34] In the meantime the tragic estrangement of Joseph and Oliver came, the latter withdrawing from the Church for a decade. During this separation both translators gave new details that were consistent with the unguarded comments of the other. And neither argued the point—both took for granted the angels' ordination. For instance, Cowdery wrote his brother-in-law that his reputation must be cleared before returning to the Church because its credibility rested on "the private character of the man who bore that testimony." He had "stood in the presence of John with our departed Brother Joseph, to receive the lesser priesthood." He had also stood "in the presence of Peter to receive the greater."[35] When prematurely aged by his lung condition, Oliver Cowdery returned to the exiled Mormons. Obviously making his peace with God before dying, he very simply reviewed what he knew about the beginnings:

> I was present with Joseph when an holy angel from God came down from heaven and conferred or restored the Aaronic priesthood and said at the same time that it should remain upon the earth while the earth stands. I was also present with Joseph when the Melchizedek Priesthood was conferred by the holy angels of God, which we then confirmed upon each other by the will and commandment of God.[36]

Eighteen years before, the first printed copies of the Book of Mormon carried a testimony of revelation printed over the names of three witnesses, Oliver being one:

> And we declare with words of soberness, that an angel of God came down from heaven, and he brought and laid before our eyes, that we beheld and saw the plates, and the engravings thereon; . . . [T]he voice of the Lord commanded us that we should bear record of it.[37]

Again we see the rhetoric of assertion, not persuasion. The public statement is forceful, but it is not descriptive in trying to overawe the reader by divine brilliance, costume, or countenance. These realistic features were given later as the Three Witnesses freely spoke and answered questions, last-surviving David Whitmer sometimes submitting to extensive cross-examination by newspaper reporters. Through decades after seeing the angel, none of the three denied their daylight experience or reduced it to a subjective level.[38] In reality there are four witnesses, for Joseph Smith had been with them. He gave the first printed details of the angelic revelation and the voice of

God to the Three Witnesses. This procedure would be odd for a conspiracy, for the three severed their membership in 1838; Joseph produced this part of his history manuscript in 1839 and did not publish it until 1842.[39] He dared to greatly enlarge the story without consulting any of them.

The world would read the witnesses' declaration in the Book of Mormon, but believers and serious investigators could feel the dimensions of the experience in Joseph's later history. There he portrayed the first "light above us in the air" and the angel's appearance as he held the ancient record, turning "over the leaves one by one, so that we could see . . . the engravings thereon distinctly."[40] He also included the words of the voice of God. The 1830 public testimony only summarized the Lord's words approving the manuscript and commanding the listeners to witness, but Joseph Smith gave the more complete and persuasive version later:

1830 Testimony	*1839 History*
	These plates have been revealed by the power of God, and they have been
that "they have been translated by the gift and power of God."	translated by the power of God. The translation of them which you have seen is correct, and I command
that "we should bear record of it."	you to bear record of what you now see and hear.[41]

In form the 1830 words are a clear condensation of sentences that would originally be spoken in an expanded form. Quotation in indirect discourse of the third person tends to be more compressed than the first version in first person. In other words, approximate quotation is generally more concise than exact quotation. Thus not all expanded accounts are interpolations.

The shift from early simple records to later complex ones tempts the critic to see fabrication. But no real analyst can ignore the purpose of the compositions he studies. The issue is not really *short* versus *long* accounts, but *beginning testimony* versus *later history*. Symbolic of all vision reports, the above seventeen words of 1830 became forty-four as the Prophet told God's message in 1839. Early visions—even those seen by Joseph Smith alone—were mostly reported in the main two stages of a shorthand declaration followed by later graphic narrative. It is beside the point to apply a strict historical measure to early Mormonism, because it first acted on the need for summary testimony to announce its new message to the world. The need for history developed as the Church grew. It then produced history at a point which, compared to other world religions, was very early, and with superbly direct information. The story of Book of Mormon translation and visions was produced mainly between the years 1832 and 1839 and hardly grew after that. There is no ongoing mythology of founding, but after those years merely summary testimony based on the narrative record.

Oliver Cowdery and Joseph Smith are consistent with themselves and with each other in discussing the visions, whether in short or extensive form. Usually they simply reiterate what they have seen, without attempts to oversell or overexplain. For instance, a Shaker community reported Oliver's testimony a year after finishing the manuscript: "He stated that he had been one who assisted in the translation of the golden Bible, and had seen the angel. . . . He appeared meek and mild."[42] Nearly two decades later his Book of Mormon knowledge was recorded on returning to the Church: "I beheld with my eyes, and handled with my hands, the gold plates from which it was translated. I also beheld the Interpreters."[43]

There are advantages in examining Joseph and Oliver through documents, for lifetime patterns appear there that could not be judged by their first converts. But those converts made decisions based on personal impressions of look and tone. One can approximate this experience through Parley P. Pratt's letter to his Canadian converts. Six years after his own conversion he was still overwhelmed by the reality of the Prophet's testimony of the beginning:

> One of the most interesting meetings I ever attended was held in the Lord's house Sunday before last. One week

before, word was publicly given that Brother Joseph Smith, Jr. would give a relation of the coming forth of the records and also of the rise of the Church and of his experience. Accordingly a vast concourse assembled at an early hour. Every seat was crowded, and four or five hundred people stood up in the aisles. Brother Smith gave the history of these things, relating many particulars of the manner of his first visions, and the spirit and power of God was upon him in bearing testimony, insomuch that many, if not most of the congregation were in tears. As for myself I can say that all the reasonings in uncertainty and all the conclusions drawn from the writings of others . . . dwindle into insignificance when compared with living testimony.[44]

RELIGIOUS CREDIBILITY

Joseph and Oliver kept private journals and wrote many candid letters, current tools from which to estimate their motives and values. Part of their credibility is that they were generally regarded by associates as honest men. As with Lincoln, public storms raged around them but personal friends were convinced of their truthfulness. Joseph's religiously divided family knew him well, and all became Mormons, confident that his word was reliable.[45] Oliver Cowdery's non Mormon community respected him as a man of honor.[46] These facts are important, though the careful student wants to confront the men as personally as did Parley P. Pratt. New manuscript sources opening up in the last few decades furnish much more information on these men, and a high proportion is personal. A main thrust of present Mormon studies is the reopening of early records. Thus there are now better tools with which to know the youthful Joseph Smith. Although secular biographers sought to do this with Freudian theory, they used guesswork instead of firsthand sources. Joseph Smith speaks personally in many documents from the early 1830s. Nauvoo manuscripts, on the other hand, often reveal his extensive responsibilities more than his inner feelings. He was then a leader directing the economic, political, social, and religious problems of thousands. Joseph's Nauvoo diaries are also inferior to his Kirtland diaries in personal reflections because the pressure of affairs made entries shorter, and they seem more the product of secretaries than previously. In the Nauvoo diaries it is harder to find the private thoughts of this busy administrator.

The best collection of the Prophet's teachings contains about four hundred pages, and a hundred of these are devoted to the New York and Ohio periods, the first half of the Prophet's direction of the Church. Moreover, this New York and Ohio selection features business letters, doctrinal expositions, and official Presidency statements. The title of the book, *Teachings of the Prophet Joseph Smith,* of course indicates its design, which as a byproduct gives a formal image of the Prophet. But the intimate view of the Prophet is found in the minutes of talks, Joseph's private diaries, and his personal letters—and much of this material is unpublished. For instance, his earliest known letter closely follows the completion of the Book of Mormon translation and effectively shows his religious concerns, not only for the typesetting of the new work of scripture, but for his family and the small nucleus of believers near Palmyra, New York. He instructs Oliver:

> Tell them that our prayers are put up daily for them that they may be prospered in every good word and work, and that they may be preserved from sin here and from the consequence of sin hereafter. And now, dear brother, be faithful in the discharge of every duty, looking for the reward of the righteous. And now may God of his infinite mercy keep and preserve us spotless until his coming and receive us all to rest with him in eternal repose through the atonement of Christ our Lord. Amen.[47]

Joseph's critics include Christian fundamentalists who should accurately label him deeply Christian, totally devoted to God and his work. The early Joseph is above all the Joseph of faith, of great humility, and of constant prayer. Two 1832 letters to his wife symbolize this. Waiting for Newel Whitney's leg to mend in Indiana, he does not tell of religious study or practical planning. Instead he tells Emma that he has "visited a grove" daily to "give vent to all the feelings of my heart in meditation and prayer."[48] Waiting for Newel Whitney to purchase goods in New York City, the Prophet does not have a taste for sightseeing or seeking out libraries. Instead he prefers private "reading and praying and holding communion with the Holy Spirit and writing to you."[49] The same year he opens his private journal with a prayer: "Oh, may God grant that I may be directed in all my thoughts; oh, bless thy servant. Amen."[50]

Oliver Cowdery's first letters are also intense with love for God and Christ, the first already quoted, written during Book of Mormon translation. Cowdery's next letter answered the one just quoted from the Prophet; it shared some practical affairs but mostly shared faith in the plan of salvation stressed in the Book of Mormon:

> My dear brother, when I think of the goodness of Christ I feel no desire to live or stay here upon the shores of this world of iniquity, only to serve my maker and be if possible an instrument in his hands of doing some good in his cause, with his grace to assist me.[51]

Six weeks later Oliver sent Joseph another letter as Father Smith travelled to summon his son on typesetting business. Knowing that they would soon see each other, Oliver wrote a short but feeling letter, again addressing some practical problems but sharing sorrow for a wicked world:

> I feel almost as though I could quit time and fly away and be at rest in the bosom of my Redeemer for the many deep feelings of sorrow and the many long strugglings of prayer in sorrow for the sins of my fellow beings.[52]

These letters disclose no intrigue—only mutual faith that their authors were engaged in a great, divine cause. Such letters cannot be written for effect, for they are unstudied and unpolished, in this respect quite different from the 1830 testimonies of the witnesses or the Book of Mormon preface. Furthermore, for a long time they lay obscure in Church letter books without any attempt being made to prove anything by them. Their recovery now recreates the earnest faith operating in Book of Mormon translation.

The glimpses in council records sustain the intense dedication shown in the earliest Cowdery-Smith letters. The atmosphere is not one of dreamy perfection; the millennium has not
arrived, but these brethren are preparing a people for it. Church
recorders captured sincere strugglings and strivings. Oliver
exhorts his brethren on "the necessity of having their hearts
drawn out in prayer to God and also realize that they are in the
immediate presence of God."[53] Joseph speaks of the potential of
faith: "And could we all come together with one heart and one
mind in perfect faith, the veil might as well be rent today as next
week, or any other time."[54] A year later the Prophet has the
same goal, urging Church leaders to pray for a special revelation of comfort and instruction: "To receive revelation and the
blessing of heaven it was necessary to have our minds on God
and exercise faith and become of one heart and of one mind."
He asked the leaders to pray "separately and vocally," which
they did; the result was the elevated and stimulating section 88
of the Doctrine and Covenants, a treasury of spiritual insight.[55]

Profound faith and reverence characterize Joseph and Oliver
in the early years of the Church. The above illustrations of
spirituality all date to 1832, in a period of about three years
after the translation of the Book of Mormon. And the same
qualities continue in their private journals through the next
three years, the peak of Oliver's prominence in the Church. The
early Joseph and Oliver are men with missions, servants of
Christ devoted to his work. This is supremely relevant in
judging their Book of Mormon translation. They are the kind of
men that God would use in such a great work. Their lives and
thoughts are in harmony with what they claimed to do. He who
invited men to ask and receive ought to respond to such seekers
after his kingdom. Their intense prayerfulness is consistent with
communion with God. Not only is their translation story
credible by numerous practical tests—the translators themselves
emerge as spiritually credible.

SUMMARY

This essay joins others in asking what intellectual tests the
Book of Mormon can meet, but that book also transcends in-

tellectual tests. It closes with the invitation to pray and know through the Holy Ghost, the invitation of every true prophet. Paul's travels are exciting reading in Luke's Acts of the Apostles. That work is respected by many tough-minded historians and classicists, who accept its rich information about ancient sea voyages, cities, and social customs. But one should step from physical authenticity to its spiritual witness that Paul and Peter performed miracles in Christ's name, and brought salvation from God to their converts. Paul warned that spiritual things must be spiritually discerned and chided the Corinthians for using only reason to determine what parts of the gospel to believe.[56] Neither Jesus nor his apostles offered the world painless belief. They challenged all to put God's cause above money, power, cheap pleasure, status, and reputation. Those who confound the logical with the respectable will not easily see why Paul said, "God hath chosen the foolish things of the world to confound the wise."[57] Early Mormon Jared Carter had no problem in believing that the Spirit might speak through the unsophisticated as he measured Joseph Smith in an 1831 meeting: "Brother Joseph, notwithstanding he is not naturally talented for a speaker, yet he was filled with the power of the Holy Ghost, so that he spoke as I never heard man speak."[58]

Religious history is blind without unflinching use of history, but empty if history cannot include religious experience. Knowing God is closely related to knowing love, ethical values, and other inner realities. Did Oliver and Joseph translate by revelation and receive testimony and authority from angels? One must judge their credibility and discern the product of their work. Their activities are verified and their lifetime testimonies unwavering. The translators' minds harmonize with their prophetic call. Moreover, their claims are phrased with the confident simplicity of men who expect to be believed. What they said is important, but so also is how they said it; lack of overstatement in their first testimonies underlines depth of conviction. Were they sincere but deceived? The counterquestion is whether God and prayer are realities. If so, Joseph and Oliver cannot be faulted in prayerfulness and Christian discipleship. Their words are impressive by every test at the beginning and by the supreme test of enduring to the end, for ridicule and persecution brought no change. Their testimony appears in many forms, including the forceful context of the dedication of the Kirtland Temple, a time of God's favor yet glowing in the records of scores who were there. One was Oliver Cowdery, who privately wrote of the visible glory that filled the temple in the evening meeting.[59] He also reported the day's dedication service with characteristic restraint. Near the end, "President J. Smith then arose and bore record of his mission." Soon after, "President O. Cowdery spoke and testified of the truth of the Book of Mormon, and of the work of the Lord in these last days."[60]

By this time documents disclose these founders' personal feelings about their testimony. A secular society hardly recognizes that decisions can be made in terms of future accountability. But the Prophet reveals this perspective in adjusting a conflict with the intense comment, "I would be willing to be weighed in the scale of truth today in this matter, and risk it in the day of judgment."[61] The Prophet and Cowdery kept journals with periodic and profound introspection. Thus Cowdery's editorial farewell rings true in saying that he had well counted the cost of trying to "persuade others to believe as myself," and he willingly faced the "judgment seat of Christ," who would see "the integrity of my heart."[62] The names of Joseph Smith and Oliver Cowdery led the rest in certifying the truth of the events and teachings of the 1835 Doctrine and Covenants, the first book to name the messengers restoring both the Book of Mormon and the two priesthoods.[63] The preface, stamped with Oliver Cowdery's phraseology, expresses their solemn view of eternal responsibility:

> We do not present this little volume with any other expectation than that we are to be called to answer to every principle advanced, in that day when the secrets of all hearts will be revealed, and the reward of every man's labor be given him.[64]

NOTES

1. Joseph Smith, "A History of the Life of Joseph Smith," 1832 manuscript that was the Prophet's first attempt to give "an account of his marvelous

experiences." Portions are dictated, but Dean Jessee has determined that significant parts are in the Prophet's handwriting. For background see Dean C. Jessee, "Early Accounts of Joseph Smith's First Vision," *BYU Studies* 9:275 (1969). This manuscript and others not noted are held by the LDS Historical Department. Documents are herein transcribed with verbal exactness but with moderate editorial correction of spelling and punctuation.

2. The outline and approximate words following are found in the recollections of Oliver Cowdery's Manchester stay in the edited publication, Lucy Smith, *Biographical Sketches of Joseph Smith the Prophet* (Liverpool, 1853), pp. 128-29. However, the quotations and personal details come from her preliminary manuscript, being prepared for publication by this author.

3. Ibid.

4. Ibid.

5. Doctrine and Covenants, current ed. 6:22-24, 1833 Book of Commandments 5:11.

6. Joseph Smith, *History of The Church of Jesus Christ of Latter-day Saints* 1:35, this volume (Salt Lake City, 1902) dictated by the Prophet and compiled under his direction. All quotations agree with the Nauvoo printing of 1842 unless otherwise noted.

7. "A History of the Life of Joseph Smith," cit. n. 1.

8. Lucy Smith, preliminary manuscript. Cp. *Biographical Sketches,* pp. 130-31.

9. *Latter-day Saints' Messenger and Advocate* 1:14 (1834).

10. *History of the Church* 1:32, 35.

11. See ibid., p. 36, D&C 8 and 9, and the 1833 first printings in Book of Commandments 7 and 8.

12. *History of the Church* 1:39.

13. Agreement of Joseph Smith, Jr., and Isaac Hale, April 6, 1829, for Joseph's purchase of the latter's thirteen-acre farm, consideration $200, with $114 due by the end of that April. In the light of the next quotation on Joseph's poverty and the risk of being turned away, it is possible that Cowdery's teaching salary secured the home for translation.

14. "A History of the Life of Joseph Smith," cit. n. 1. Part of this quotation was used in the opening paragraph of this article to show Joseph's need of a full-time scribe. His prayer sought this assistance and also relief from financial pressure.

15. *History of the Church* 1:47, the final "which" following the 1842 text. These 1839 memoirs are supplemented by Joseph's 1842 reflections (*HC* 5:124): "Joseph Knight, Sr., . . . was among the number of the first to administer to my necessities, while I was laboring in the commencement of the bringing forth of the work of the Lord."

16. Reuben Miller, Journal, Oct. 21, 1848. For background on Miller's capability and interest in Cowdery, see Richard Lloyd Anderson, "Reuben

Miller as a Recorder of Oliver Cowdery's Reaffirmations," *BYU Studies* 8:277 (1968).

17. Dean C. Jessee, "The Original Book of Mormon Manuscript," *BYU Studies* 10:276 (1970). Recent attempts to equate the unidentified scribe with Solomon Spaulding were a bubble burst by the careful analysis of Jessee in the *Deseret News, Church News,* Aug. 20, 1977, pp. 3-5.

18. Statistics are calculated from inventory of pages in Jessee, *BYU Studies* 10:273, cit. n. 17.

19. Cit. n. 9 above.

20. Quoted phrases are from a special "Preface" subscribed "The Author," an explanation of the 116-page loss that appeared in the 1830 edition but is not carried into current editions. The Prophet repeated such language many times in summarizing his translation, examples of which are in Richard L. Anderson, "By the Gift and Power of God," *Ensign,* Sept., 1977, p. 79.

21. Oliver Cowdery to Hyrum Smith, June 14, 1829, Fayette, New York, Joseph Smith Letter Book 1. For a convenient transcription, see Lyndon W. Cook, *The Revelations of the Prophet Joseph Smith* (Provo, Utah 1981), p. 29. Correct "unto Zion" there to "unto you."

22. 2 Corinthians 12:7, where Paul resumes the first person after indirectly narrating a great vision to avoid claiming "glory" for himself. Except for charges of his enemies, he would not have listed his sacrifices (11:18-33) or cautiously summarized the greatest of his "visions and revelations of the Lord" (12:1-7).

23. 1 Corinthians 9:1, a letter written about A.D. 56. This is before the composition of Acts, which could not be written until some six years afterward, the date of events in its last chapter. In 1 Corinthians 15:8 Paul also testifies of seeing Christ without giving any particulars.

24. Luke's history of Paul's vision is in Acts 9, and Paul's two speeches on his vision are in Acts 22 and 26. For dating, cp. the previous note.

25. D&C 20:73 gives the current LDS baptismal formula, "Having been commissioned of Jesus Christ, I baptize you in the name of the Father, and of the Son, and of the Holy Ghost. Amen." The beginning phrase dates from the 1835 Doctrine and Covenants, before which time manuscripts and printed versions read "having authority given me," the same claim of being "commissioned" but with different wording. The ordinance sections of D&C 20 were put together in 1829 by Oliver Cowdery, who relied heavily on the Book of Mormon manuscript. His document begins by saying he wrote it by "a command of God" and closes with "written in the year of our Lord and Savior 1829—a true copy of the articles of the Church of Christ. O.C." The baptismal formula exactly follows 3 Nephi 11:25 and shows that the first baptisms of the restored Church asserted a special appointment from God not claimed in orthodox Christian baptisms. Both the Prophet and David Whitmer wrote of baptisms during 1829. For a transcription of the full Cowdery document, see

Robert J. Woodford, *The Historical Development of the Doctrine and Covenants* (BYU Ph.D. Dissertation, 1974), the first pages concerning D&C 20. For the traditional baptismal formula, see Mt. 28:19-20.

26. D&C 18:9, the same wording of the 1833 Book of Commandments. The revelation came in June, 1829, which suggests that they had by then received apostolic authority, which was not fully used until the 1830 organization of the Church. In Acts 8:12-20, confirmation of the Holy Ghost by the laying on of hands requires a higher authority than does baptism.

27. *Painesville* [Ohio] *Telegraph,* Nov. 16, 1830.

28. "A History of the Life of Joseph Smith," cit. n. 1. This 1832 source is now the earliest priesthood restoration reference, supplementing Richard L. Anderson, "The Second Witness of Priesthood Restoration," *Improvement Era,* Sept., 1968, p. 15. There correct "1842" to 1839 on p. 15, and correct "1833" to 1835 on p. 20.

29. D&C 27:8, 12-13, first printed in this form in the 1835 edition. As the preface indicates, the revising committee was the First Presidency, listed in the order of Joseph Smith, Oliver Cowdery, Sidney Rigdon, and F. G. Williams. Cp. the close of this article, including n. 63.

30. Quotations are from Cowdery's preface to his historical installments, *Latter Day Saints' Messenger and Advocate* 1:13 (1834).

31. *Latter Day Saints' Messenger and Advocate* 1:15-16 (1834), also found in recent editions of the Pearl of Great Price, the end of the Joseph Smith section. A fraudulent pamphlet with Cowdery's name imitates and diminishes this confident language, but no copy before 1906 has been found, nor was it referred to in the 1848 discussion on Cowdery returning to the Church. For a survey of this problem, see Richard Lloyd Anderson, *Investigating the Book of Mormon Witnesses* (Salt Lake City, 1981), pp. 172-73. Cp. Anderson, "The Second Witness," *Improvement Era,* Sept., 1968, pp. 20, 22.

32. For the Prophet's problems in starting his history, see Dean C. Jessee, "The Reliability of Joseph Smith's History," *Journal of Mormon History* 3:30-34 (1976).

33. *History of the Church* 1:39-42.

34. These seven accounts are in records or journals of Kirtland and Nauvoo. One is the "History of the Life of Joseph Smith," cit. n. 1; the remaining six are in Anderson, "The Second Witness," *Improvement Era,* Sept., 1968, pp. 15-16. The Dibble recollection on p. 18 is subtracted as not contemporary.

35. Oliver Cowdery to Phineas Young, Mar. 23, 1846, Tiffin, Ohio, Photofacsimile in Anderson, "The Second Witness," *Improvement Era,* Sept., 1968, p. 21.

36. Miller, Journal, Oct. 21, 1848.

37. "The Testimony of Three Witnesses," at the end of the 1830 edition of

the Book of Mormon, reprinted with minor grammatical corrections in the introductory section of current editions.

38. See Anderson, *Investigating the Book of Mormon Witnesses,* particularly chs. 4, 6, and 8.

39. According to *History of the Church* 1:18-19, on May 2, 1838, Joseph Smith had completed the history up to getting the plates from the angel. He may have continued to the witnesses' revelation during that year. The earliest manuscript is apparently recopied, since it was written by James Mulholland, the Prophet's scribe a short time during 1838 and for many months during 1839, during which time events were written up to the fall of 1830. Thus Joseph related the witnesses' vision no later than 1839. See Dean C. Jessee, "The Writing of Joseph Smith's History," *BYU Studies* 11:450 and 441 (1971).

40. *History of the Church* 1:54-55.

41. Ibid., p. 55. (Quotation marks added by author.)

42. Journal of Ashbel Kitchell, ms. at the Shaker Museum, Old Chatham, N.Y. See Anderson, *Investigating the Book of Mormon Witnesses,* p. 55, where a fuller quotation is given.

43. Miller, Journal, Oct. 21, 1848.

44. Parley P. Pratt to LDS leaders in Canada, Nov. 27, 1836, Kirtland, Ohio, called to my attention by descendant Steven Pratt.

45. See Richard Lloyd Anderson, "The Trustworthiness of Young Joseph Smith," *Improvement Era,* Oct., 1970, p. 82.

46. See Anderson, *Investigating the Book of Mormon Witnesses,* ch. 3: "Oliver Cowdery: Non-Mormon Lawyer." Cp. Anderson, "Oliver Cowdery, Esq.: His Non-Church Decade," Truman G. Madsen and Charles G. Tate, Jr. (eds.), *To the Glory of God* (Salt Lake City, 1972), p. 199.

47. Joseph Smith, Jr., to Oliver Cowdery, Oct. 22, 1829, Harmony, Penn., Joseph Smith Letter Book 1.

48. Joseph Smith, Jr., to Emma Smith, June 6, 1832, Greenville, Indiana, Chicago Historical Society ms. This and the next letter quoted are scheduled for publication by the author in 1983 in a source book on the letters of Joseph and Emma Smith.

49. Joseph Smith, Jr., to Emma Smith, Oct. 13, 1832, in the archives of the Reorganized Church of Jesus Christ of Latter Day Saints. Cp. n. 48.

50. Joseph Smith, Journal, Nov. 27 or 28, 1832, this entry and the opening pages identified as being in the handwriting of Joseph Smith by Dean C. Jessee. He is preparing a scholarly edition of this diary and other personal writings of Joseph Smith.

51. Oliver Cowdery to Joseph Smith, Jr., Nov. 6, 1829, Manchester, New York, Joseph Smith Letter Book 1.

52. Oliver Cowdery to Joseph Smith, Jr., Dec. 28, 1829, Manchester, New York, Joseph Smith Letter Book 1.

53. Far West Record, p. 20, Dec. 6, 1831, Randolph County, Indiana.

54. Ibid., p. 11, Oct. 25, 1831, Orange, Ohio, also cit. Joseph Fielding Smith (ed.), *Teachings of the Prophet Joseph Smith* (Salt Lake City, 1977 ed.), p. 9.

55. Kirtland Council Minute Book, Dec. 27, 1832, cit. Cook, *Revelations of Joseph Smith,* p. 181.

56. Cp. 1 Corinthians 2:9-14 with 1:18-25.

57. 1 Corinthians 1:27.

58. Jared Carter, Autobiography, narration of June 3, 1831, meeting. Cp. Davis Bitton, *Guide to Mormon Diaries and Autobiographies* (Provo, Utah, 1977), p. 62, Jared Carter entry.

59. Leonard J. Arrington, "Oliver Cowdery's Kirtland, Ohio, 'Sketch Book,'" *BYU Studies* 12:426 (1972), Mar. 27, 1836 entry.

60. *Latter Day Saints' Messenger and Advocate* 2:281 (1836).

61. "Sketch Book for the Use of Joseph Smith, Jr.," Jan. 16, 1836, Joseph Smith's speech to the Twelve. It appears with slight modification in *History of the Church* 2:373.

62. Editor's "Address," *Latter-Day Saints' Messenger and Advocate* 1:120-121, the quotation linking three representative phrases in a long but eloquent statement.

63. The first edition of the revelations was largely destroyed by the 1833 mob, and its publication in Missouri away from Joseph Smith probably contributed to an absence of information about the heavenly messengers. The main appearances had already been summarized in the Prophet's private 1832 autobiography. Two features of the 1835 Doctrine and Covenants moved to publicize the founding events. First, present Section 20 was changed from its later chronological position as Section 24. In 1835 it became Section 2, the featured position after the revealed preface. There it prominently testified to the revelation of the Book of Mormon through the "holy angel whose countenance was as lightning" and the inspired process of Book of Mormon translation. (See present D&C 20:1-16.) The second feature perfecting the restoration record was the printed listing of the main messengers, adding a section to present D&C 27 listing Moroni as the Book of Mormon angel, and John the Baptist and Peter, James, and John as the angels of priesthood restoration.

64. Close of preface to the 1835 edition of the Doctrine and Covenants, the title page indicating that it was "compiled by" Joseph Smith, Jr., Oliver Cowdery, Sidney Rigdon, and Frederick G. Williams, all of whose names appear in that order below the preface, dated Feb. 17, 1835. For Cowdery's parallel phraseology, compare his farewell address as editor, *Latter-Day Saints' Messenger and Advocate* 1:120 (1835). He would be measured by "the strict principles of righteousness," and was filled "with the expectation and assurance that before the Judge of all and an assembled universe I must answer for the same." The full preface to the 1835 Doctrine and Covenants is conveniently quoted in *History of the Church* 2:250-51.

Index